The
EVERYTHING
Psychology Book

Dear Reader:

I'll admit it: I had to drag myself to my very first psychology course. It was just another required course I had to suffer through. But then something remarkable happened; I became hooked. It quickly became my favorite class, and I found myself wanting to learn more and more, to delve deeper into the studies and to further my education in "psychology." I no longer saw psychology as a required course but a lesson in life.

It is my hope that you, too, will view psychology as a lesson in life and hunger for those answers it gives us. Whatever your preconceived notion of psychology may be, I ask that you put it aside and just read. You will soon find yourself absorbed in this world where questions are answered and an understanding of yourself and others is developed. Far more than just an academic study, psychology is a real-world study whose information can be applied to your everyday life.

Lesley Bolton

Welcome to the EVERYTHING Series!

These handy, accessible books give you all you need to tackle a difficult project, gain a new hobby, comprehend a fascinating topic, prepare for an exam, or even brush up on something you learned back in school but have since forgotten.

You can choose to read an *Everything*® book from cover to cover or just pick out the information you want from our four useful boxes: e-questions, e-facts, e-alerts, and e-ssentials.

We give you everything you need to know on the subject, but throw in a lot of fun stuff along the way, too.

We now have more than 400 *Everything*® books in print, spanning such wide-ranging categories as weddings, pregnancy, cooking, music instruction, foreign language, crafts, pets, New Age, and so much more. When you're done reading them all, you can finally say you know *Everything*®!

QUESTIONS?
Answers to
common questions

FACTS
Important snippets
of information

ALERTS!
Urgent
warnings

ESSENTIALS
Quick
handy tips

PUBLISHER Karen Cooper

DIRECTOR OF ACQUISITIONS AND INNOVATION Paula Munier

MANAGING EDITOR, EVERYTHING SERIES Lisa Laing

COPY CHIEF Casey Ebert

ACQUISITIONS EDITOR Lisa Laing

DEVELOPMENT EDITOR Elizabeth Kassab

EDITORIAL ASSISTANT Hillary Thompson

Visit the entire Everything® series at *www.everything.com*

THE
EVERYTHING
PSYCHOLOGY
BOOK

Explore the human psyche and
understand why we do the things we do

Lynda L. Warwick, Ph.D., and Lesley Bolton

Adams Media
Avon, Massachusetts

An Everything® Series Book.
Everything® and everything.com® are registered trademarks of F+W Media, Inc.

Published by Adams Media, a division of F+W Media, Inc.
57 Littlefield Street, Avon, MA 02322 U.S.A.
www.adamsmedia.com

ISBN 10: 1-59337-056-3
ISBN 13: 978-1-59337-056-5

Printed in the United States of America.

J   I   H   G

Library of Congress Cataloging-in-Publication Data
Bolton, Lesley.
The everything psychology book / Lesley Bolton.
p.   cm.
(An everything series book)
ISBN 1-59337-056-3
1. Psychology. I. Title. II. Series: Everything series.
BF121.B58   2004
150–dc22   2004004807

This book is available at quantity discounts for bulk purchases.
For information, call 1-800-289-0963.

Contents

Acknowledgments

I'd like to express my deepest thanks to Angelique Pinet, Brooke Bolton, and Lora Bolton for all their help in the writing of this book.

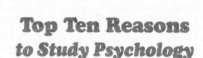

Top Ten Reasons
to Study Psychology

1. To achieve a better understanding of yourself, including your thoughts and behaviors.

2. To understand the biological as well as psychological processes of the human mind.

3. To learn how to cope with stressors and environmental factors beyond our control.

4. To be able to recognize the symptoms of mental disorders.

5. To better understand how we relate to others and why we form certain relationships.

6. To understand how our environment affects us and how we affect the environment.

7. To be able to determine the difference between normal and abnormal.

8. To understand the stages of human development and how they affect us both mentally and physically.

9. To be familiar with the treatments available for mental disorders and other psychological problems.

10. To gain insight into the behavior of others.

Introduction

▶ EACH OF US HAS an interest in psychology. How can we not? Psychology surrounds us; it is a part of our world and a part of us. From the toddler who gets on his parent's last nerve by asking "why?" repeatedly and demanding answers, to your next-door neighbor who is asking herself "why?" over and over in an attempt to understand the complications of her life, we all have a desire to understand ourselves and the happenings in our environment. Psychology is what helps us answer those questions.

Psychology is an ongoing study devoted to discovering, understanding, and explaining human nature—the behavior and mental processes that make us who we are. As psychology encompasses a complex network of study, one book couldn't possibly cover all the information available; however, the goal of this book is to give you a working understanding of the important basics, laying a foundation for further study if you so choose.

Whether you realize it or not, you've already begun your study of psychology with all those questions you ask yourself on a daily basis. You are inherently curious about your feelings, behaviors, and motives as well as those of others. You are often exploring your environment and evaluating how you fit in with it. You are constantly receiving sensory perceptions and processing them. All of this, and more, is part of psychology.

To set the stage, you will learn about the different branches of psychology and how each has made its own contributions to our knowledge of modern psychology. It is very interesting to observe how theories have developed and evolved throughout the years. You may even be shocked by some of the treatments used in the past. As this is a constantly evolving discipline, it is important to take what we've learned in the past and expound on it.

We will also take a look at the biological and psychological processes of the brain and how these work in conjunction to make us who we are—from personality to intelligence and motivation to emotion. As humans, we are very complex beings capable of amazing feats of the mind. No two people are exactly alike, and we will explore the reasons for differences.

Of course, a book on psychology wouldn't be complete without the exploration of mental disorders. This is a fascinating yet frightening topic. Movies, television, and the media give us glimpses into the lives of those suffering mental disorders, but these are only glimpses and are often inaccurate. For instance, people have a tendency to confuse schizophrenia with multiple personality disorder, though these two disorders are completely different. The world of mental disorders is unknown to most of us, yet it affects so many. By studying these disorders, their causes, their symptoms, and their treatments, we can delve deeper into the human psyche.

Psychology opens the door to self-awareness. You will find many answers for why you feel and behave the way you do within these pages. However, there is always room for more study. Once we are better able to understand ourselves, we can then begin to understand others and the world around us. So, let's get started!

Psychology— Yesterday and Today

It's likely that psychology is more than you think it is. Just about everything we do has been or is being studied by psychologists, often from more than one perspective. If not, it's on the list. Psychology's goal is to understand human behavior objectively and in its entirety.

What Is Psychology?

Psychology is a broad and diverse area of endeavor, one that has evolved from relatively humble beginnings in the nineteenth century into a science that is now concerned with a great many different aspects of our lives. Modern psychology is comprised of many specialty areas that are interwoven into a complex network of research and practice. There is no such thing as "the psychologist," and it's unlikely that two psychologists will give you the same definition of their discipline. To get a thorough appreciation of the many different things that psychologists do, you'll just have to read this book.

FACT

People often confuse psychology with psychiatry. They are not the same. Whereas psychology can be read as "soul science," psychiatry reads as "soul healing" (healing comes from the Greek *iatreia*). Psychiatrists are medical doctors who focus exclusively on understanding and treating mental and behavioral disorders. Many psychologists also study and treat such disorders, but psychology is a far broader discipline.

However, it is helpful to have some kind of working definition. Here's one that is general enough that most psychologists would go along with it: Psychology is a science that studies the behavior of living organisms, with emphasis on animals and especially humans. Like most such definitions, some notes on the key elements are in order:

- The term *psychology* has its origins in the Greek words *psyche* (soul or self) and *logos* (logic and, in turn, science).
- Psychology is indeed a science, one that stresses careful observation and experimentation in the quest for objective evidence to back up its claims.
- *Behavior* refers to anything an organism does, whether it can be observed directly or must be inferred.
- Observing behavior includes measuring it with increasingly sophisticated techniques and equipment.

- Behaviors that can only be inferred—so far—include thinking, feeling, being motivated, and the many other "unseeable" activities that go on in our minds; but in studying these behaviors, psychologists must back up what they say with directly observable evidence.
- Psychologists have been known to study plants, and certain areas of psychology study nonhuman animals in their own right, but the goals are most often to understand humans and put this understanding to good use.

What Do Psychologists Do?

There was once a distinction between psychologists who did "basic" research oriented toward knowledge for its own sake—like a physicist seeking to understand the mechanics of the universe—versus those who did "applied" research oriented toward solving individual and societal problems—like a chemist trying to develop a more effective drug for a pharmaceutical company to market. In turn, those who did basic research were "experimental" psychologists and those who did applied research were usually "clinical" psychologists.

In recent decades, however, this distinction has become somewhat blurred. Of the major varieties of psychologists noted in the following, any might be found doing basic research, applied research, or a mix of the two. About half of all psychologists fall into the first category. The remaining half consists of small percentages of the others in the list—plus more to come later in the book.

- **Clinical psychologists** study and treat mental and behavioral disorders, typically the more serious ones. Clinical psychologists often specialize in working with people of different age ranges or who have specific disorders, and psychotherapy and psychological testing are a large part of the work they do.
- **Counseling psychologists** typically work with people who have less severe disorders, people who are having problems with their marriage or other aspects of their lives, or those who want guidance with regard to choosing a vocation.

- **Cognitive psychologists** come in many varieties, but they have in common an interest in understanding basic mental processes such as how we think, learn, and remember.
- **Social psychologists** are primarily interested in how individuals influence and are influenced by others, including how a person's behavior may vary from one social situation to the next.
- **Personality psychologists'** interests sometimes overlap with those of social psychologists in that they are concerned with how others influence who we become; however, they focus more on understanding stable personality characteristics that tend to change little from one situation to the next.
- **Developmental psychologists** study how people grow and change throughout the life span, from conception to death. They often specialize in a certain age range, or an aspect of development such as personality, cognition, or intelligence.
- **School psychologists** and **educational psychologists** work with children in academic settings, with regard to issues ranging from individual adjustment problems to the educational process as a whole.
- **Industrial/organizational psychologists** focus their efforts on work settings and are concerned with issues ranging from job performance to organizational processes and structures as a whole. Some are concerned with human factors such as the "fit" between people and machines.
- **Forensic psychologists** work on a variety of issues involving judicial and correctional systems. One specialty in this area is evaluating "insanity" pleas.
- **Cognitive** and **behavioral neuroscientists** are the newest on the scene. They study relationships between brain, mind, and behavior, and are trained extensively both in psychology and physiology.

As you probably noticed, psychological disciplines often overlap. Beyond what is noted in the previous list, cognitive psychology cuts across most, if not all, the other disciplines listed, as do elements of social psychology and developmental psychology. Modern psychology is indeed a complex network of specialties and interests, although there is a trend worth bearing in mind as we explore research from these and other areas in detail: For the last couple of decades or so, psychologists have increasingly been acknowledging that it is the "whole" person who should be of primary interest, not just specific aspects of development or behavior. However, putting it all together is still very much a work in progress.

Ethics in the Practice of Psychology

In the United States, psychologists must be licensed to practice psychotherapy with individuals or to work with organizations. Licensing ensures that they are properly trained and up-to-date on their particular discipline, and it likewise ensures that they adhere to a strict code of ethics in working with their clients. The code of ethics is specified by the American Psychological Association (APA), the largest organization of U.S. psychologists, and it spells out in detail what psychologists should and should not do in keeping with their professional obligations to safeguard their clients' rights and dignity as human beings.

The APA code also specifies that sexual intimacy between a client and a psychologist is strictly forbidden. So if your therapist "comes on" to you, only two possibilities exist. Your psychologist is violating the code, or your therapist is not really a psychologist or other legitimate therapist. In either case, contact your state psychological association.

Aside from the ethical requirement that a psychologist be competent to perform the services and not misrepresent this, perhaps the most important ethical consideration in the practice of psychology is confidentiality. For example, if you're in psychotherapy, your psychologist cannot divulge any of your personal information without your written consent. To do so would be grounds for a lawsuit and loss of licensure at the least.

There are a few exceptions. One is if, say, a judge issues a court order overriding your confidentiality, perhaps in a criminal case. Another is if you make a statement to the effect that you intend to harm yourself or others. A third is the sharing of scientific knowledge: Your psychologist can write about or otherwise share information about your case, as long as it is done in a manner that in no way identifies you personally. But for the most part by far, your privacy is a cornerstone of your relationship with a psychologist. Different states have different exceptions to confidentiality; for instance, in Massachusetts, psychologists must break confidentiality if a client tells them about the abuse of a child or an elderly person.

Psychology in the Early Years

It is generally agreed that Wilhelm Wundt (1832–1920) founded psychology in 1879 when he established the first "psychological" laboratory at the University of Leipzig in Germany. Wundt set out to study the human mind using a method called *introspection*. In this approach, specially trained individuals attempted to look inside their minds and describe what went on in response to events they were exposed to, such as lights and sounds.

What's wrong with this picture? Although introspection as a research method survived for a few decades and was briefly popular in the United States, it was far too subjective. The introspectors often reported conflicting information and there was no way to verify what any of them said (remember the scientific requirement of objectivity noted earlier).

Introspection has survived in a different form. In some versions of psychotherapy, clients or patients are asked to report their innermost thoughts and feelings, as we'll see in Chapter 17.

Introspection was also the approach used by William James (1842–1910) in the United States, in writing his *Principles of Psychology* (1890)—which for most psychologists marks the beginning of modern psychology. James went into great detail in describing his thoughts and feelings and relating them to psychological processes such as perceiving, emotionality, and memory. Though subjective, many of James's observations have held up reasonably well as later verified by scientific research.

James firmly believed that psychology should be the "study of mental life." He also proposed—in accord with the views of Charles Darwin (1809–1882) on physical evolution—that the human mind as it is today, evolved as a result of successive adaptations by our distant ancestors. This view, which was called *functionalism,* would soon fall into disfavor, but it resurfaced in the later twentieth century as an increasingly popular line of theory and research now known as evolutionary psychology. We'll discuss evolutionary psychology and other biological approaches to understanding behavior in Chapter 3.

Psychoanalysis

Meanwhile, in Austria, Sigmund Freud (1856–1939) was working on his psychoanalytic theory, a work that would span some forty years. We'll return to Freud in detail at various points in the book, but an overview of his theory here is helpful in understanding where psychology went next.

The prevailing view in the late nineteenth century was that humans are rational beings, removed from other animals because of logic and morality. To Freud, humans were anything but rational, instead driven by selfish "animal" impulses (such as desires for nourishment and sex, and what Freud thought was a built-in impulse to commit aggression). Freud alleged that these impulses are biological in origin, and they demand satisfaction even though they are part of what he called the unconscious mind. His was a hedonistic view, stating that we exist to seek pleasure and avoid pain.

We do have "animal" needs that must be satisfied just to survive. These include needs for oxygen, food, and liquids. We also need sex. Although some people might rank this right up there with survival needs, sex has more to do with reproducing our species. Many people manage to get by without being preoccupied with it, contrary to what Freud thought.

When thwarted, impulses cause emotional problems. Along with the fears and guilt over misdeeds—real and imagined—that we accumulate and that become unconscious because they are too painful to think about, they exert pressure on us to behave in maladaptive ways. This is especially the case with desires and guilt of a sexual nature, which Freud saw as primary determinants of behavior. Thus, life is a constant struggle to satisfy, or more often to try to contain, our impulses and guilt if we are to give the appearance of being rational and moral and to be able to live together in relative harmony.

Freud developed his theory through his treatment of typically mildly disordered patients, which eventually yielded the treatment approach he called psychoanalysis. Some of Freud's ideas have survived, but much of his theorizing—especially the part about sex being our "prime mover"—has been discounted. However, he is still regarded as one of the most influential figures in all of psychology, and he was the first to attempt a comprehensive theory of personality.

FACT

Have you ever referred to someone as "anal"? If so, you probably meant that the person is stubborn, demanding, and very picky. It's a Freudian term to describe personality characteristics that supposedly result from faulty toilet training. Other Freudian terms and concepts are also still with us. Some make sense; more don't.

Behaviorism

What is best called *strict behaviorism* is an extreme view that only observable behavior is fit subject matter for psychology as a science. Strict behaviorism was a reaction both against introspection and psychoanalytic theory, each of which attempted to deal with the inner and unobservable workings of the mind. It softened somewhat over the years, but the basic idea of studying only what can be seen or measured dominated U.S. psychology for most of the first half of the twentieth century.

J. B. Watson (1878–1958) is often credited with being the founder of strict behaviorism, but he's an unlikely candidate. In the early 1920s Watson did become the spokesperson for this approach, but the real credit goes to two researchers who preceded him by years. These were E. L. Thorndike (1874–1949) in the United States and Ivan Pavlov (1849–1936) in Russia.

Thorndike's Cats

Thorndike's most noteworthy contribution was his "law of effect," which he derived from work with laboratory animals—primarily cats. In brief, he proposed that any behavior that is followed by a satisfying state of affairs (such as getting food) tends to be repeated, and any behavior that is followed by an unsatisfying or unpleasant state of affairs (such as experiencing pain) tends not to be repeated. "Satisfying" and "unsatisfying" may not sound like terms a strict behaviorist would use, but Thorndike got around that by defining *satisfying* as something an animal typically approaches and *unsatisfying* as something an animal typically avoids—a nicely behavioral solution. Thorndike's work laid the groundwork for the operant conditioning approach of B. F. Skinner (1904–1990), who ranks alongside Freud among the most influential psychologists of all time and whose work is discussed in Chapter 9.

Pavlov's Dogs

Pavlov's contribution was what is now called *classical conditioning*, which started out somewhat mentalistic but wound up strictly behaviorist. Pavlov's work is also an example of what scientists call serendipity, or accidental discovery. He was originally a renowned physiologist studying digestive processes in dogs, but as legend has it, he became distracted by the observation that his dogs developed a tendency to salivate before food was placed in their mouths. That is, they learned to anticipate food, in much the same way that we might salivate a bit when we approach a restaurant that we like.

Behaviorism Today

Strict behaviorists are oriented toward discovering principles that apply to the behavior of all organisms, human or otherwise, which is no longer a popular approach—nor is the idea that only observable behavior can be studied scientifically. Nevertheless, they had a major if extreme impact on psychology with their emphasis on scientific method. Nowadays there are few strict behaviorists, but the legacy of this approach is alive and well. As opposed to shunning behavior that cannot be directly observed, psychologists now embrace it. But the bottom line is still observable, verifiable evidence.

The contributions of Thorndike, Pavlov, Skinner, and their many adherents have been reinterpreted and are better understood in cognitive terms, with regard to what laboratory animals and people "think" in situations that involve conditioning. But this does not mean that principles of conditioning are outmoded. They still explain a great variety of behaviors—for humans as well as laboratory animals.

Strict behaviorism was a reaction to the nonscientific approaches that preceded it. In turn, the approaches that followed were in large measure reactions to strict behaviorism, psychoanalytic theory, or both. And added to that is the impact of modern technology, which allows for measuring behavior at a level of precision that the early theorists could only dream about.

Humanistic Psychology and Positive Psychology

By the middle of the twentieth century, some personality theorists had long been arguing that there is more to being human than simply satisfying or controlling animal desires, or seeking pleasure and avoiding pain. Both psychoanalytic theory and strict behaviorism were limited to these factors in explaining human behavior. They had little to say about positive and uniquely human desires such as helping others, belonging to family and society, and becoming all that you can become as a person.

Enter the humanistic psychologists, the best known of whom were Carl Rogers (1902–1987) and Abraham Maslow (1908–1970). Their credo was that humans are different from other animals in important ways. Although we certainly have needs in common with other animals and can be quite selfish at times, there's more to being human. We have goals in life, we have a need to grow and fulfill ourselves psychologically and feel good about it all, and we have a need to find happiness that goes beyond satisfaction of basic needs. To the humanists, the positive thinking and hoping that both the psychoanalysts and strict behaviorists ignored are the most important aspects of human behavior.

Then came positive psychology, which is an approach that runs parallel to that of the humanists but has a different emphasis. In the view of Martin Seligman, a prominent proponent of positive psychology, far too much emphasis has been placed on understanding undesirable and maladaptive aspects of human behavior—such as disorders and criminal behavior—and far too little has involved understanding the good things that people do—the things that lead to happiness, well-being, and being functional members of society. It isn't that undesirable behaviors aren't important; it's just that desirable ones are too. The details and impact of humanistic psychology and positive psychology are discussed further in Chapter 14.

QUESTION?

As humans, are we basically just selfish animals or are we more? The answer depends on your observations as well as those of the theorists. If you believe that people are hedonistic at the core, we're basically just animals. If you believe that people have concerns that go beyond their own needs, we're more. Give it some thought.

Cognitive Psychology

Cognitive psychology took off in the 1960s, having been launched by the information-processing model developed by Allen Newell (1927–1992) and Herbert Simon (1916–2001) some years earlier. As noted, cognitive psychology and its scientific approaches to studying mental processes have now been incorporated into virtually all areas of psychology. We'll see its effects throughout the book.

Newell and Simon did indeed launch a "cognitive revolution" with their model, which is based on computer analogies. Simply put, human information processing begins with input from the external environment, which is then stored temporarily in the conscious mind—for immediate use, such as when we look up a number and make a phone call—or is processed further and stored permanently for future use—such as making the call again from memory. The stages involved are thus encoding, storage, and retrieval, and the complexities of how we accomplish this are the subject of Chapter 10.

FACT

The information-processing model doesn't completely describe what humans do. Your computer uses serial processing; only one bit of information at a time is processed, even when your computer is multitasking. In contrast, the human mind is capable of parallel processing: thinking about more than one thing at a time.

Biological Psychology

Other areas of psychology that are having increasingly broad impact across the major psychological disciplines fall under the umbrella term *biological psychology*. This refers in general to researchers who study relationships between behavior and any aspects of bodily functioning, but foremost among them nowadays are those who search for direct links between behavior and the brain or behavior and the mind. Those who stay fairly close to observable brain-behavior relationships are called *behavioral neuroscientists*. Those who extend their study to the as-yet unobservable processes of the mind are called *cognitive neuroscientists*.

Both use highly sophisticated brain scanning and monitoring equipment to study what goes on in the brain in response to external events or while certain tasks are being performed. Their research includes accurately assessing which areas of the brain are active in a given situation and how the flow of information through the brain takes place. Their approach is being applied to areas such as understanding the physiological bases for learning and memory, emotionality, and mental and behavioral disorders.

Culture, Ethnicity, and Diversity in Modern Psychology

In the early years of psychology and continuing into the latter part of the twentieth century, it was mostly taken for granted that all human beings are the same where psychological functioning is concerned. At the same time, almost all psychologists were white North Americans or Europeans, and they mostly studied white people like themselves. There were some exceptions, such as research that compared whites and blacks or females and males, but even this was narrowly focused on topics such as intelligence.

By and large, psychology ignored the effects of culture, which is the aggregate of the practices and the beliefs and generally the heritage of differing groups of people. They likewise paid little attention to ethnicity, which includes a person's culture but traditionally adds biological heritage and considerations such as "race." The same went for diversity, which emphasizes ethnicity as well as gender, sexual orientation, age, and anything else that might consistently distinguish people psychologically.

Many scientists now believe that "race" has no scientific basis whatsoever. One important reason is that all modern humans appear to have originated in Africa, which means that we all have the same ancestors. Another is that so-called racial characteristics aren't clear-cut—you'll find almost every imaginable combination of skin color, facial features, and so on. In all, there is only one human race.

People often use the terms *culture* and *society* interchangeably, but there is a distinct difference. As noted, culture consists of beliefs, heritage, and the like—largely abstract things. In contrast, a society is an organized group of people—a physical thing. Thus, it has been observed that culture is to a society as personality is to an individual.

In the last couple of decades, psychologists have come to appreciate the potential impact of these considerations and a flood of research on cultural differences in particular has ensued—indeed, so much so that researchers are still grappling with how to sort it out. A major finding, however, is that there are consistent psychological differences between people who live in individualist cultures, such as Western societies in which individual accomplishments are emphasized, versus collectivist cultures, such as Asian societies in which the emphasis is on group accomplishments. Research comparing the two has had its greatest impact on social psychology, as we'll see in Chapters 18 and 19.

How to Become a Psychologist

Having surveyed what psychology is, what psychologists do, and where it all came from, you might be wondering how people get to be psychologists in the first place. There are several routes; here's the most common one. First, you major in psychology as an undergraduate student, also taking as many natural science, math, and computer courses as you can work in to your schedule. And you make very good grades throughout.

That's actually the easy part. Next, you apply to graduate programs in psychology, many of which also require that you score high on the Graduate Record Exam (GRE). You will also need strong letters of recommendation from faculty members whom you somehow managed to get to know as an undergraduate. Work experience in psychology, especially any research experience that you managed to gain as a lab assistant helps a lot too. Basically, you do everything you can to prepare yourself and make yourself a strong candidate—competition is fierce and only a very small percentage of applicants are admitted. If you are applying to be a clinical psychologist, it also helps to get volunteer or practicum experience working in human services, such as homeless or domestic violence shelters.

So you're in! Now comes the really hard part: You have to do the work, and you're likely to find that it's quite difficult and demanding—especially during the first year, which is always the hardest. In all, you have to really *want* to be a psychologist, and while in graduate school you have to devote your life to it.

If all goes well, you eventually receive your Doctor of Philosophy (Ph.D.) degree, which is the most common one for psychologists. If your degree is primarily clinical, it probably took you three or four years in the graduate program plus another year of internship in a mental health setting—not counting how much additional time it took you to do your dissertation. If your degree is primarily experimental, the time was much the same except for the internship. But especially if your primary interest is research, either clinical or experimental, you'll probably want to continue past the Ph.D. with at least a one-year "post doc" to continue your training and help you get established.

Chapter 2

How Psychologists Know What They Know

Like other scientists, psychologists prefer experiments that assess what causes what, and they conduct and publish thousands of these each year. However, experiments aren't always possible. Fortunately, psychologists have various methods that mostly rely either on observation or on people's self-reports of their thoughts and feelings. Where necessary, psychologists also conduct experiments with laboratory animals.

Experiments—The Cornerstone of Psychology

The basic idea of psychological experimentation is that the researcher manipulates certain aspects of a situation to see what happens to the behavior of participants or subjects as a result. What the researcher manipulates are called *experimental conditions.* If the experiment is conducted according to proper procedures, and if the participants' or subjects' behavior differs as a result of the experimental conditions, the researcher can conclude that the manipulation caused the difference.

When humans are involved in psychological research, they're called *participants.* When laboratory animals are involved, they're called *subjects*. If you're curious, terms and many other aspects of talking and writing about psychology are specified in *The Publication Manual of the American Psychological Association (5th ed.).*

An Example Experiment

Here's a classic experiment on children and their learning of aggression conducted in the 1960s by Albert Bandura—a prominent social-learning theorist. Three groups of young children saw a film in which an adult "model" beat up and shouted at a Bobo doll in highly specific ways. The film was the same for all the children except for the ending: One group saw the model rewarded (praised) for doing a good job of beating up Bobo, one group instead saw the model punished (scolded) for beating up Bobo, and one group saw the model experience no consequences.

Next came what was called the *performance phase* of the experiment. Each child was allowed to play with a Bobo alone and the question was how many of the model's behaviors the children would imitate. So far, no surprises. Children who had seen the model punished imitated few behaviors; children who had seen the model either be rewarded or experience no consequences imitated significantly more.

Finally came the *learning phase,* in which each child was offered rewards for imitating the model's behaviors. Surprise: The differences between the groups disappeared and the children all imitated the behaviors at a high level. That is, all the children had learned how to mistreat Bobo in detail; the ones who saw the model punished simply didn't display this learning until the right time, when there was an incentive for doing so instead of—in their minds—the possibility of punishment. An important implication of this experiment and many related ones that followed is that when children watch violent TV shows and movies, it doesn't much matter if the "bad guys" get it in the end. Children (and adults) still learn how to commit violence and aggression. Later, they may use this learning if the occasion seems to warrant it, especially if they don't think they will be caught and punished.

QUESTION?

What is a Bobo doll?
Once popular as a toy on which children could harmlessly "vent" their aggressive urges, a Bobo is a soft plastic blowup with a grin on its face and a weight in the bottom. When struck, it goes over and then bounces back up for more.

Elements of a Good Experiment

Psychological experimenters must attend to certain principles and adhere to fairly specific procedures. Otherwise, the results may be difficult if not impossible to interpret or may not be meaningful. The following is a partial list of important considerations in conducting experiments, using Bandura's experiment for reference:

- Participants are typically randomly assigned to experimental conditions in the hope that each group will be equivalent in any important respects. Bandura randomly assigned children in the hope that the groups, overall, would be equivalent in aggressiveness.
- Each group has exactly the same experiences except for differences in the experimental conditions. In Bandura's experiment, all the children saw the same film except for the ending.

- If the groups aren't equivalent and treated the same except for experimental conditions, the result is confounding—something other than the conditions might instead be responsible for the results. For example, Bandura's experiment might have been confounded if one group saw the film in the morning and the others in the afternoon, because the afternoon groups might be tired and pay less attention.

- What happens in an experiment must be relevant to the topic under study. The term for this is *operational definition,* and it was reasonable for Bandura—in studying aggressive behavior and imitation—to define these as exposure to an aggressive model and the extent to which the children beat up Bobo.

- Operational definitions also determine the extent to which an experiment reflects what happens in the real world, which is called *external validity.* Most would agree that Bandura's definitions and results shed light on children's observational learning of aggression that might apply to many real-world settings.

ALERT!

Even when these considerations are followed, no researcher should make sweeping generalizations based on a single experiment. We can only say that children learn aggressive behavior through observing it because Bandura's experiments have been replicated extensively by others. That is, similar studies have been conducted with different children, in different settings, with different procedures, and with various other forms of aggressive behavior.

Observational Studies

Careful, accurate observation is essential to experiments and most psychological research, but sometimes it is conducted for its own sake— perhaps simply to detail what people and other animals normally do. *Naturalistic observation* means observing behavior in everyday settings, which could be a school playground, a shopping mall, a freeway, a remote village, a jungle, etc. For example, a researcher might gain insight into what factors are involved in people helping and cooperating with each other simply by observing situations in which they do and comparing these to situations in which they don't. The researcher also would then be in a better position to design experiments to determine what produces helping and cooperating or interferes with it.

Laboratory observation is also a useful tool. Laboratory settings can be either simulations of natural settings or completely artificial. The advantages of observation in a laboratory setting are that a researcher has much more control over what behaviors occur and, as applicable, can use sophisticated instrumentation. A classic example of laboratory observation using instrumentation is the 1960s research of William Masters and Virginia Johnson on the sexual arousal cycles of men and women, in which the researchers took physiological measurements while their participants were having sexual intercourse. Their basic findings about differences between men and women in this respect are still relevant today.

FACT

A question remains about whether the participants in the Masters and Johnson studies were representative of all adult human beings. Probably they were, because basic physiology differs little from one woman or one man to the next. But ask yourself: Would you be willing to have sex while being hooked up to electrodes and watched? Might the participants have been "different" in some important way?

Case Histories and Interviews

A case history is an in-depth study of an individual. Freud based his psychoanalytic theory in part on the case histories of his patients, and they are still used as a prelude to clinical diagnosis and treatment. Case histories consist of interviews with the person, perhaps also with the person's family, and sometimes a combing-through of the person's academic records, legal records, and work history—with the person's permission, of course. Case histories are also at times the method of choice in studying the origins of relatively rare mental and behavioral disorders.

Either way, the goal is to construct a thorough and rich picture of the person's life history and past and present functioning, and a case history's thoroughness is its advantage. The main disadvantage is that—like all psychological research methods except experiments—it cannot determine cause and effect.

Researchers have found that people with "split" or "multiple" personality disorder (currently called *dissociative identity disorder*) often have a history of having been abused as children, which makes it tempting to conclude that abuse is the cause. But there is no way to be sure.

Interviews can be part of a case history or they can serve more immediate purposes in clinical practice. A mental status exam is one; its purpose is to determine a client's current functioning, and it includes relatively informal questions that assess things like bodily functions (Do you sleep well? How's your appetite? Any problems with your sex life?), emotional state (Have you been feeling depressed or anxious lately?), cognitive functioning (Count backward from 100 by 7s. What did you have for breakfast this morning?), and general orientation (What day is it? Where are you and why are you here?). Your general practitioner probably uses some of these questions during your checkup as a screen both for physical complaints and mental problems.

Self-Report Questionnaires and Surveys

Interviews are a form of self-report, but the term more often refers to "paper-and-pencil" questionnaires that researchers have people fill out. They take various forms, such as a simple *Yes, No,* or a more sophisticated *Strongly Agree, Agree, No Opinion, Disagree, Strongly Disagree* in response to statements designed to tap your beliefs, attitudes, preferences, habits, mood, and more. Psychological researchers often use questionnaires to screen experiment participants, also to assess the results of experiments. Questionnaires have the advantage that the answers can easily be turned into numbers for computer analysis—for individuals, or in the case of surveys, for large numbers of people.

FACT

The National Household Survey on Drug Abuse (NHSDA) conducts a survey each year. Workers knock on the doors of thousands of randomly selected households and ask the person who opens the door to complete the survey regarding her or his use of certain substances of abuse. The person completes the survey, seals it in an envelope, and is assured that her or his personal responses will remain strictly confidential.

Questionnaires do of course have their disadvantages as a research tool. Where sensitive topics such as a person's use of drugs, sexual behavior, or attitudes toward his or her employer are concerned, participants may not risk answering truthfully for fear that the responses won't really be kept confidential. A more general problem is that people may not be able to remember their behavior accurately even if they want to respond truthfully. Assuming that it's a number larger than zero or one or so, can you remember exactly how many times you've had sex in the past year? Some people would have difficulty remembering even the past month.

Psychological Tests

Some psychological tests are also self-reports. This time, however, the distinction is that the term applies to inventories of items that have been given to large numbers of people and carefully polished. They are also subjected to statistical analysis so that when they are given to an individual, the researcher or clinician has a much better idea of what the results mean.

There are two general types of psychological tests: those that assess one or another type of ability and those that assess personality. Ability tests come in two varieties: Intelligence tests assess your intellectual/ cognitive functioning and achievement tests assess the progress you've made in acquiring academic or other skills. Clinicians often include intelligence tests in diagnosis; researchers use them the same way that they use self-reports as noted earlier. Achievement tests assess progress during grade school, and some are intended to predict success in college or other advanced training. Personality tests assess relatively stable personality characteristics, using various forms of self-reports. They also are used in diagnosing and researching mental and behavioral disorders. Popular personality tests are discussed in Chapter 13.

The Essential Role of Statistics

Modern psychology couldn't get by without statistics. Some of these simply describe research data and stop there. An example is correlation, which yields a single number that indicates the extent to which two variables are "related." Another example is the set of often-complex statistical computations that help researchers decide whether the results of their experiments are likely to be "real."

A variable is literally anything in the environment or about a person that can take different values. The amount of light or noise in a room is a variable—it differs from one room to the next. Height and weight are variables, as are intelligence, personality characteristics, and a host of observable behaviors, because these differ from one person to the next.

Correlation

In correlation, the resulting number can range from 0 to +1.00 or 0 to −1.00. Where it falls indicates the strength of the correlation. The sign of the correlation indicates its direction. A correlation of 0 is nonexistent; a correlation of either +1.00 or −1.00 is perfect.

For example, to assess the correlation between height and weight, a researcher would measure the height and weight of each of a group of individuals and then plug the numbers into a mathematical formula. This correlation will usually turn out to be noticeable, perhaps about +.63. The

".63" tells us that it is a relatively strong correlation, and the "+" tells us that height and weight tend to vary in the same direction—taller people tend to weigh more, shorter people less. But the correlation is far from perfect and there are many exceptions.

FACT

What the correlations you encounter in this book mean vary somewhat according to the application, but here's a rule of thumb: A correlation between 0 and about +.20 (or 0 and –.20) is weak, one between +.20 and +.60 (or –.20 and –.60) is moderate, and one between +.60 and +1.00 (or –.60 and –1.00) is strong.

As another example, a researcher might assess the extent to which people's blood alcohol content (BAC) is related to their ability to drive. The participants might be asked to drink and then attempt to operate a driving simulator. Their BACs would then be compared with their scores on the simulator, and the researcher might find a correlation of –.68. This is again a relatively strong correlation, but the "–" tells us that BAC and driving ability vary in an opposite direction—the higher the BAC, the lower the driving ability.

Inferential Statistics

For descriptive statistics such as correlation, the "mean" or average, and some others we consider in context later in the book, the purpose is to describe or summarize aspects of behavior to understand them better. Inferential statistics start with descriptive ones and go further in allowing researchers to draw meaningful conclusions—especially in experiments. These procedures are beyond the scope of this book, but the basic logic is helpful in understanding how psychologists know what they know.

Again recalling Bandura's experiment of observational learning of aggression, consider just the model-punished and model-rewarded groups. It was stated that the former children imitated few behaviors and the latter significantly more. What this really means is that, based on statistical analysis, the difference between the two groups was large enough and consistent enough to be unlikely to have occurred simply by "chance." That is, it would have been a long shot to obtain the observed difference if what happened to the model wasn't a factor. Thus, Bandura and colleagues discounted the possibility of chance alone and concluded that what the children saw happen to the model was the cause of the difference in their behavior.

This logic may seem puzzling to you, and it isn't important that you grasp it to understand the many experiments that are noted throughout this book. Indeed, it isn't mentioned again. The point of mentioning it at all is to underscore that people are much less predictable than chemical reactions and the like, and therefore have to be studied somewhat differently—usually without formulas.

Psychologists study what people tend to do in a given situation, recognizing that not all people will behave as predicted—just as the children in the model-rewarded group did not all imitate all the behaviors. In a nutshell, the question is simply whether a tendency is strong enough—as assessed by statistics—to warrant a conclusion about cause and effect.

Ethics in Psychological Research

Just as there is a tight code of ethics that governs how psychologists practice their profession with clients (Chapter 1), there is a code that governs how they conduct their research that is mandated by the APA and public law. This applies to research both with humans and laboratory animals. The following is a list of primary ethical considerations in psychological research with humans:

• Psychologists must never knowingly conduct research that has the potential for immediate, significant harm or lasting harm of any kind; they can make their participants uncomfortable or upset, but only mildly and only if the research question justifies it.

- Research participants always take part entirely voluntarily, without coercion, and they can stop participating at any point without penalty—they don't even have to say why.
- A major aspect of voluntary participation is informed consent. Participants must be told in advance what to expect in experiments or other research efforts, and it must be made clear to them that they can stop participating at any time.
- Although participants must be told what to expect, they don't necessarily have to be told the true nature of the experiment—they can be deceived in this respect, because people may behave quite differently if they know what an experimenter is really interested in.
- When deception is used—as it often is in research with humans—participants must be thoroughly debriefed afterward, which means that they are told the true nature of the experiment and are allowed to ask questions and express any concerns they have.
- As in psychological practice, all information about a particular participant's behavior is strictly confidential and every effort must be made to keep it that way.
- Institutional review boards (IRBs), comprised of professionals, evaluate all proposed research to determine if there are potential ethical problems with any of the research practices. IRBs may suggest changes and they can withhold approval for the research to be conducted.

In accord with these ethical principles, by far most psychological research with human participants is benign. It is possible, however, for psychologists to conduct approved research with the best of intentions and inadvertently have things turn out other than they had planned. We'll see some examples of this later in the book.

Psychological research with laboratory animals—especially research that is harmful to them—has steadily declined in recent years. When it is conducted, the harm is kept to the absolute minimum necessary to answer the research questions at hand.

In research with laboratory and other animals, the principles regarding the potential for harm are of course not as strict. Important research—particularly that of an experimental nature and that risks significant harm—can be conducted only with nonhuman animals. Nowadays, however, the question is always whether it is truly warranted. The main consideration in using laboratory animals for research is that they must be treated humanely, which includes caring for them responsibly and attending to their health and needs.

ALERT!

Should you find yourself in a psychological experiment, say, in response to an ad in your local media, remember the part about quitting at any point without penalty. Participants usually are paid, and what the principle means is that you must be paid in full if you begin an experiment—whether or not you complete it. Withholding payment would be coercion.

Chapter 3

The Biology of Psychology

Our biological functioning is a constant hum of activity, most of which we aren't aware of. Normally, this activity is orderly and coordinated as we go through our days and live our lives. Here we take a look at the role of the nervous system, the role genes play, and some ideas on where it all came from in an evolutionary sense.

Neurons and What They Do

Neurons are the starting point in understanding the human nervous system. The nervous system is comprised of many billions of neurons—some estimates go over 100 billion—and they come in many varieties, each with a highly specialized function. However, neurons do have some essential things in common.

The Basic Structure of a Neuron

Like other cells, neurons have a cell body with a nucleus and other structures that keep them alive. Also like other cells, the nucleus contains genes that cause a neuron to become what it is in the first place. Early in life—mostly during the prenatal period—these genes also cause neurons to reproduce as the nervous system matures.

The remaining structures are involved in processing information. A neuron receives signals from other neurons at branches called *dendrites* and at smaller receptor sites on the cell body. It sends signals to other neurons via its axon terminals. In between is the axon, which, when conditions are right, generates a signal to its terminals. Many axons also have a myelin sheath, which serves a purpose similar to that of the insulation on an electrical wire.

Neural Transmission

Neurons aren't directly connected to other neurons. A neuron's axon terminal and another's dendrite or receptor site "connect" via a synapse, which contains a minuscule gap across which neurotransmitters flow. Within the human brain in particular, a given neuron may synapse with thousands of other neurons, giving rise to many trillions of such interconnections—a level of complexity that staggers the imagination and helps us see why unraveling the workings of the nervous system is such a formidable task.

Neurotransmitters are minute biochemicals; there are perhaps several hundred different kinds. Some neurotransmitters stimulate the next neuron in line, while others inhibit it. When the balance of neurotransmitters present at the synapses of a neuron is sufficiently favorable, the axon "fires" and releases neurotransmitters to still other neurons, and so on in endless cycles of activity.

FACT

A "nervous breakdown" is not what it might seem. If your central nervous system were to break down like a car engine, you wouldn't run at all, and that would be the end of things. Instead, typically because of extreme stress, you lose the ability to think clearly and control your emotions—with proper care, this usually lasts for only a few days or weeks.

On a larger scale, an abundance or shortage of certain neuro-transmitters in different areas of the brain affects our thought processes, emotionality, and overall level of arousal. One way psychologists know this is that alcohol and other "psychoactive" drugs—including medicinal ones—affect the brain through altering the levels of specific neuro-transmitters. For example, "depressant" drugs alter certain neurotransmitter levels with the general effect of slowing down brain functioning, whereas "stimulant" drugs alter certain levels and speed it up. Another way neurotransmitters are implicated is through their association with certain mental disorders.

The Central Nervous System

The central nervous system consists of the spinal column and the brain. The spinal column primarily houses a "cable" of nerves (bundles of neurons) through which the brain communicates with the rest of the body; this cable is called *the spinal cord*. The brain is best thought of as the "executor" of the nervous system as a whole.

The Spinal Cord

The spinal cord consists of neurons that (1) relay sensory information to the brain, keeping the brain aware of external stimulation and internal bodily functioning, and (2) transmit information from the brain eventually to muscles that generate movement and to internal organs to control their functioning. The spinal cord also contains tiny interneurons (which link the sensory and motor neurons) that can bypass the brain. The knee-jerk reflex is an example: A doctor's tap to the patellar tendon of the knee causes it to jerk, and the connection is a direct one through the spine. The jerk tells the doctor that the connection is intact.

The Brain

The vast number of interneurons of the brain itself constitutes the center of the entire nervous system. They receive and transmit information through the spinal cord and in other ways, but by far the greater part of their activity is processing information through their myriad synapses. Somehow, this constant and incredibly intricate activity gives rise to consciousness and "mind."

It may seem obvious to say that the brain is the location of mental activity, but this was not always thought to be the case. For example, some of the ancient Greek philosophers attributed mind and "soul" to the liver. And at various points in history, the location was thought to be the heart. The ancient Egyptians even threw away the brain of a mummy, assuming it would not be important in the afterlife!

The brain consists of a number of areas that are now known to be involved in specific functions, both bodily and mental. Although the brain always works as a whole, certain areas are more active than others when different activities are taking place. We'll return to the complexities of what these areas are and what they do in Chapter 4.

The Peripheral Nervous System

Through their connections with the spinal cord and in some cases directly, the neurons of the peripheral nervous system are the rest of the chain that carries information to and from the brain. In contrast to interneurons, these can be quite long—extending much of the length of the body. Those that relay information to the central nervous system are called *afferent neurons* and those that relay information from the central nervous system are called *efferent neurons*. Based on function, the peripheral nervous system is subdivided into the somatic nervous system and the autonomic nervous system.

The Somatic Nervous System

The afferent neurons of the somatic nervous system relay signals from sensory receptors in the eyes and ears, plus those involved in taste, smell, touch, and certain internal sensations. The somatic nervous system's efferent neurons relay signals to the many skeletal muscles, ranging from those that produce "gross motor" activity such as walking, running, and jumping, to those that produce "fine motor" activity such as manipulating objects with the fingers. The brain coordinates the somatic nervous system and, for example, enables us to hear something, turn to look at it, and perhaps reach out and touch or grasp it.

The Autonomic Nervous System

The afferent and efferent neurons of the autonomic nervous system monitor and help regulate the internal workings of the body, such as breathing, heart rate, and the many other activities necessary to life. It is also important to your overall level of arousal and your emotional state: feeling up, feeling down, feeling "wired," feeling "laid back." An extreme example is the fight or flight reaction.

In addition to the presence of threat or danger, any strenuous activity can halt digestive processes. This is the reason for the long-standing observation that you shouldn't go swimming after eating. The life-threatening stomach cramps you may experience are a result of digestion temporarily shutting down.

Given the appropriate signals from the brain and working in concert with the endocrine system (discussed in the following section), its sympathetic division initiates a variety of changes that help prepare the body to cope. When the danger is over, the parasympathetic division counteracts these effects and brings the body back to a normal state.

Most of the time, the interplay between the sympathetic and parasympathetic divisions helps maintain homeostasis, a sort of "steady state" within the limits necessary for the body to stay alive. Much like the way a thermostat tries to maintain a constant temperature in a house, homeostatic reactions try to maintain vital bodily states. For example, if your temperature starts to become too high, you perspire and the liquid cools your body a bit. If your temperature starts to become too low, you shiver and the heat generated by the muscle activity warms you up a bit.

The Endocrine System

The endocrine system works very closely with the nervous system, although it is not classified as part of it. Endocrine glands secrete a variety of hormones, which are biochemicals that travel through the bloodstream. The "master gland" is the pituitary, which secretes some hormones that directly affect emotionality and arousal, and some that stimulate other glands to secrete theirs. The onset of puberty and menopause are examples of complex processes that are governed by hormone levels.

FACT

The effects of hormones take a while to wear off. Thus, if you get a whiplash in a traffic accident, you initially don't feel much pain but it becomes excruciating later when the endorphins subside. If you have a terrifying near miss, your "adrenaline rush" may produce so much arousal that you have to pull over for a while to get yourself under control.

During the fight or flight reaction, the pituitary releases endorphins, which are natural painkillers that work at the synaptic level and reduce the sensation of pain—highly adaptive if someone or some thing is assaulting you. The pituitary also stimulates the adrenal glands to secrete epinephrine (formerly called adrenaline), a hormone that is the agent by which the sympathetic nervous system increases heart rate, blood sugar level, and red blood cells, in each case providing you with more energy—highly adaptive if you decide to run or fight back.

Genes and What They Do

Genes are segments of the deoxyribonucleic acid (DNA) that is present in the nucleus of each of the roughly 200 different kinds of cells in the body (here, neurons are simply one kind). Your first reaction to genes is perhaps that they are involved in sexual reproduction and heredity, or that genes help determine what we look like. Both are true, but these aren't their only functions or necessarily their most important ones. A small but significant number of genes synthesize the proteins that make life possible in the first place. That is, they make it possible for us to live and then reproduce.

QUESTION?

What is DNA?
It's a number of "clusters" of six specific molecules, where molecules are compounds one step above atoms. In turn, a gene is a segment of DNA that can contain from hundreds to millions of these clusters.

Proteins

Proteins are molecules that perform a multitude of crucial functions both within cells and throughout the body. Humans have over 200,000 known proteins, with more undoubtedly waiting to be discovered. All are important, and an absence or malformation of a single kind can cause severe physical and mental disorders such as those discussed. Here are a few commonly occurring proteins and what they do:

- *Enzymes,* the most common, break down or otherwise process biochemicals; this occurs within cells, also within internal organs—the enzymes in your digestive tract break down the food you eat into molecules that your body can use.

- Red blood cells contain the protein *hemoglobin,* which binds with oxygen and transports it through the bloodstream to cells and especially the brain.
- *Collagen* is a protein essential to the formation of skin, bones, blood vessels, and the walls of a number of internal organs.
- *Actin* and *myosin* are specialized proteins that enable your muscles to move.
- Hair is made of a specialized protein called *keratin,* as are fingernails and toenails.

Genes and Chromosomes

Genes exist in larger collections called *chromosomes.* These are distinctly visible under a microscope, but only when their genes come together during cell division and reproduction. Humans normally have twenty-three pairs of chromosomes with thousands of genes each, where—with some notable exceptions—one member of each pair comes from the mother and the other from the father. All of the chromosomes on the first twenty-two pairs—called *autosomes*—are alternates with regard to their genetic contents. That is, for each gene on one chromosome there is a counterpart on the other that can perform the same function. The members of the pairs are called *alleles.*

The twenty-third and smallest pair determines sex, so these are called the *sex chromosomes.* In females, who are said to be XX for this pair, the arrangement is the same as with the autosomes—there are corresponding alleles on each chromosome. However, males are XY, denoting that the Y chromosome is different. It is much smaller than the X and contains far fewer genes, so that many of the X chromosome genes have no corresponding allele on the Y chromosome.

Gene Expression

Many genes play an important role in what you look like, how intelligent you may become, and perhaps even aspects of your personality. Increasingly, as work on the human genome continues, researchers are linking specific genes to psychological functioning and behavior. "Linking," however, is an important qualifier. In many cases, your genotype, which is your genetic makeup, does not entirely determine your phenotype, which is who and what you actually are. The link between genotype and phenotype can range from simple to exceedingly complex.

Simple Dominance-Recessiveness

Some characteristics are determined by a single gene and are affected little if at all by the environment that you experience. An example is the texture of your hair, which is directly determined by a single gene. The allele for curly hair—let's call it *C*—is dominant over the recessive allele for straight hair—call this *S*. This means that whenever either or both of the alleles for hair texture are C, the person will have curly hair, and only when both alleles are S will a person have straight hair.

Suppose both parents are CS for hair texture. Thus, their child can be CC, CS, SC, or SS for these alleles. The child will then have a 75 percent chance of having curly hair (3 combinations out of 4) and only a 25 percent chance of straight hair (1 out of 4). If either parent is CC, no SS combination is possible.

Environmental factors can intervene, of course. This is a bit of a stretch, but your parents or you can apply "straighteners" to curly hair or "curlers" to straight hair. Your phenotype is then different from your genotype—at least until your hair grows out.

Partial Dominance-Recessiveness

Allele combinations can also display partial dominance and recessiveness. A classic example is the sickle-cell trait, which occurs primarily among people of black African ancestry and is believed to have developed originally because it enhanced the chances of survival. Here, the partially recessive gene that produces "sickle-shaped" red blood cells—which are less efficient than normal ones at transporting oxygen—are at the same time highly resistant to the mosquito-transmitted malaria that is rampant in Africa's wet regions. Thus, a person in these regions who has one allele for normal red blood cells and the other for sickled ones has a better chance of survival than does a person who has all normal blood cells. A mix of the two works best in an environment where malaria is a strong possibility.

People with the mix of red blood cells tend to experience joint pains from time to time and need to avoid high altitudes where the oxygen content of the air is low. But they survive. In contrast, those who have all sickled cells as a result of both alleles being the recessive for the trait have much more severe symptoms and cannot survive without regular transfusions of normal blood.

Alleles that fall in the category of codominance are neither dominant nor recessive. The result is a blend of the two, which happens in blood types. If a person has one allele for A positive and the other for B positive, the person's blood type will be AB positive.

Genotype, Phenotype, and Polygenic Expression

Even where one pair of genes is concerned, genotype doesn't always determine phenotype. Hair type, blood traits, and blood type aren't affected by environmental factors, but many other physical characteristics are. For example, genes may set the stage for how tall or heavy or muscular a person may be, but environmental considerations such as nutrition and exercise are important factors too. Malnutrition, especially during early childhood, can make the phenotype much less than what it was genetically set to be. Exceptionally good nutrition, exercise, and so on can instead enhance the phenotype.

An additional complication is polygenic expression, which is characteristic of psychological traits such as intelligence and personality. The prevailing view is that a multitude of yet to be identified genes are responsible for complex characteristics such as these, and in turn that these are strongly affected by the environment in which a person grows up. We'll take a further look at the interaction between heredity and environment at various points in the book.

Evolution and Humans

The scientific view is that we as "modern humans" evolved in much the same way as other forms of life did. But from there, much remains to be explained about why and how we developed our proclivity for walking upright, thinking abstractly, using language, manipulating objects to make increasingly sophisticated tools, and—jumping to the present—developing technology that until fairly recently would have defied anyone's imagination. In addition, the story often changes with new "finds" by paleontologists and physical anthropologists who study fossil records and by biogeneticists who attempt to trace the evolution of human DNA. Here we'll look at factors in evolution with emphasis on humans.

FACT

We belong to a family called Hominidae, a line that began some 5 to 7 million years ago when our ancestors diverged from those of chimpanzees. Our exact line of descent isn't known, but it appears that we emerged relatively recently—some 150,000 years ago, more or less. *Homo sapiens sapiens* distinguishes us from *Homo sapiens neanderthalensis* (the Neanderthals), who preceded us but "vanished" about 35,000 years ago.

Darwin's Survival of the Fittest

Darwin explained evolution in terms of natural selection, in which the fittest have the best chance to survive and reproduce. This is called *direct fitness.* But profound though the concept was, Darwin had no biological basis for how this might happen—an understanding of the operation of genes was still decades away.

In the modern and more complete view of Darwin's survival of the fittest, hominids across the millennia either were subjected to changing environments or they migrated and subjected themselves to change. Change is the key. It often meant living in different environments such as jungles versus open savannahs and dealing with radically different climates. It meant finding different plant and animal food sources—plus catching or scavenging the latter. And it meant coping with different predators, of which there were many.

Thus, those of our ancestors who were best able to adapt and survive long enough to reproduce were more likely to pass along their genes to future generations. Those who were least able were less likely to reproduce their genes. Across generations, then, the gene pool would gradually change to favor adaptive characteristics in a given population, in accord with the environment in which they had to live.

Why would some individuals be more fit than others? As noted earlier, children aren't exact genetic blends of their parents. We return to several ways that this happens when we look at the reproductive cycle in Chapter 20, but one important way is mutation. At times and seemingly at random, the DNA that makes up genes changes in subtle ways, some of which are adaptive. Chance is again the key. If a person happens to inherit a mutation that is highly adaptive for a given environment, the odds are that the individual will have more children and likewise more successful ones—thus having a major impact on the gene pool down the line.

Indirect Fitness and Inclusive Fitness

Lacking information about the role of genes, Darwin couldn't see another important way that some characteristics get passed along and others don't. In addition to direct fitness, there is the concept of indirect fitness, and the two taken together constitute inclusive fitness. As elaborated by modern geneticists and evolutionary psychologists, indirect fitness works as follows. Anything you do that increases the survival chances of your offspring, or of relatives such as your sisters and brothers and their offspring, passes along at least part of your genes—the ones that you and they have in common. To a lesser but still significant sense, this also applies to members of your tribe or clan—who, at least in prehistoric times, would also share some of your genes.

Thus, for example, whatever genes might be involved in a tendency to help and cooperate with others can also be passed along. Indirect fitness therefore explains how a tendency toward altruism—helping others without regard to yourself, perhaps to the point of self-sacrifice—could have evolved in humans. More generally, it helps explain how we have evolved to be the highly social creatures that we are. Ⓔ

Chapter 4

Brain and Mind— What Makes Us Human

The brain is the center of the nervous system and initiates activities that range from regulating bodily functioning to somehow allowing us to think, feel, plan, and dream. First, we'll look at ideas about where it came from; then we'll look at its structures and functions. Finally we'll ponder how consciousness and mind might best be conceptualized in scientific terms.

Origins of the Human Brain

Why the early hominids walked upright—which is associated with their divergence from chimpanzees' ancestors—remains a matter of debate. It certainly was convenient, in that it allowed hominids to use their hands for manipulating tools and wielding weapons instead of simply for getting around. They could also carry things while they traveled. Travel and migration may have been necessary because of environmental change that sent early hominids out of dense jungles and into open savannahs, and therein lies another advantage of being upright as opposed to down on all fours: They could see both food sources and threats a lot farther away on the horizon.

How this relates to the evolutionary growth of the human brain remains unclear, except that theorists generally agree that walking upright came first. Something about that was accompanied by growth of the brain. Tool use may have been involved, although the fossil record indicates that increases in brain size and complexity don't correspond to the development of truly sophisticated tools—these didn't start appearing until around the time of *Homo sapiens sapiens*.

QUESTION?

Is the human brain still evolving?
Perhaps the best answer is "yes," that the evolution of the brain is being driven by ever more sophisticated technology that bigger brains can more easily grasp. The problem, however, is that more technologically capable people don't necessarily have more children—at least not yet!

A better candidate is the early formation of social hierarchies and the increasing intelligence necessary to survive and prosper in social interactions. It may be that as some hominids became smarter in developing social skills and "climbing the social ladder," others had to become smarter, too, just to keep up and not be less fit and have their genes drop out of the pool. As generations passed and natural selection exerted itself, there may have been an ever-escalating trend toward higher intelligence and therefore pressures that led to the development of a brain capable of this intelligence. We may, of course, never know.

The Hindbrain

Regardless of what drove human brain structures to their present state of development, the order in which this took place is reasonably well understood. The most primitive and earliest-to-develop part of the human brain is the hindbrain, which is involved in heart rate, breathing, digestion, and other basic activities ultimately administered by the autonomic nervous system, plus reflexes such as sneezing and those involved in balance and motor coordination. Such activities are necessary to the life of many animals, including some relatively low on the scale that have a hindbrain comparable to that of humans.

The Midbrain

Next came the midbrain, which is intimately involved in transmitting visual and auditory information to a portion of the hindbrain as well as controlling eye movements. As discussed in the next chapter, vision is our primary sense. Other animals that also are primarily visually oriented show a corresponding development of the structures of the midbrain. Last came the structures of the forebrain, much of which is what makes us distinctly human. As hominids developed into our present form, the fossil record indicates a steadily increasing growth of the size of the forebrain.

The Forebrain's Structures and Functions

As we continue to work upward in the brain, we encounter the thalamus, which sits on top of the midbrain. The thalamus is involved in sleep and arousal (as are the hindbrain and midbrain to an extent), and it also processes visual and auditory sensory information—as well as much of the information that reaches the brain from the nervous system as a whole. Closely intertwined with the thalamus is the hypothalamus, a particularly interesting structure because it processes information regarding bodily needs, sex, and emotionality. The hypothalamus "controls" the autonomic nervous system and the endocrine system, so it plays an important role in homeostasis.

Above and around those structures is the limbic region, which works along with the hypothalamus. It also contains the hippocampus, a structure that is intimately involved in the formation of memories. And above this is the cerebrum, the area of the brain that is most highly developed in modern humans. We'll return to more specific functions of the brain at various points in the text.

The Cerebrum

The cerebrum comprises about 80 percent of the human brain, and it is extensively convoluted—wrinkled and folded—which allows much more of it to fit in the skull than would otherwise be the case. The outer cerebral cortex or "bark" of the cerebrum is grayish in color and contains some two-thirds of the neurons of the nervous system. The inner layer is whitish and consists of the myelinated axons of these neurons as well as glia—cells that sustain them and play various roles in neural transmission. Like neurons, glia come in a wide variety of types.

FACT

A blow to the brain or an infection can cause irreparable damage. The neurons of the central nervous system don't regenerate, and when damaged, whatever function they served is lost. However, the human brain does display considerable plasticity—the ability to shift functions to other areas and recover them to an extent.

The cerebrum consists of a left hemisphere and a right hemisphere, which are connected by a set of neural pathways called the *corpus callosum*. The brain is essentially symmetrical down its middle. The areas toward the rear of the cerebrum are the occipital lobes, where visual information enters the higher areas of the brain.

Along the middle and sides are the temporal lobes, which process auditory information, and the parietal lobes, which include the somato-sensory area. The latter receives bodily sensations such as from our sense of touch, and it transmits signals that make bodily movement occur. Interestingly, the left side of the body is "mapped" to the right parietal lobe and the right side to the left. This is true of all motor control and all the senses except vision, which, as discussed in Chapter 5, is a partial exception.

But much of the lobes consists of higher association areas. Association areas throughout the brain—especially in the frontal lobes, which consist entirely of association areas—are the most highly developed in humans. These are the areas that are responsible for distinctly human brain activity such as complex and abstract thinking, reasoning, and remembering.

The association areas of the frontal lobes appear to be most involved in higher human thought processes. One obvious line of evidence is that as hominids evolved, the size and shape of the front part of the skull and therefore the frontal lobes increased the most. Even the Neanderthals had a more "sloping" forehead than we do.

Traditional Approaches to Studying the Brain

Neuroscientists have been "mapping" the brain's functions since the nineteenth century. This began with studying loss of behaviors as a result of accidental damage to people's brains. For example, Paul Broca (1824–1880) helped determine that the brain's language centers are primarily in the left hemisphere by studying patients with damage to relatively specific areas of the brain—damage that resulted in speech problems. Wilder Penfield (1891–1976) took a more sophisticated approach called *electrical brain stimulation,* in which tiny and harmless electrical currents are sent through areas of the brain to see what thoughts or other behaviors result. His participants were people who were undergoing necessary brain surgery.

Roger Sperry (1913–1994) took another approach. His participants were people who had their corpus callosum severed as a treatment for severe epilepsy, which has the effect of isolating the hemispheres. Sperry then presented various types of stimuli to only one hemisphere at a time, demonstrating that the hemispheres aren't exactly mirror images. Each performs some functions better than the other.

ALERT!

Research on hemisphere specialization led some to speculate that differences in ability might result from being predominantly a "left-brain" or "right-brain" person. For example, a left-brain person was said to be better at logical reasoning, a right-brain person at artistic or creative endeavors. However, research generally has not borne out this notion.

In the years since, numerous researchers also have used systematic brain lesions (tiny cuts) to study changes produced in laboratory animals such as rats. This research, for example, yielded evidence that areas of the hypothalamus are involved in homeostatic behaviors such as eating. Rats with lesions to one area won't stop eating even when they become obese. Rats with lesions to another area won't eat at all. Still other lesions to the hypothalamus increase or decrease sexual interest.

Neuroscience and Brain Imaging— The Modern Approach

The development of computerized tomography (CT), or "cat scans," heralded a major change in the way neuroscientists study the brain. CT is basically an x-ray procedure that produces pictures of "slices" of the brain taken from rotated angles. The pictures have limited resolution, but CT can be highly effective in spotting brain damage and tumors. Magnetic resonance imaging (MRI) is better: Here, higher-resolution pictures are produced by sending pulses of radio waves through the brain to a magnetic coil.

However, neither approach can provide information about ongoing brain activity and functions. The truly remarkable breakthroughs came with the advent of more sophisticated techniques and computers capable of imaging brain activity as it occurs.

Positron Emission Tomography

In addition to oxygen, the brain runs on a steady supply of glucose (blood sugar), and positron emission tomography (PET) takes advantage of this by the injection of glucose treated with harmless amounts of radioactivity. As this glucose is metabolized by neural cells, special detectors placed on the head record the activity, and computer enhancement yields color images of the level of the activity in different areas of the brain. As a simple example, different areas might be more active when participants are looking at an object, engaging in thinking about it, or talking about it. However, the time required for metabolism produces delays of a minute or more between when the brain activity occurs and when it is displayed, which limits the accuracy of PET. Given the speed at which neural impulses travel—about 100 miles per hour—the researcher is always looking at the past instead of the present.

Functional Magnetic Resonance Imaging

Functional magnetic resonance imaging (fMRI) is much better and is the method of choice until something even better comes along. Here, precision detectors transmit information about areas of naturally occurring oxygen metabolism in the brain for computer enhancement, and the delay is seconds instead of a minute or more.

It appears that brain-imaging technology will provide the basis for the lie detectors of the not so distant future. If specific areas of the brain are consistently active or certain types of ERPs (event-related potentials) appear when people lie, brain-imaging techniques could be much more reliable than today's polygraphs.

Because no "invasive" radioactive substances are involved, fMRI can also be used with any kind of participants—including infants. And the resolution is much finer, although the precision is still on the order of at least a few hundred thousand neurons that might or might not be doing the same thing. It's a safe bet, however, that researchers will continue to refine this method.

Quantitative Electroencephalography

Electroencephalography has been around for a long time. Originally, it consisted of placing two or three electrodes on the skull to measure overall brain electrical activity, such as during wakefulness or varying levels of sleep. In its present form, called Quantitative Electroencephalography (QEEG), the number of electrodes has greatly increased, a skullcap standardizes their location, and the much more localized measures are subjected to computer analysis. This yields event-related potentials (ERPs), that is, minute electrical changes that are studied to localize brain activity—with only milliseconds of delay. This speed also allows QEEG to be used to mark timing as a cross-reference for fMRI, thus increasing its accuracy.

What Is Mind—Earlier Views

Throughout the ages, philosophers have pondered the nature of "mind" and especially its relationship to physiology. The issue has likewise been debated within psychology since the discipline's inception—except for the strict behaviorists who simply dismissed mind altogether as inappropriate for scientific study. First we look at some historical notes on what is known as *the mind-body problem;* then we look at what modern psychologists and neuroscientists have to say.

René Descartes (1596–1650), the first modern philosopher and also a good candidate for the founder of modern physiology, took what came to be a well-known position called *dualism:* Mind or "soul" and body are distinct, separate entities, but they interconnect at some physical point in the brain. Descartes took this to be the smallish pineal gland in the midbrain, whose function in humans remains poorly understood even today. Through this gland, he decided, the inborn "animal" spirits of the body—plus sensory experience—enter the thought processes of the mind, which in turn sends commands for motor activity and the like outward. Thus, mind took on an existence all its own, as did "consciousness."

Descartes coined the famous expression *Cogito, ergo sum* ("I think, therefore I am"), which he took as the starting point in his philosophy. A less known but quite insightful quote from his writings is, in translation, "It is not enough to have a good mind. The main thing is to use it well."

William James later had a good bit to say about mind and consciousness—along with where the latter in particular came from both in humans and other animals. Basically, his view was that it enhanced fitness. As humans, we think about the events we experience, we make decisions, we make things, we change things—in each case enhancing our chances of survival by allowing us to adapt. In James's view, then, consciousness is essential to survival. Without it, we would instead be plants.

What Is Mind—Views Based on Neuroscience

Early researchers sought the "location" of consciousness in the brain, but they didn't get far because they lacked the necessary equipment and methods to study brain activities. It appears that their approach was also misguided. Virtually all psychologists and neuroscientists now agree that mind and consciousness have a purely physical basis in the brain. They take the form of neural pathways, that is, intricately interconnected networks of neurons that vary in their activity levels in accord with the kind of mental activity that is occurring.

Brain imaging is of course the means by which theorists and researchers have arrived at this conclusion. The phenomal experience of the mind, which means the subjective and personal experience that occurs when you think about things or engage in other conscious processes, has neural correlates in the electrochemical processes of the brain and its many billions of neurons. "Neural network theory," which attempts to pull together mental events with corresponding brain activity, has a long way to go in presenting a coherent picture of mind and conscious processes. One problem is achieving the necessary level of resolution, as noted earlier: fMRI, for example, as yet can only look at bundles of hundreds of thousands of neurons at a time. But the basis is a sound one and most agree that a coherent picture will eventually emerge.

FACT

Most cat owners believe that their pets have a mind and are conscious. Whereas Descartes restricted mind to humans and saw other animals mainly as "automata" or machines, James endowed other animals with minds as well. Consistent with the views of modern neuroscientists, it appears that your cat does have a mind, and a mind of its own, too.

So mind and consciousness are the constant hum of neural activity that becomes discernible during the prenatal period and continues uninterrupted until you die. Soul is another matter. If you equate soul with mind, then death brings a halt to soul as well. But if you separate soul as some special kind of matter that exists beyond brain activity—as Descartes did—then soul in some form might live on. Your position here is entirely one to be made by you or those whose teachings you respect—life after death is as yet beyond the purview of science.

Chapter 5

How We Experience Our World

Psychologists have long studied principles of how we become aware of and interpret events in the world around us. In this chapter, we'll explore vision, audition, and the other senses, each of which plays an important role in daily functioning and survival.

Sensation and Perception

Sensation is the process by which the sensory receptors detect and then transduce, or "transform," incoming stimulation from the external world—or from within the body—into neural impulses. These are then relayed to various areas of the central nervous system for further processing, which constitutes perception. Perception includes higher cognitive processes such as discriminating, recognizing, interpreting, and understanding the incoming information, and it is closely integrated with other cognitive processes such as learning and memory. In other words, perception is how we "make sense" of the ongoing events in our world so we can function in it as well as acquire and accumulate knowledge about it.

Sensory Thresholds

Each of our senses responds to a different and specific kind of stimulation, but the senses do have some things in common. In addition to transduction, they have absolute thresholds—minimum levels of stimulation necessary to trigger them in a given situation. For you to hear a sound, for example, it has to occur at some minimum intensity that will trigger the receptors in your ears. The senses also have difference thresholds, which refers to the amount of change in stimulation necessary for the change to be discernible. For you to hear a change in the intensity of a sound, it has to be sufficient to trigger a change in the neural impulses being sent by the receptors in your ears.

Sensory Adaptation

Sensory adaptation is another process that is characteristic of all the senses. As receptors are continually exposed to the same stimuli, their thresholds increase and you become less aware of the stimulation—or perhaps entirely unaware of it. For example, as you sit in your chair and read this, you are unaware of the chair and the clothing in between pressing against your body—unless something calls your attention to it, such as this sentence may have. This characteristic of the senses is extremely important in allowing us to focus our attention. We couldn't function if we were constantly distracted by sensations such as the feel of shoes or a wristwatch, the drone of an air conditioner, sounds from outside on the street, and so on.

FACT

It may occur to you that as you stare at something, your field of vision doesn't dim or go blank as sensory adaptation would predict. But vision is no exception. The receptors of the eyes never receive the same stimulation for long because of their automatic and rapid back-and-forth movements that we are entirely unaware of.

From a different perspective, what the senses also have in common is that how they work at the receptor level, where the information they transmit goes, and what perceptions they ultimately produce are relatively well understood. However, what goes on in the brain in between is not. Neuroscientists are in hot pursuit of how the specialized areas of the cortex process incoming stimulation from the senses, but they are only beginning to unravel these mysteries.

Of course, if sensory stimulation is too intense, relatively little adaptation takes place and you can't ignore it. The sound of a jackhammer on a sidewalk just outside your window is unlikely to "go away." Similarly, the loud and steady bass *thumpa-thumpa-thumpa* of someone's stereo in an apartment next door can be impossible to adapt to and ignore.

The Eyes and Visual Sensation

The human eye is a highly intricate structure with over 100 million receptors that respond and emit neural impulses when stimulated by light. More specifically, they respond to the "wavelengths" of light, where wavelength is exactly what it implies. It is measured in nanometers (billionths of a meter), and what is called our *visible spectrum* is the range from about 400 to 700 nanometers. What we see as purples and violets are the shorter wavelengths; below that are the ultraviolets that we can't see without special equipment. Our reds are the longer wavelengths, above which are the infrareds that we again normally can't see.

After some additional processing by other neurons in the eye, impulses from the receptors travel out the back of the eye via the optic nerve and eventually to the occipital lobes of the brain. In between is the optic chiasm, which is responsible for the partial exception to the opposite-side brain mapping noted in Chapter 4. Here, vision is "split" so that the left visual field of each eye is sent to the right occipital lobe and the right visual field to the left. The evolutionary significance of this may be that if one eye is lost, the entire visual field will still be projected to both occipital lobes from the other eye.

How the Eye Works

Light enters the fluid-filled eye through an outer surface called the *cornea,* which is like the outer glass of a TV camera. Next it passes through an aperture called the *pupil,* which is expanded or contracted by the iris to allow for the intensity of the light—again, much the way a camera works. The lens of the eye, however, works differently. The ciliary muscles control the lens, causing it to "accommodate" and thicken or flatten to bring objects near or far into focus—something that the glass lens of a camera can't do. Finally, the retina is the rear of the eye where the visual receptors are located. Problems with the eye's structures cause many correctable visual problems, including the following:

- A *cataract* is a visible clouding of the cornea that limits the amount of light that can enter the eye, which greatly interferes with vision.
- An irregularly shaped cornea constitutes an *astigmatism,* which interferes with focusing.
- *Myopia,* or "nearsightedness," occurs when the focal point is in front of the retina instead of directly on it; distant objects appear fuzzy.
- *Hyperopia,* or "farsightedness," occurs when the focal point is behind the retina; nearby objects appear blurred.
- *Presbyopia* is a stiffening of the lenses that interferes with accommodation.
- *Glaucoma* is a severe disorder in which the pressure of the fluid within the eye becomes too high and can cause damage to the retina.

The Retina and Its Light Receptors

The retina consists of several layers of interconnected neurons. The deepest layer contains the rods and cones that are the actual light receptors, and the mostly transparent layers above combine signals from these and pass them along to the optic nerve. Rods and cones are named in accord with their shape, and they perform quite different functions.

Rods are by far the most abundant of the 100 million or so receptors and they are sensitive to the intensity (brightness) of the incoming light. Thus, rods are predominantly active in low light, such as on a moonlit night, when we see things mainly in black and white and shades of gray. If you go from a brightly lit area to a dark one, such as when you enter a dark movie theater, you may have to fumble for a seat because it can take up to 30 minutes for your rods to adapt and reach their maximum sensitivity.

The time that is normally required for dark adaptation is why many vehicles—including military ones—have reddish or orange panel lighting. Rods aren't activated by the longer wavelengths of this light, so your eyes remain dark adapted, say, when you're driving down a lonely road at night.

The eye contains only a few million cones, which are concentrated in the fovea—the area of the retina that is the main focal point of the lens. Cones have a much higher threshold for light than rods do, so they are inactive in the dark. Given sufficient light, however, cones have the ability to differentiate wavelengths and are therefore responsible for color vision. There are three kinds of cones, each of which emits signals in response to different wavelengths of light; the interplay between these sets the stage for the experience of color.

You probably know that in low light, you can see an object more clearly if you look just to the side of it. This is because the center of the human fovea contains no rods—only cones. So when you look slightly away, more of the low-light detecting rods that surround the fovea are stimulated and your vision improves.

Visual Perception

Visual perception begins with specialized neurons in the visual cortex of the occipital lobe. Somehow, these neurons interact to give rise to mental images that include shapes, groupings, location, movement, and especially color. Perceptual principles that are based on properties of visual stimuli have been around for quite some time and are the focus here.

Gestalt Principles of Perception

The Gestalt psychologists naturally spent much of their time researching how we perceive "wholes" from partial and sometimes fragmentary visual information. One of the clearest illustrations of their idea that the whole is more than the sum of the parts is the principle of closure. For example, a line drawing of a familiar object such as a human face can omit many details but still easily be perceived as a face—even if parts of the outline are missing.

Another principle is proximity. Here, similar objects that are uniformly spaced tend to be seen as one group. Spread out the objects in trios, however, and the perception will be that there are several groups.

FACT

Similarity is the principle that we tend to perceive groups of objects in accord with the extent to which they are similar. A matrix of circles is seen as just that—a bunch of circles. But if we make some of the circles squares instead, the circles and squares are perceived as separate groups.

Finally, figure-ground is a basic but somewhat more complicated principle of visual perception in which we attend to part of a visual stimulus as the figure and ignore the rest of the image as the background. The classic "vase and faces" reversible figure provides an example. If you happen to attend first to the light area, you see a vase against a dark background. If you instead attend to the dark area, you see two faces in profile looking at each other.

Perceiving Location

We perceive the location of things and how far away they are in two basic ways. One is binocular vision, which is based on our normally having two eyes that are separated. When we cast our eyes on an object, each eye therefore has a different perspective—that is, the object is seen from two slightly different angles of view. At the same time, the object is projected to slightly different areas of each retina. The visual cortex then integrates the differences in neural impulses from the eyes and determines "where," including "near" or "far."

The other way is monocular cues. With only one functional eye, we can still use certain information to determine location. Or with both eyes, we use these monocular cues in conjunction with our binocular vision to determine location in a two-dimensional scene such as a TV picture, a movie, or a cartoon. One such cue is interposition. If one object partially blocks the view of another, we perceive the first object as being closer.

Another is relative size. Other things equal, an object that is larger than another seems closer. Cartoonists in particular make extensive use of height in field. An object that is at the bottom of a cartoon panel appears closer; one toward the top appears farther away.

Among the many other monocular cues is linear perspective. Two lines that begin at the bottom of an illustration and then draw closer near the top appear to be receding into the distance. This perception corresponds to looking down a pair of railroad tracks.

Perceiving Movement and Motion

An obvious way that we perceive movement and motion is that retinal stimuli change as an object crosses our visual field. A less obvious one is that if our eyes move to "track" the object, the muscular changes generate neural impulses that the brain can also use in determining movement. We also perceive ourselves as moving by using these cues in addition to bodily ones such as kinesthesis and equilibrium, discussed later in this chapter.

Our ability to detect very small movements in our environment is especially keen, and this may have an evolutionary basis. To our ancient ancestors who lived in the wild, any sort of movement signaled the possibility of danger and being killed and eaten, so those who were less alert to movement were less likely to pass along their genes.

However, cues for movement can be quite misleading. If you're flying in a plane, it may very well seem that the clouds are passing by and the plane is actually standing still. Similarly, while sitting in a carwash with your vision partly obscured by suds and water on the windows, you may get the impression that you and the car are moving and the carwash machinery is standing still—especially if your car is being rocked a bit by the brushes. These kinds of effects occur because you lack an absolute reference point for what's moving and what isn't.

Perceiving Color

Light waves have three properties that are involved in all visual sensation and perception. Wavelength as discussed earlier determines hue, the technical term for color. Intensity determines brightness. And the "blend" of wavelengths determines saturation—relatively pure colors such as vivid greens or reds contain a narrow band of wavelengths, whereas softer colors such as pastels contain a broader mix. Each of these properties of light interacts to influence the colors we perceive.

The rudiments of how we experience color have been understood reasonably well since the nineteenth century. In essence, the three types of cones and the cells in the eye that they synapse with generate different rates and combinations of neural impulses. Via the optic nerve, these impulses go next to the thalamus for further processing and recombination by several kinds of specialized cells, and from there they enter the brain through the visual cortex for even more processing that researchers are still trying to figure out.

FACT

Objects don't actually have color in a real sense. What we experience is wavelengths that are reflected from objects instead of being absorbed by them. The pigmentation of a bright yellow canary, for example, absorbs all wavelengths of light except those for yellow, which bounce off and enter our eyes.

It is known, however, that the processing is based on complementary colors, which are pairs that when combined produce white or gray. An example is red-green, and the idea is that the processing cells for red-green generate either red or green signals—depending upon the information from the cones—but not both at the same time. Thus, the myriad colors we experience are not neurologically "canceled out" down the line.

The Ears and Auditory Sensation

The apparatus for the ears is mechanical up to the point where sounds are transduced into neural impulses. The sound waves that stimulate our ears are produced when, for example, something in the world around us clicks, rings, vibrates, or scrapes against or hits something else. Each produces cyclical displacements of molecules in the air—that is, contractions and expansions of the air. Although you can't see these waves, you can get a clear idea of how sound is produced if you remove the front cover of a speaker system, turn up the volume, and watch what the bass and midrange speakers do.

One instance of expansion and contraction is a cycle, and sound waves are measured in cycles per second called *hertz* (Hz)—in honor of a prominent physicist. People vary considerably in the levels and the range of sound waves they can detect, but the typical range is 20 to 20,000 Hz. This is also the range that home electronics manufacturers try to cover as faithfully as possible, although modern systems often go below and above this range just to make sure that everything on a CD is reproduced.

Repeated exposure to extremely loud sounds can cause permanent damage to the structures of the ear and diminish hearing in certain ranges. Think about this the next time you're tempted to stand in front of the speakers at a rock concert.

How the Ear Works

Sound waves enter through the pinna—the part we can see—and travel through the auditory canal to the tympanic membrane, or eardrum, which they cause to vibrate. The vibrations are amplified by several bony structures called the *ossicles* and transmitted to the cochlea (which, because of its coiled shape, derives from the Greek for "snail"). Within the fluid-filled cochlea the vestibular canal carries the vibrations in the form of ripples to the basilar membrane, where thousands of tiny hair cells move in response to the ripples and perform the transduction into neural impulses. From there, the thousands of receptor neurons of the auditory nerve relay the signals to the thalamus and eventually to the auditory cortex of the temporal lobes. Partial or complete hearing loss can occur anywhere along the way, such as through the following:

- Obstruction of the auditory canal.
- Inflammation of the auditory canal because of infection.
- Puncturing of the eardrum.
- Fusion or other damage to the ossicles.
- Less-efficient hearing associated with aging.
- Damage to the hair cells of the basilar membrane by viral infections or exposure to very loud sounds.
- Damage to the auditory nerve.

Most of these conditions are correctible either through medical intervention or use of a hearing aid. The last two are not. Damage anywhere from the basilar membrane on is irreversible.

Auditory Perception

Three qualities of the sound waves that enter the ear interact to determine what we hear. The first is frequency in Hz, which determines pitch—from bass sounds, which have the slowest frequency and therefore the longest waves, to treble sounds with the highest frequencies and the shortest waves. The second is the amplitude, or strength, of the wave, which determines loudness. The third is complexity, or timbre, which accounts for the "richness" of what we hear. For example, most musical instruments produce multiple frequencies of sound called *harmonics* even when a single note is played.

Timbre accounts in large part for how we tell the difference between a guitar and a violin when the same note is plucked. In turn, the richness of the harmonics generated and resonated by such instruments determines their quality.

Discriminating Sounds

Our perception of loudness depends mainly on how many of the hairs on the basilar membrane are being stimulated, but our perception of pitch is more complex. One long-standing observation—called place theory—is that different areas of the basilar membrane are maximally sensitive to different frequencies. We therefore experience pitch in accord with which receptors are being stimulated and sending signals to the auditory cortex.

However, more recent research indicates that the timing of the neural impulses being generated is important as well. That is, different tones produce different patterns or "bursts" of neural impulses independently of the area of the basilar membrane being stimulated, thus also providing information about frequency to the auditory cortex. The auditory cortex then somehow combines this information to determine our perception of pitch in response to frequency.

Localizing Sounds

How we determine where sounds are coming from is straightforward, at least at the level of the auditory receptors. Any sound that isn't precisely centered in front of or behind the ears stimulates the receptors differently in two ways. One is intensity: A sound to the right, for example, will be louder in the right ear than in the left. The other is timing: A sound to the right will reach the right ear slightly sooner than the left. Again, however, how this information is processed in the auditory cortex remains under investigation.

Smell and Taste—The Chemical Senses

Olfaction (smell) and gustation (taste) are senses that respond to minute traces of chemical molecules that foods and many other substances emit. In humans, there are perhaps 10 million olfactory receptors in the nasal cavities that respond to specific odorants or combinations of them when they enter the nasal tracts from the surrounding air. The number of receptors stimulated determines the strength of the smell. The particular combination stimulated determines the quality of the smell, which of course can range from pleasant and enticing to thoroughly obnoxious.

Signals from the olfactory receptors fan out to a number of areas of the brain, and compared to the other senses, they take a much shorter route. They also go to an area deep in the cortex called the *amygdala,* which is intimately involved with emotional responses—we therefore very quickly feel pleasure or disgust in response to an odor. All of this is consistent with the view that smell is our oldest and most basic sense in terms of evolution, and it is likely that our ancient ancestors had a much keener sense of smell than we do—as do dogs, cats, and many other animals that rely more on smell than on vision or hearing.

In gustation, chemical molecules from substances we eat enter the saliva and stimulate taste buds concealed in small bumps on the tongue and also fan out to areas of the brain. We have about 10,000 taste buds, which are maximally responsive to molecules that give rise to "sweet," "salty," "sour," or "bitter" tastes. But the delicate experiences of flavor that we're capable of depend on a complex interplay between taste and smell, as anyone who's ever had a stuffy nose is aware of. When you have a cold, for example, you can still sense the four basic tastes, but that's about it.

FACT

Many animals have special glands that emit chemical molecules called *pheromones* to signal their readiness to mate and arouse sexual interest in potential partners. Humans also emit pheromones—our underarms, for example, contain glands that are especially active in secreting them. Some theorists have proposed that our pheromones also stimulate sexual interest, but so far the jury is still out.

All of our senses tend to decline as we age, and smell and taste are no exception. Older people may remark that foods prepared the same way as when they were younger don't taste as good, and they may find themselves using more sugar, salt, or other spices to compensate.

The Skin Senses

The receptors for the skin senses lie just below the surface and come in several varieties. These include receptors that respond to mechanical pressure (touch), temperature, and pain. Signals from these receptors go to the somatosensory areas of the parietal lobes.

However, the experiences of touch, temperature, or pain are not the result of a simple correspondence between the kind of stimulation and the neural impulses sent by the specific receptors. Pain, for example, can result from extreme stimulation of either of the other kinds of receptors, such as when you accidentally hit your thumb with a hammer or burn yourself with a match. Sensitivity to pain also varies considerably from one individual to the next, and people can learn to "control" pain with practice—especially if they have no choice because of bodily damage or disease. The experience of pain is therefore a function of higher thought processes as well as stimulation to the skin.

Kinesthesis and Equilibrium

The receptors for kinesthesis are mostly in muscles, tendons, and joints. They send information to lower areas of the brain about bodily movements such as reaching out and grasping something, walking, or standing, as well as bodily position. The brain then coordinates this information automatically, allowing us, for example, to walk without consciously thinking about specific movements of our legs.

FACT

Many people experience a temporary sense of dizziness and loss of balance after they spin around rapidly while standing or being on certain amusement park rides. This is caused by disruption of the functioning of the senses of kinesthesis and equilibrium, which spinning ballet dancers and ice skaters somehow learn to overcome.

The receptors for our automatic sense of equilibrium or balance are in and around the fluid-filled semicircular canals just above the cochlea of the inner ear. These are bundles of tiny hairs similar to those of the auditory apparatus, but they transmit impulses to lower areas of the brain regarding movement and the positioning of the head and body with respect to gravity. It is through the senses of kinesthesis and equilibrium in interaction that we "know" where we are and what we are doing, even though we aren't aware of how we know it.

Chapter 6

Emotions—Feeling Up, Feeling Down

The gamut of emotion one human being is capable of experiencing can certainly make a person feel like he's on a roller coaster—going up, coming down; becoming excited, then fearful; anxious and tense, then joyful and relieved. This chapter looks at the attempt to define what an emotion is by exploring both the physical and nonphysical factors that contribute to its genesis.

rsus Motives

tand the similarities and differences between emotions
ortant to establish a guideline for what an emotion
combine mental and biological aspects of emotion
,ysiological, subjective, cognitive, and reactive elements
.n emotion. Each of these elements will be discussed in
.ail later on in this chapter.

Like motives, emotions can set behavior into action and direct its
course to achieve a goal. Some can also be directly associated with
motives—the same activity fulfills a need as well as provokes an emotional
response. Eating, for example, is the result of a motive to satisfy hunger,
as well as a possible means to experience joy. But as similar as emotions
and motives may be, it's important to recognize their differences in order
to understand their effects on our lives.

Initiating a Response

One of the major differences between emotion and motive is how the
response is triggered. External occurrences cause emotions to surface
internally as a reaction to the situation, whereas internal occurrences such
as thirst elicit direct activity toward an external objective such as water.
Where emotion is a psychic and physical reaction that is subjectively
experienced, motive is a need or desire that propels a person to act.

ALERT!

Results from surveys conducted by the Centers for Disease Control
concluded that during a period of almost ten years the proportion
of the population with obesity increased 61 percent. Emotional
eating is a major contributor to these statistics because both
overweight and obese individuals have reported their food intake
is more extensive during intensely emotional situations.

However, this observation is not set in stone. Have you ever flipped
through a magazine and, after coming across a photograph of a
delectable, honey-glazed baked ham with all the trimmings, suddenly

realized that you were hungry? Looking at food, whether in a magazine or on the shelf at the grocery store, can trigger what you think is hunger. But is it truly hunger if you weren't even hungry before you picked up the magazine? As we'll discuss in Chapter 7, hunger is a basic need of survival but when it becomes confused with emotion, the need to survive is replaced with the need to feel good, and the mental and physical aspects of hunger can become indiscernible.

Looking at the photograph of the ham may have brought back memories of how delicious it tasted the last time you ate it, so your initial response was emotional—tasty food is enjoyable—but in order to justify your need for eating the ham you had to *assume* you were hungry.

Activating the Autonomic Nervous System

Another difference between emotions and motives is that emotions may indirectly stimulate the autonomic nervous system, in which dramatic physical changes progress rapidly, such as increased heart rate, muscle tension, dry mouth, or "butterflies" in the stomach, while motives may not. The sympathetic division of the autonomic nervous system controls these symptoms and is responsible for the following internal changes as well:

- Individual breaths become shorter and occur faster.
- Pupils become dilated.
- Levels of perspiration rise, while saliva and mucous dispersion decreases.
- Energy is produced due to an increase in blood sugar levels.
- Accelerated blood clotting occurs to prepare for wounds.
- Skin hairs rise, producing "goose bumps."

These homeostatic imbalances occur especially when fear or anger is experienced at extreme levels. When anger is expressed, the sensation of rising body temperature feels as if the blood is "boiling" and the face becomes so red it seems as though you might "blow your top." In fact, this type of anger causes one literally and physically to "lose his cool" causing the body to begin restoring itself to its normal state by bringing down its temperature via perspiration.

FACT

Arrectores pilorum, or hair erector muscles, contract when stimuli such as cold or fear create discharge. As a result of the tiny contracting muscles, hair follicles rise above the skin, developing what we call goose bumps.

Again, this notion is not without exception. When a person is suffering from the physical torments of relentless hunger and the motivation to obtain food cannot be satisfied, emotions such as depression and sadness can ensue.

The Physiology of Emotion

Internal, physical reactions to emotion occur when our autonomic nervous system is called into action. Depending on the emotion and its intensity, the body's energy distribution either increases or decreases. When anger or fear is experienced, the pulse quickens and shortness of breath and trembling may take place, while emotions such as heartache, grief, and regret may cause the body to slow down significantly. When this takes place, we fall into a depression, resulting in excessive sleeping and physical weakness.

The James-Lange Theory of Emotions

How we are able to differentiate emotions is the subject of much debate. William James and Carl Lange (1834–1900) theorized that it is the physical actions and reactions that determine the subjective experience of an emotion. Common sense tells us that we run from danger because we're afraid. In complete opposition, James's notion focused on the physiological aspect of emotion, holding the position that we are afraid because we run and we are excited because we shout. Lange's ideas were similar, only he took it further and included autonomic responses as well. He suggested that not only are we afraid because we run, we are afraid because our heart is beating rapidly. Arriving at these conclusions at about the same time, the two positions were combined and the James-Lange theory was born.

Arguments Against the James-Lange Theory

Walter Cannon (1871–1945) strongly disagreed with the James-Lange theory for several reasons. First, he argued that due to the body's lack of nerve-sensitive organs, visceral changes are too slow to take place and therefore are not contributing factors in felt emotions. Second, emotions that are experienced after epinephrine injections are not true emotions as much as they are physical affectations (accelerated pulsations, sweaty palms). Cannon's final argument acknowledged that the autonomic patterns of emotions are often too similar to be a source of distinction—for example, fear, anger, and love all incite a faster heartbeat. This suggests that other factors are at work in differentiating emotions.

The Brain's Role in Emotion

Although technological advancements have been able to detect internal differences from one emotion to the next, it doesn't hold true for all emotions. Additional factors play a major role in emotional responses, and one of those factors is how the brain creates and recognizes facial expressions.

Emotions that are universal, such as happiness or anger, utilize distinctive muscles to express those emotions. This implies that the neurological system that makes this possible was part of human evolution, allowing nonverbal communication through facial signals and recognition of those signals to be valuable to hunting and survival techniques.

Located in the right cerebral hemisphere, this neurological system is not our only aid in the process of enabling us to express emotion. Variations in voice projection (pitch, tone, and stress), which are also controlled by a specific neurological system housed in the right cerebral hemisphere, make it possible for us to scream or laugh.

Varieties of Emotions

Emotions vary in intensity, and our interpretation of day-to-day situations through cognitive appraisal dictates the quality and type of emotion we experience. In Schacter and Singer's *Psychological Review* (1962), an experiment was conducted to determine if cognitive appraisal indeed would create a subjective response regardless of autonomic behavior.

What is cognitive appraisal?
It's an individual's personal estimation of events or situations in relation to her or his goals and beliefs. It also affects the significance and level of intensity at which the emotion is experienced as well as the seriousness of the threat.

Preconditioned Appraisals

Subjects were injected with epinephrine and given specific information regarding the effect the drug would have on them. Some of them were told the drug would make them euphoric while others were told it would make them feel angry. In actuality, all subjects experienced the same physical reactions to the drug, including increased heart rate, sweaty palms, and rapid breathing. Each subject was then directed to a waiting room where he or she encountered a confederate posed as another subject who had also been injected with the drug. If the real subject had been told he or she would experience euphoria, then the confederate would act out that emotion by amusing himself with paper airplanes, wastebasket basketball, etc. In the rooms where subjects were told they would feel angry, the confederate would display that behavior by complaining or storming out of the room.

FACT

In addition to stimulating autonomic nerve action, epinephrine is used to reverse advanced stages of the same action, which occurs when a potentially life-threatening allergic reaction called *anaphylaxis* severely attacks the body by affecting skin, respiratory and gastrointestinal tracts, and the cardiovascular system.

Since the autonomic responses of both anger and euphoria are similar (increased heart rate, fidgety behavior, and breathing patterns), the injection worked in conjunction with the preconditioned mindset (anger or euphoria) to elicit a total emotional experience. Those who encountered the euphoric confederate generally recorded their feelings as happy, while the subjects who came in contact with the angry confederate recorded negative feelings.

Assessing the Situation

Rather than subscribing to the theory that emotion is rooted solely in physical reactions, the previously outlined experiment suggests that both autonomic arousal and the interpretation of the situation that causes the arousal are key factors in producing an emotional response. In fact, our perception of life experiences becomes even more important in determining the emotion and, in turn, the physiological repercussions of that emotion.

A single occurrence, then, can provoke a full range of emotions depending on the person experiencing the event. For example, if a young woman marries a very attractive young man with a severe drinking problem, her feelings may be primarily joyous. At the same time, her rival might experience sadness, her parents anxiety, and his parents relief. Each person's assessment of the same experience triggered a completely different emotion, although all parties involved most likely had a shared anatomic response: tears!

Explanations of Emotionality

A direct relationship between physiological stimulation and emotionality can be established by taking a look at the following experiment in which subjects with spinal cord injuries described the intensity of emotion they experienced after the injury as compared to the level at which emotions were felt before it.

Subjects with spinal cord lesions of varying degrees of damage were selected and evaluated. As noted at the beginning of this book, the origin of some autonomic changes can be traced to the sympathetic division of the nervous system, so any feelings below the section of the spinal cord that is damaged cannot be transmitted to the brain.

The following list illustrates the location of lesions on the spinal cord that each group of subjects suffered:

- Near the neck, at the cervical level
- Lumbar region
- Lower thoracic level
- Upper thoracic level
- Near the base of the spine, at the sacral level

Subjects were asked to compare situations involving fear, anger, grief, and sexual excitement that occurred before the injury to those that occurred after. Results showed that those with lesions highest on the spinal cord experienced the least amount of emotionality because a large portion of the autonomic nervous system was unable to communicate sensation to the brain.

Unlike occasions that took place before the injury, some subjects related that although they were able to verbally and facially express emotion, the level of intensity was noticeably minimal due to the absence of physical reaction. When the body is incapable of regulating blood temperature, increasing energy, or producing perspiration, a complete emotional experience cannot be felt.

Aggressive Behavior

Innovative technological advancements result in many positive improvements to our society as a whole as well as in relation to other societies, but they consequently lead to inevitable negative aspects such as weapons of mass destruction. In return, the presence of aggressive behavior in our society continues to rise in part because of our continual exposure to it via the media, movies, and video games and also in part because of our innate, primitive drive toward instinctive aggression.

Behind the Wheel of Aggression

Freud's psychoanalytical theory that almost all of humankind's actions can be traced to sexual instinct is formulated around the idea that unfulfilled sexual desire leads to frustration, which is expressed by aggression. In *Frustration and Aggression* by Dollard, et al. (1939), Freud's theory is further enhanced by the *frustration-aggression hypothesis,* which proposes that whenever something prevents a person from achieving a goal, it's perceived as an obstruction, whether animate or inanimate, and needs to be injured, hence the aggressive drive.

FACT

If aggression echoes the hallmarks of a person's most basic drive in that it takes the form of energy that will continue to exist until its goal is reached, an ultimate end-result must occur. Following the theory that all things are created of matter and matter cannot be destroyed but rather only transferred, the aggressive behavior will continue to gain momentum until it finds a way to be released.

Steering the Wheel of Aggression

Almost all reported instances of violence, whether in newspapers or on the local news network, fail to give the complete history of the aggressor. More often than not, the chain of events that led up to the eventual crime becomes pertinent information in attempting to trace the nature of aggressive behavior. The snowball effect, which begins with repressed frustration and leads to a buildup of destructive behavior patterns that manifest themselves in a variety of hostile ways, comes to an end with an ultimate barbaric act. If the root of this eventual act is not discovered, understood, and treated, the cycle may be triggered and the sequence will begin all over again.

From a biological standpoint, arousing specific regions of the brain causes equally specific aggressive reactions. Stimulating different regions of a cat's hypothalamus causes the cat to react either in a wild display of aggression by hissing and striking out or in a sophisticated form of premeditated hunting that results in the prey's death. Monkeys on the other hand follow a hierarchy of dominance and act accordingly based on recollections of past experiences.

Driving Is a Learning Process

The *social-learning theory* holds the belief that aggression is a learned response as opposed to an inherited instinctual one. This puts us in the driver's seat where the action that is necessary to drive is something that is learned by observation, imitation, and practice—all components of the social-learning theory.

Studies researching the effects of observation on nursery school children involved an experiment where the children watched adults display a range of aggressive actions toward an oversized, inflated doll. In addition, two films were shown to a different set of children. One film showed an adult behaving aggressively toward the doll, while the other film portrayed a cartoon carrying out similar aggressive responses. Kicking, punching, pushing, shoving, and throwing are some of the actions that were viewed live and on television.

Since parents possess the most influential power over their children by constantly being observed in natural settings, the way they treat violence and the frequency with which they resort to aggressive behavior is likely to be imitated by their children.

Two control groups were also set up, in which one set of children observed nonaggressive behavior and another set of children simply observed nothing. When put to the test, the two groups of children who viewed the assailing behavior mimicked the behaviors they observed, whereas the other two groups did not.

Violence on Television and Its Effect on Children

As seen in the previous experiment, young children often imitate viewed aggression because they associate people on TV with being role models for adulthood. Children believe the action is justified because a "grownup" did it, and therefore understand it to be a part of "growing up" in today's society. Television violence's effect on children results in aggressive behavior for a number of other reasons, including the following:

- **Elevated levels of arousal.** Osborn and Endsley's *Child Development* (1971) shows how children are more apt to become emotionally aroused while viewing violent programs by measuring the increase in their galvanic skin responses. The increase is notably higher when viewing violent behavior.
- **Excessive exposure leads to desensitizing people to violence.** The shock of violent behavior subsides after repeated incidents of violence are experienced, thus stunting our ability to react appropriately and effectively to real-life situations and provide help when needed.
- **Mixed messages on settling conflicts.** Children don't often recognize whether a situation is fictional or based in reality, so when they see the timeless struggle of good versus evil played out on television by their favorite cartoon characters, they also develop a positive image of how good triumphs over evil through violent means.

Do We All Have the Same Emotions?

Some emotions are indeed universal in scope. Happiness, anger, fear, and sadness produce similar facial expressions, which are recognizable in cultures outside of Western civilization. This shared reaction illustrates Darwin's belief that emotions are instinctive responses that evolved from a crucial need to develop multiple survival techniques.

Although certain emotions are shared, individual expression of that emotion is what makes it appear to be different. Each person's reaction to a situation is subjective, and how that situation is interpreted is based on personal beliefs, past experiences, and physical capabilities. The level of intensity at which the emotion is felt and the individual's dramatic expression of it is what make our communication of emotions different.

Motives—Why We Do the Things We Do

Our needs are pretty basic when viewed from an instinctual and evolutionary standpoint. It's the internal processes propelling us to act that become complicated when examined more closely. Here we'll distinguish between the different types of motives we respond to; how we recognize them cognitively, physiologically, and emotionally; the dangers of misinterpreting their signals; and their role in our sexual behavior.

Varieties of Motives

Motives that have not been learned, such as the need to acquire physical things, are called basic motives, distinguishable in that we share them with other animals. They can be broken down into three classes: survival (hunger and thirst), social (sex and maternal expression), and curiosity (conscious investigation).

Since survival motives are directly dependent on a healthy physical state, homeostatic systems are crucial in picking up on body signals that warn of an imbalance and disruption of the internal mechanisms. The ability of the body to adapt to constant change allows it to recognize, for example, when blood sugar levels reach a point below what is healthy. Once this recognition occurs, a cry for help is put out (need) and the appropriate drive is stimulated, causing the organism to perform the actions that are necessary (obtaining food high in sugar) in returning blood sugar levels back to normal.

Diabetes is a life-long disease that occurs when there are high levels of sugar in the blood. It can be caused by too little insulin (type 1), resistance to it (type 2), or both. Type 2 diabetes is usually developed during adulthood. Currently, there is no cure for diabetes.

The Brain's Role in Motivation

Regulation of body temperature, specific metabolic processes, and other autonomic activities all take place in the brain's hypothalamus region, which also determines blood temperature by way of sensors. These sensors are additionally present inside the mouth, skin, spinal cord, and brain allowing us to differentiate between hot and cold.

Setting the Thermostat

The anterior, or frontal, portion of the brain is responsible for making sure body temperature remains consistently normal by following a process similar to that of a thermostat. Existing temperature is "read" by sensors and compared to what the normal temperature should be. If the readout turns up an irregularity, specific physiological adjustments will attempt to correct the problem by producing sweat when hot and shivers when cold. In addition, external behavioral adjustments may be prompted, for example, covering up with a blanket when you're cold and tossing the blanket to the side when you're warm.

Although both physiological and behavioral adjustments occur in the hypothalamus, the differences between them are as follows:

Behavioral
Willful acts of selfishness
Drive elicits the response
External conditions are influenced
Housed in the lateral area of the hypothalamus

Physiological
Uncontrollable physical acts
Need elicits the response
Internal conditions are influenced
Housed in the preoptic area of the hypothalamus

Behavioral and physiological adjustments, as different as they are, work together toward the shared goal of regulating the body's temperature, a process necessary to survival. Temperatures too high above or too far below the norm of 98.6° Fahrenheit (F) must be treated immediately, otherwise organs may become permanently damaged or death may result.

ALERT!

Hypothermia (body temperature below the norm) must be treated when temperature drops below 95°F, and becomes fatal when it drops below 90°F. Fever is when body temperature rises above normal, but doesn't become much of a concern until it reaches at least 100°F.

Severe weather conditions when not guarded against can cause the body to go into shock For example, Alaska's lowest average temperature during winter (between December and February) is −15.7°F. A person cannot simply walk outside with only one layer of clothing and a heavy jacket without experiencing instant frostbite and symptoms of hypothermic shock.

FACT

The point at which temperature freezes is determined by using water as a guide. Since water freezes at 32°F, "below freezing" temperature is any degree below that number.

In contrast, Arizona's climate can reach temperatures as high as 120°F, so if a person takes a day trip to the middle of the desert with only a short supply of water, the body's ability to keep cool is dominated by extreme external temperatures that cause it to "overheat" and suffer from heat stroke. Drastic irregularities in body temperature result in various degrees of physical decline.

When the body reaches certain degrees of temperature, specific reactions are experienced as shown here (temperatures are measured in Fahrenheit):

- 82.7° muscle failure
- 91.4° unconsciousness
- 107.6° breakdown of central nervous system
- 111.2° death

The Physiology of Motivation

Our survival is directly dependent on two fundamental operations: body temperature and sufficient water supply. Homeostatic processes ensure these operations run smoothly and when necessary activate emergency systems in an effort to restore balance to the body. When these systems fail—temperatures are too high or too low for too long, or dehydration is present for several days—death is inevitable.

Blood Temperature

Since protein is one of the major components that propel a cell's activity, when it becomes dormant in temperatures above 113°F, cells cannot perform their responsibilities. Similarly, when water inside cells freezes, ice crystals develop and ultimately shut them down.

When temperature is not at the desired level, physiological adjustments (in addition to possible behavioral adjustments) are automatically induced in a variety of ways including sweating, panting, and shivering. The skin's capillaries expand and contract to control blood by either producing excessive amounts of it beneath the surface of the skin (expansion) or reserving the depleting supply of it for organs (contraction). Excessive heat is then released through sweat glands located on the body in the form of sweating, as seen in humans, horses, and cows, or through sweat glands located on the tongue in the form of panting, as seen in dogs, cats, and rats. The act of shivering resolves heat shortages by creating warmth.

Internal Water Supply

Water is essential to our existence because it transports nutrients and oxygen to tissues and helps purge wastes from the body. When dehydration is detected, our basic motive of thirst is triggered and replenishment becomes our primary goal. Because constant water loss is a natural function of the body, it is kept in check by maintaining intracellular and extracellular fluid.

Depletion of intracellular fluid occurs when water outside a cell contains higher quantities of sodium than water inside a cell. The cell then becomes dehydrated and shrinks, sending the message that an adjustment needs to be made.

Kidneys play an important role in this adjustment. Before water is released through urination, the antidiuretic hormone (ADH) is unleashed allowing water instead to be retrieved and directed to the bloodstream.

Extracellular fluid loss is caused by excessive amounts of blood loss as well as loss of sodium through sweating. The kidneys become key players in regulating fluids by restoring blood volume to normal levels. They do this by constricting blood vessels, which allow blood loss to take place, through the release of an enzyme into the bloodstream.

Since it is impossible to decide when these fluids are fully restored without being monitored by machines, satiety sensors (found in the intestines) do all the work for us by telling the body it has enough water to regulate dehydrated cells.

The Hunger Motive

One element alone doesn't make us hungry; rather several occurrences working together to provide the body with energy trigger the motive to eat. Homeostasis contributes by regulating metabolism and digestion via monitoring supplies needed to produce nutrients, while satiety sensors (as first encountered in relation to the thirst motive) serve as lookout stations set up to detect when supplies are on the way. On a more abstract level, external influence and culture-specific rituals can sometimes stimulate our desire to eat by recalling memories of how certain foods or celebrations made us feel euphoric.

Homeostasis Gets the Ball Rolling

One of the main reasons we experience hunger is that our body tells us it is so. Much like a new mother learns to distinguish between her baby's cries for hunger, cries for discomfort, and cries for sickness, a person who is "in tune" with his body learns to differentiate between hunger pangs and nervous rumblings. If we listen to our bodies, the hunger subsides; however, if we ignore the signals our bodies give off, more signals will be given—physical weakness and lethargy, for example.

While all this action takes place externally, a different kind of internal action is responsible for what eventually produces the hunger pangs we experience. In order for our cells to function properly, nutrients must be made available. This is the primary goal of digestion.

Food goes in, breaks down into simpler compounds, and gets recycled into concentrated forms of energy. Glucose, or the primary sugar found in blood, is a major source of energy for the brain and can be regulated either by obtaining it from the liver's storage supply or by eating food.

It's imperative that we listen to our bodies. Our bodies give us signs of well-being or lack thereof all the time. Should there be something physically wrong, you can help a doctor diagnose the problem and find the appropriate treatment much more easily if you understand what your body is telling you.

Sensors Make Sense

Now that we know we're hungry, how do we know when we're full? In other words, how is the body informed that nutrients will eventually be present if digestion itself takes four hours to complete? Remember, nutrients are products of digestion, so take a moment if you will to imagine eating for four hours at a time each time the body tells you food is needed. Like most, you probably got full just thinking about the first two hours!

Sensors located in the stomach and liver let the body know that nutrients will be coming shortly. Lucky for us, eating three meals a day doesn't take up half our day.

Abstract Motivation

The desire to eat food we know tastes good is often mistaken for the need to eat it. After consuming a satisfying, seven-course meal that made you feel "stuffed," why would you continue to eat when dessert is brought to the table? You already fulfilled your body's request for food, so it certainly has nothing to do with your need for it.

An abstract idea concerning eating habits involves "the holidays," a three-month period in which massive quantities of food are readily available at almost any given time at any given place. Halloween starts us off with the ritual of providing candy to trick-or-treaters, but when candy is left over, the purchaser usually ends up eating it or bringing it to the workplace, thus making it more available. One of the rituals performed during Thanksgiving is to prepare an overabundance of food and eat as much of it as we can stand throughout the day. And don't forget the leftovers that usually last for about a week thereafter! A tradition similar to this one repeats itself a few weeks later at Christmas parties and New Year's Eve celebrations. Why do we continue to prepare so much food year after year when we know it physically is not necessary? Because these rituals are part of the customs that define our culture and society, and since we are members of that society our participation in the rituals is an expression of celebration.

Memory can provide a possible explanation. Remembering how you felt the last time you ate dessert might trigger your desire to feel that way again if the reaction was favorable. And, considering the amount of sugar most desserts are made with, the "rush" one feels after eating dessert is similar to the feeling of euphoria.

Eating Disorders

The physical need for food is a normal function of our body to remain in healthy, working condition, and more important to stay alive. Although it is the primary motivator that directs us to consume food, emotions, behaviors, and attitudes are also important contributors. Anorexia, bulimia, and binge eating are all examples of eating disorders; however, the one most prevalent in our society is obesity.

Genetically Inherited Obesity

Body fat is stored in fat cells and genetic inheritance is one of the factors that dictate the number of fat cells an organism has. Members of an obese family are more likely to produce additional obese members, thus perpetuating the cycle. Research shows that in addition to the number of fat cells we have, the size of fat cells can cause us to become obese.

Overeating during the stages of infancy can contribute to the size of fat cells, but overeating, at this stage, is controlled by our guardians who most likely inherited nursing practices from one of their own family members.

QUESTION?

What is the main cause of obesity?
Perhaps one of the reasons obesity affects so many people in our society is that there are several causes. To complicate things even further, the complexity of these causes are both physical and nonphysical, including genetics, environment, sociology, nutrition, psychology, and metabolism.

Emotion as a Motive

When hunger is confused with other feelings, emotional eating ensues. One hypothesis suggests that this mixup established its roots in infancy when our caregivers interpreted most of our cries as cries for hunger, thereby frequently mistaking anxiety for hunger. Another hypothesis suggests that because caregivers regularly comforted the infant with food, obese adults innately mimic that behavioral response because it seems to calm them down. As mentioned earlier, when we associate euphoric feelings with eating, the act of eating becomes something desirable rather than something needed.

Metabolism and Exercise

The lower the metabolism, the fewer the calories spent and, incidentally, the higher the body weight. Dieting slows metabolism as well, which helps explain the "breaking even" point during dieting that may halt weight loss.

Exercise helps maintain a regular metabolism, and when it is absent from an obese person's life, it may cause a domino effect of repeated inactivity. Excessive body weight makes it difficult and uncomfortable to exercise, so the opportunity to burn a substantial amount of calories is lost. Fat tissue then replaces lean tissue causing a reduction in the person's basic metabolic rate. This combination of unspent calories and reduced metabolism makes for rapid weight gain that can become dangerously out of control if not addressed right away.

The Motive for Sex

Whereas survival motives such as thirst and hunger occur in relation to the self, social motives like sex mostly involve another person. Another notable difference is that thirst and hunger develop as physical reactions to an internal imbalance that needs to be corrected in order to survive. Social motives do not need to be regulated in order for survival to continue; their influences are hormonal and environmental.

FACT

Hermaphrodites are individuals who were born with both male and female genital tissues—ovaries and a penis, for example. An imbalance in prenatal hormones is responsible for this abnormal development and occurs when there is an excess of the genital development hormone androgen in the female fetus or not enough of it in the male fetus.

Hormonal Changes

Puberty occurs somewhere between ages eleven and fourteen and causes us to think in depth about our own sexuality for the first time. Hormones in females (estrogen) produce breasts, "shapely curves," and genital advancement, while hormones in males (testosterone) produce development of facial and underarm hair, voice changes, muscle definition, and genital growth.

These natural changes prepare the body for sexual interaction by displaying obvious external developments that tell the world (potential mates) it's ready to reproduce. While teenagers may become physically mature, all too often their response to their own sexuality involves choices that have not been analyzed with maturity, and all too often result in circumstances they were not yet prepared for.

Environmental Influences

Different cultures have different levels of tolerance for the same behaviors, such as premarital sex, masturbation, or homosexuality. The same behavior, such as intercourse with a girl who hasn't reached puberty, may be punishable by death in some cultures, but more acceptable in others.

Even further, specific attitudes differ significantly between men and women and involve emotion, self-worth, desire, and frustration. The following list of sexual attitude differences between men and women was developed after asking college students to list their concerns with all aspects of sexuality and was taken from Tavris and Offir's *The Longest War: Sex Differences in Perspective* (1977). The students who were surveyed were young and single.

Women

Fear of pregnancy.
Fear of rape.
Fear of being conquered and then regarded as of no further use.
Fear of being rejected if they said no.
Masturbation was acceptable.
Fear that they would physically repulse their partners.
Fear of losing self-respect.
Fear of becoming too attached when the feeling was not mutual.
Feelings of guilt about premarital sex.
Pressure to have sex even when they did not want to.
Fear of not satisfying their partners.
Embarrassment or concern over not being orgasmic.

Men

Finding partners who were open to varying sexual experiences.
Always having to be on the hunt.
Not being able to have sexual relations when they wanted to.
Women who tease, without wanting to engage in sexual activity.
Women's refusal to take responsibility for their own sexuality.
Women who used their sexual attractiveness in a manipulative fashion.

The excessive modesty of women (they wanted the lights off).
Passive women.
Aggressive women.
Necessity to say you loved the woman even if it was not true.
Being expected to know all about sex.
Inability to communicate feelings or needs during sex.

Sexual Orientation

In the past, homosexuality was considered to be either a mental illness or a sexual abnormality related to hormonal imbalance. Multiple studies have shown that homosexuals can be as well adjusted as heterosexuals, and experiments involving hormonal manipulation by injection seemed to affect only the person's sexual drive and not his or her preference.

The cause for homosexuality still remains to be discovered; however, new theories are constantly being developed and tested. Some ideas include relationships with the father, relationships with the mother, and relationships with peers during sex-drive maturation. At any rate, homosexuality has become more accepted; same-sex marriage in some parts of the world is legal and even encouraged.

Transsexuality is not received with as much acceptance as homosexuality, mainly because it is viewed as a form of betrayal—the reality of the situation is kept hidden. If a man is attracted to a woman who turns out to be biologically male, he may feel as if his sexual orientation has been challenged without his permission—after all, he was just sexually attracted to a man! True, some transsexuals are immediately upfront about their natural sex, but with today's surgical, technical, and pharmaceutical advancements, it becomes increasingly difficult for us to determine what sex a person is based on external appearances alone. Ⓔ

Altered States of Consciousness

People have been trying for eons to alter their states of consciousness, whether for enlightenment, relaxation, or escape. As a result, several different ways of accomplishing this have been discovered. This chapter will discuss what consciousness is and the different ways in which consciousness is or can be altered.

Levels of Consciousness

Before we can begin to discuss the different levels of consciousness, you'll need to have a firm grasp on just what consciousness is. The easiest way to understand consciousness is to think of it as awareness. It is your awareness of yourself and your environment. There are varying degrees of how aware you are of materials and things going on within your body and your environment; these varying degrees determine the levels of consciousness: conscious, preconscious, unconscious, subconscious, and nonconscious. Let's take a look at each in detail.

Conscious

Conscious is the term used to describe your active awareness. For example, if you stub your toe on your way to answer the door, you are actively aware of the coffee table that you just ran into. You are aware of the pain shooting up from your injured toe. You are aware of the swear word escaping your mouth. You are aware of the sound each time the doorbell rings. You are conscious of all these things.

Preconscious

The preconscious stores memories that you do not have a use for at the present moment, but that you can retrieve in the future if needed. You are aware of these memories, but it is not an active awareness until a trigger requires you to retrieve a memory and put it to use, thus becoming conscious of it. For example, you know when your birthday is, but you aren't actively aware of that information until you need to retrieve it. It stays within your preconscious, and then when someone asks you when your birthday is, you activate that memory, bring it to your conscious, and answer the question.

Subconscious

The subconscious handles the information and mental processes needed to perform routine activities that do not require conscious thought. For instance, let's say you are writing a paper for a psychology class. While you are conscious of the words you are typing, your subconscious handles the typing itself. You have already learned how to type and that information was stored in your subconscious, so your fingers can find the appropriate keys in an automatic response to the words you want to type.

Unconscious

The unconscious is what stores those memories we are unaware of. You may be wondering how the unconscious is even known to exist if the information stored there is unknown to the individual. Often, these memories can be brought to the surface when a person is taken into an altered state of consciousness, such as in hypnosis. During hypnosis, an individual can recall unconscious memories, such as a conversation that the individual heard but was unaware of hearing while under anesthesia in an operating room.

FACT

The unconscious was a subject of constant study with Freud. He thought that the unconscious stored all memories, thoughts, and emotions that were too troubling to allow into the conscious. He considered it a realm of secrets that held the key to unlocking an individual's true identity, desires, and personality.

Nonconscious

The nonconscious part of your mind stores information that you are not aware of but is necessary for you to live out your daily life. For example, you get up every morning, carry out your daily activities, and sleep at night, and all the while your heart is beating. You are not aware of the information being mentally processed within your body to maintain that heartbeat, but you don't have to be, as your nonconscious handles that.

Sleep

Sleep is a state of consciousness that is essential to our daily mental and physical functions. While no one has been able to determine exactly why we sleep, studies have shown that sleep allows our body to restore itself after a time of wakefulness. During sleep the body has time to repair itself (repair cells, strengthen the immune system, digest and store the mental processes required in learning) after the damaging effects of everyday activities.

Until the early 1950s when the electroencephalograph (EEG) was invented, sleep was thought to be a time-out period during which the brain shuts down. However, the EEG made it possible to study the brain waves of people sleeping and found that the brain was anything but shut down during sleep. By recording the electrical activity of the brain, researchers were able to determine that the brain goes through four stages of activity during sleep:

1. **Stage 1**—During the first stage, you begin to relax and your body prepares for sleep. According to the EEG, your brain first emits alpha waves, which show a slow, regular rhythm. As you drift further into stage 1, the waves become more irregular. You are in a state of light sleep from which you can easily be awakened.
2. **Stage 2**—During the second stage, your brain emits irregular, short bursts of waves that contain peaks, called *sleep spindles*. Even though you are asleep at this stage, you may not think you are. Background noise isn't likely to awaken you.
3. **Stage 3**—This third stage takes you progressively deeper into true sleep. Your brain still emits the irregular pattern of stage 2, but also occasionally throws in slower waves with high peaks, called delta waves. Your body has relaxed to the point that your pulse rate and breathing slow down. You are more difficult to arouse during this stage.
4. **Stage 4**—During the fourth stage, the alpha waves of stage 2 have all but left the scene and the delta waves have taken control. You are in a deep sleep and it will require an outside stimuli such as a loud alarm clock to awaken you.

Once you reach the final stage, you will travel backward through the stages until you reach the first. However, instead of entering the period of semiwakefulness, your body enters REM sleep. REM sleep gets its name from the rapid eye movement characteristic of this stage. The EEG shows that during REM sleep, your brain is just as active as it is when you are wide-awake during the day. During REM, your blood pressure rises, your heartbeat increases, you breathe faster, and you will likely dream.

You will alternate from REM sleep to stages 2, 3, and 4 several times throughout the night. As the hours pass, the time spent in the stages often gets shorter and shorter and time spent in REM gets longer and longer.

Sleep Disorders

Even though sleep is a necessary element for mental and physical well-being, only approximately a third of Americans get the recommended eight hours of sleep a night. While most of us would say that we often feel sleepy at some point during the day (perhaps after a large meal or when facing a project you aren't wanting to start), some people suffer from sleep disorders, which inhibit their ability to sleep properly.

Insomnia

Insomnia is the most well known sleep disorder and is characterized by the inability to fall or stay asleep. People who suffer insomnia desire and feel the need for sleep but for some reason are unable to get the amount of sleep their bodies need. Insomnia can be caused by a variety of reasons. It can be the result of psychological factors such as anxiety, worry, or depression; biological factors such as the effect of stimulants used before bed, arthritis, or hot flashes during menopause; or environmental factors such as noises emitted from loud neighbors, trains, or traffic.

ALERT!

While insomnia may seem to be just a nuisance, if you are unable to resolve the problem (such as avoiding caffeine or keeping a regular bedtime and rising schedule), see your doctor and discuss the problem. Sleep is vital to your mental and physical health, so take whatever measures you can to ensure proper rest for your body.

Sleep Apnea

Sleep apnea is a sleep disorder in which a person's breathing stops for a moment, causing the person to choke, gasp, and wake up momentarily. The person will fall back asleep once normal breathing resumes and often doesn't even realize he or she has woken up. This can happen hundreds of times a night, thus interrupting the stages of sleep and causing exhaustion. Sleep apnea is a serious disorder and is potentially life-threatening. It can also cause an irregular heartbeat or high blood pressure.

Narcolepsy

Narcolepsy is a sleep disorder in which a person suffers unpredictable attacks of daytime sleepiness. The urge to sleep is irresistible and can last anywhere from five to thirty minutes for each attack. Though this disorder has been the subject matter for several comedy skits, the condition is a serious neurological disorder and can cause the individual harm depending on what the person is doing when the attacks occur. For instance, a narcoleptic person may suffer an attack while driving and cause a serious accident.

Why Do We Dream?

The answer to this question is debatable, and you will find a wide range of answers, depending on whom you ask. Many scientists will tell you that while dreaming is an altered state of consciousness, the dream itself is a by-product of the brain's electrical discharges and wave patterns—a result of the brain's activities to restore the body during sleep. Neurons are fired during the electrical discharges, and depending on where they end up, differing images within the dream will occur. For instance, if neurons are fired in the part of the brain that maintains your balance, you may dream that you are falling and may even jerk in your sleep to try to keep your balance.

However, this explanation isn't accepted by all. Some psychoanalysts believe, as Freud did, that dreams are an outlet for people to live out their desires—desires that may not be socially acceptable—or resolve conflicts. Dreams have an underlying meaning that the dreamer is unaware of. Each element of the dream is symbolic of the individual's innermost wishes, conflicts, and/or motives. Though dreams may have a deep-rooted psychological meaning, there isn't a reliable and objective way to interpret one's dreams.

FACT

Many cultures believe that dreams are prophetic and/or contain messages from the spirit world. Therefore, dreams are elevated to a high level of importance and are interpreted in all seriousness. In this way, dreams can have a direct impact on the lives of several or all members within the culture.

Still others believe that dreams are a direct result of life's experiences and are an unconscious continuation of a person's conscious thoughts and activities during the day. During these dreams a person may express anxiety or worry over a problem that is current in his life. He may also be able to solve that problem or find the root of the problem by interpreting the images, thoughts, and emotions of the dream.

Of course, there are more explanations than those offered here. Individuals, scientists, and cultures are continuously studying and interpreting dreams. However, no one explanation has been substantially proven as the reason we dream.

Hypnosis and Its Uses

Hypnosis is a procedure in which a hypnotist suggests changes in the feelings, perceptions, thoughts, or behavior of the subject. Many consider a hypnotized person to be experiencing an altered state of consciousness. Those under hypnosis are open to the suggestions of the hypnotist but are not under the hypnotist's control. In other words, hypnosis is not a form of mind control, regardless of what you may have seen in the movies. The subject is nearly always fully aware of what is happening and cannot be forced to do anything against his will.

Hypnotizability

Not all people can be hypnotized. Even the best of hypnotists cannot hypnotize a subject if he doesn't want to be hypnotized. Whether or not a subject enters a hypnotic state is dependent upon the subject more than on the hypnotist. People vary in degrees of hypnotic responsiveness. Those who are able to lose themselves in books and movies, or have active imaginations, are good candidates for hypnosis. Those who are grounded in the real world at all times are not likely to be nearly as responsive to hypnosis. This susceptibility is in no way tied to personality traits such as gullibility or submissiveness.

Uses for Hypnosis

Contrary to popular belief, hypnosis is not a guaranteed way to bring to the surface suppressed memories, not even of alien abductions or childhood abuse. Because the subject is highly responsive to the hypnotist's suggestions, he or she may be led to answer questions or recall "memories" in a particular way depending on how the suggestion is given. Or perhaps the subject has a vivid imagination and plays out a role from that imagined state. He or she may believe that the experience is real, when in actuality it is merely a product of his or her imagination.

If you ever get the chance, check out a stage hypnotist's show in an entertainment venue. It can be very entertaining. You may even choose to become a participant and experience it for yourself—all in the name of research, of course!

Of course, hypnosis can sometimes successfully stimulate the memory, though the results aren't 100 percent error-proof. For instance, a crime victim may be able to recall the image of the perpetrator's tattoo under hypnosis while in a conscious state she could not. However, if she had an imagined perception of that image, then she may recall it during hypnosis with complete conviction though it may be in error.

Studies have shown, however, that hypnosis can be quite effective in the medical arena. Hypnosis has been used to alleviate pain, stress, and anxiety, and reduce nausea in chemotherapy patients. It has even been used to anesthetize patients who are undergoing surgery. Some psychologists are able to use hypnosis to break unwanted habits such as nail biting or to increase self-esteem by boosting a subject's confidence in herself and her abilities.

Meditation

Meditation, a self-induced altered state of consciousness, has been practiced throughout the world in several different cultures. It has recently gained popularity in the United States, perhaps because of its calming effect on the individual in this stress-filled society. Surely you've seen yoga classes and instructional books and videos popping up everywhere. (Yoga is a system of exercises designed to bring on a meditative state.)

The premise behind meditation is to get your body into a relaxed position and allow yourself to clear your mind of all worries, anxiety, and troublesome thoughts. As your body relaxes and your mind clears, your blood pressure lowers, your mental activity slows down, and your alertness is enhanced. People who have incorporated meditation into their daily or weekly schedules have reported that they are better able to cope with stress, feel more emotionally stable, and even experienced physical health benefits.

Psychoactive Drugs and Their Effects

Psychoactive drugs are those that work on the brain to alter mood, behavior, thinking, and perception. Using these drugs is probably the most common way individuals alter their states of consciousness. There are four major classifications of psychoactive drugs: depressants, hallucinogens, opiates, and stimulants. Let's take a closer look at each of these and their effects on the individual.

FACT

Marijuana is typically given its own category. While it does have some hallucinogenic properties, it is also thought to contain a mild stimulant even though the effects mimic those of depressants. The effects of marijuana can vary depending on dosage. Smaller dosages typically create a euphoric feeling while larger doses can cause hallucinations. It can impair your coordination, create feelings of anxiety, and slow down reaction times.

Depressants

As the name implies, depressants slow down the activity of the central nervous system. The most widely used depressant is alcohol. Other depressants include tranquilizers and barbiturates. Because they slow down mental and physical activity, depressants can make a person feel calm and less stressed. They also relieve anxiety and tension. While this may seem like a bonus, depressants can also impair your judgment and coordination and reduce your inhibitions, causing you to act in a way you normally wouldn't. Large doses of depressants can cause insensitivity to pain, convulsions, blackouts, and irregular heartbeats.

Hallucinogens

Hallucinogens interfere with your normal thought processes, altering your perceptions and affecting your senses. Popular hallucinogens include lysergic acid diethylamide (LSD), psilocybin (mushrooms), and mescaline (peyote). The effects of hallucinogens vary from person to person, and also vary with each use. When a person uses hallucinogens, he is often said to be "tripping." This trip could range anywhere from a pleasant period of enlightenment to the most hellish of nightmares. Hallucinogens can cause sensory hallucinations (hence the name), the most common being visual hallucinations.

Opiates

Opiates impair your ability to respond to and/or feel sensations, most notably pain. As such, you may receive a prescription from your doctor for an opiate to be used as a painkiller. Of course, opiates are also used for recreational purposes, though illegally. The most common opiates include opium, heroin, methadone, and morphine. The effects of opiates vary, but most experience a sudden euphoric feeling, or "rush," at first. This feeling is then often followed by a state of relaxation in which anxiety decreases.

While you may not like to think of yourself as a drug-user, if you have that daily cup of coffee or smoke cigarettes, you are in fact using drugs. The caffeine in coffee and the nicotine in cigarettes are both stimulants.

Stimulants

Stimulants are the opposite of depressants. They speed up the activity in the central nervous system. Stimulants include, but are not limited to, cocaine, methamphetamine hydrochloride (speed), and amphetamines (uppers). Because they speed up mental and physical activity, they often create a feeling of excitement, higher energy levels, and confidence. However, large doses can create anxiety and hallucinations, and can even cause convulsions and death.

Drug Abuse and Dependence

Not all drug use is abuse; after all, some drugs are prescribed and used for medicinal purposes. Drug use turns into abuse once it disrupts a person's daily activities or functions and/or interferes with a person's interaction with society or family and friends.

Many drugs are addictive, whether psychologically or physically. As drug use continues, the body can develop a tolerance to it. Once that happens, the drug's effect on the body lessens, and the user will have to take more of the drug to get the same effect. This can continue into a vicious cycle of dependence. It can even reach a point to where the user only feels normal when he or she is using. The hold on the user is so strong that if he or she were to try to cut back, the body would suffer a withdrawal, which is far from a pleasant experience. Withdrawal symptoms can include abdominal cramps, sweating, nausea, muscle spasms, insomnia, and depression.

Drug abuse and dependency is a problem that unfortunately runs rampant in our society today. While the use of psychoactive drugs will alter your state of consciousness, the potentially long-lasting negative effects can far outweigh the pleasant effects you may temporarily experience. If you are looking to alter your state of consciousness to achieve enlightenment, for recreation, or for an escape, there are other better and less harmful ways of accomplishing this.

Some people are more at risk of becoming addicted to drugs than others. There are several factors that contribute to your risk of becoming addicted, such as the drug you choose to use, your family history, your genetic makeup, your personality, and your ability to cope with stressors.

Chapter 9

Conditioning and Learning

To better understand ourselves and others, we need to take a look at how we learn our behaviors and why we do the things we do. This chapter will discuss the various learning processes psychologists study and how they affect our lives. You will also learn how cats, rats, and dogs played a part in our knowledge of learning behavior. Curious? Read on.

Habituation—The Most Basic Form of Learning

To learn how we learn, it is best to take a look at children between the ages of eighteen and twenty-four months. They have a hunger for knowledge that cannot be touched by even the most studious of adults. They are driven to learn by experience and observation. If you have had a child, you are fully aware that he will pick up anything he can get his hands on and possibly even mouth it. While this may be an annoyance to a parent, it is a part of the learning process for a child.

While a child might not be able to tell you what she is studying and what she wants to learn, through observation we can figure it out rather easily. Pay attention to a child who is surrounded with several objects. You will notice that she will quickly turn her attention to those objects that are new to her. Once she becomes acquainted with one new object, she will discard it and turn her attention to another. This process is called habituation and is the most basic form of learning. A child becomes habituated to an item, gets bored with it, and seeks out an unfamiliar object, thus creating a cycle of learning.

FACT

Through observation, we also know that babies have the ability to remember. When given a choice between two objects, a baby will glance at the object he is already familiar with and then reach for the object he has not seen before. He remembers already learning about the first object.

Habituation shows us that we have an innate desire to learn about and experience new things. It also shows that we are able to distinguish differences in objects, patterns, colors, and textures and remember those differences. While habituation is the earliest and most basic form of learning, it is not the only process through which we learn.

Conditioning

Behaviorists view learning as a change to or influence on a person's behavior due to experience. In other words, experience is the best teacher. The type of learning behaviorists focus on is conditioning. Conditioning is a learning process in which an environmental stimulus elicits a response, and an individual learns from the association between that stimulus and response. The association is what conditions, or modifies, our behavior and we therefore learn to behave in a certain manner toward the same stimulus in the future. There are two types of conditioning: classical conditioning and operant conditioning. If this seems confusing, don't worry. We'll take a closer look at each of these types of conditioning to help you better understand how it works.

Classical Conditioning

Classical conditioning was discovered, rather accidentally, by Ivan Pavlov. As mentioned before, Pavlov was studying the digestive processes in dogs. He inserted a tube into a dog's mouth in order to measure the amount of saliva the dog produced, using food to stimulate the flow of saliva. After visiting the lab several times for this procedure, the dog began to salivate before the food was in his mouth. The saliva was stimulated by the sight or smell of the food or even the sound of footsteps bringing the food. While Pavlov first considered this to be an obstacle to his experiment, he quickly realized that the dog's salivating was a conditioned response to its anticipation of being fed. As the dog had not done this before, he recognized that the response had been learned through experience. He dropped his study of the digestive system and turned to studying this response.

Though Pavlov is the one who coined classical conditioning and was awarded the Nobel Prize for his work in this field, some say that it was actually a student of his who pointed out that the dog was salivating before he had been given the food.

This is essentially the idea behind classical conditioning. By definition classical conditioning is the process by which a normally neutral stimulus becomes a conditioned stimulus, eliciting a response in an individual, or in this case a dog, due to its association with a stimulus that already elicits a similar response. Let's take a closer look at how this works.

How It Works

There are four components to classical conditioning. Breaking it down, the first two components are an unconditioned stimulus (US) and the unconditioned response (UR). The unconditioned stimulus in Pavlov's study was the dog's food. The food was the stimulus that automatically elicited the unconditioned response, salivation. These two factors are automatic. In other words, they were not conditioned, or learned.

The next two components make for an interesting study. In Pavlov's study, he paired the ringing of a bell with the distribution of the food, thus pairing a conditioned stimulus (CS) (bell) with an unconditioned stimulus (food). Eventually, he took away the US and only provided the CS. The CS by itself still produced the unconditioned response, thus making the UR a conditioned response (CR). In other words, the dog salivated when it heard the ringing of the bell even though there wasn't any food present. These two components were conditioned, or learned.

ALERT!

The neutral stimulus must come before the unconditioned stimulus in order for it to become a conditioned stimulus. In other words, the bell was rung before the food was given, which made it act as a signal that the food was coming. Had the bell followed the distribution of the food, it would not have been a signal and therefore would not have become a conditioned stimulus.

This process of a neutral stimulus becoming a conditioned stimulus is the basis for classical conditioning. Of course, you have to throw experience in there. A dog isn't likely to salivate after the bell is rung when paired with food just one time. The dog must experience this pairing regularly and repeatedly in order to make the association between the two stimuli.

Features of Classical Conditioning

Conditioned responses in classical conditioning aren't necessarily permanent responses. They can be unlearned, or extinguished. For instance, Pavlov's dog could have been reconditioned to have no response to the ringing of the bell. Had someone rung the bell regularly without following it with food over the course of several sessions, the dog would no longer have salivated to just the ringing of the bell, as it did not signal the coming of food. In which case, the conditioned response would have been extinguished.

Classical conditioning can also produce stimulus generalization and stimulus discrimination. Stimulus generalization occurs when an individual has the same conditioned response to a stimulus that is similar though not the same as the conditioned stimulus. In other words, if a child is bitten by a Rottweiler, he may fear all dogs, not just Rottweilers. Though not all dogs are the same, the stimuli are similar enough to elicit the same response. On the other hand, two similar stimuli may produce different responses, which is called stimulus discrimination. To use the previous example, another child may be bitten by a Rottweiler but is able to distinguish the difference between a Rottweiler and a poodle, and will therefore not produce the same response (fear) toward the poodle as she would toward a Rottweiler.

Applications of Classical Conditioning

Classical conditioning has affected your life, whether you realize it or not. Many of our emotional responses to sights, sounds, objects, or people can be tied to classical conditioning. For instance, let's say a former love interest always wore a particular brand of cologne. Should you smell that particular scent even years later, you may experience a sense of sadness as though you were reliving the loss of that person in your life, because you associated that scent with that person. Perhaps your family bakes a particular dessert on holidays. You may feel a surge of excitement when you catch a whiff of that scent because you associate it with past feelings of excitement.

FACT

Emotions can be a very powerful force. They can cause us to think or act in ways we would never dream of otherwise, sometimes even superseding our rationale. Advertisers try to make use of our emotional responses, thus classical conditioning, to get us to buy their products. For instance, think back to all the commercials you saw sporting the American flag following the September 11 attacks. Associating patriotic feelings with a particular product is good business!

Classical conditioning can produce both positive and negative responses, depending on the association made. Take, for instance, a thunderstorm. If a child were to hear the rumbling of thunder and then witness a tree being struck by lightning just a second later, he may fear that rumbling sound during future storms. However, a child who heard that same rumbling of thunder while he was cozily enveloped in his father's arms may later hear the rumbling of thunder and experience pleasant emotions, as the association was one of contentment.

Operant Conditioning

Another type of learning studied by behaviorists is operant conditioning. Operant conditioning is a process by which an individual's response is followed by a consequence (either positive or negative), and that consequence teaches us to either repeat the response or decrease its occurrence. The main difference between classical conditioning and operant conditioning is that in classical conditioning, the learning process is reflexive and is not dependent upon consequences, whereas in operant conditioning, the learning process is more complex and reliant upon the type of consequences the response elicits. In other words, the learning process results in different types of voluntary behavior. You can't decide whether or not to salivate, but you can decide to go to work if you like getting paid.

Cats and Rats

Edward Thorndike introduced and laid the foundation of operant conditioning in his experiment with cats. In this experiment, Thorndike built a puzzle box in which he placed a hungry cat. He then set a bowl of food outside the box where the cat could see it but could not get to it unless the cat was able to escape. The escape route was triggered by a mechanism that the cat had to work. Of course, the cat had no idea it was supposed to trigger this mechanism, so it ran about, bounced off the walls, and cried—in short it tried everything it knew to try to get to that food. Eventually, the cat accidentally tripped the mechanism, thus escaping and reaching the food. Thorndike placed the cat back in the box several more times, and each time it took the cat less time to find the trigger. After several times in the box, the cat eventually learned to trip the mechanism immediately to escape and get its reward. Thorndike thus came to the conclusion that the cat's behavior was controlled by the consequences: tripping the mechanism and getting the food, not tripping the mechanism and being stuck in the box.

In Thorndike's day, this wasn't known as operant conditioning. Instead, he had termed his theory the *law of effect*. This theory basically stated that a consequence had an effect on the behavior of an animal or individual and that if the consequence was good, then that particular behavior would be repeated in the future.

Burrhus Frederick (B. F.) Skinner took this idea and elaborated on it. Skinner used rats instead of cats for his experiments. He created a "Skinner box" in which he placed a rat. The box held a device that delivered pellets of food when a bar was pressed. Much like Thorndike's experiment, the rat at first scurried about without any purpose or motive behind its actions. Instead of waiting for the rat to accidentally press the bar and learn on its own, Skinner rewarded the rat with food as it got closer to performing the appropriate response (pressing the bar). Gradually, Skinner was able to shape the rat's behavior and teach it to press the bar. Eventually, the rat was intentionally pressing the bar for food as fast as it could. Skinner said that to understand a person, one must look outside the person, at the consequences of his or her actions, instead of trying to figure out the inside of the person. In other words, the person's past and current consequences are what shape that person's behavior.

How It Works

Operant conditioning is reliant upon the behavior being reinforced, either positively or negatively, which in turn will determine whether the behavior increases or decreases its likelihood of future occurrences. According to Skinner there are three types of consequences to a response: reinforcers, punishment, and neutral consequences. Reinforcers increase the likelihood that the response will occur again. Positive reinforcement is when you add a good thing after the behavior, like a treat. Negative reinforcement is when you take away something bad after the behavior, like the seat-belt buzzer that stops when you put your seat belt on. The important thing to remember is that reinforcements always increase the likelihood of behaving occurring again, whether they are positive or negative. Punishment decreases the likelihood that the response will occur again. For instance, if you touch a hot burner, and your finger gets burned, you are not likely to repeat the behavior. Of course, there are also neutral consequences. These have no bearing on whether the likelihood of a response will increase or decrease. These are typically ignored and do not affect any of your decisions.

Applications of Operant Conditioning

Examples of operant conditioning surround us in our daily lives. Think for a moment about why you do the things you do. Our lives are filled with reinforcers and punishers. You go to work because you get paid to do your job. Would you still go to work every day if that reinforcer wasn't in place? Probably not. When you drive to work, you likely stay within a reasonable approximation of the speed limit (at least we hope so) because if you didn't, you could get a speeding ticket, have to pay a fine, and risk having your insurance rates rise or risk getting into an accident. Do you drink coffee in the morning? This too can be a form of operant conditioning. After all, you drink the coffee because the caffeine helps to wake you up, right? Or perhaps you simply like the taste or the warmth it provides. Regardless, the effects of the coffee are reinforcers, increasing the likelihood that you will continue to drink the coffee each morning.

Operant conditioning can lead to bad habits. For instance, smoking is a bad habit and harmful to your health, so the punisher (deterioration of your health) should ideally decrease the likelihood that you will continue smoking, right? Well, unfortunately, many find that the reinforcers of smoking (relaxing feeling, feeding the body's addiction, etc.) outweigh the punishers and therefore continue the habit. Also, the reinforcer is closer in time to the behavior, where the punisher is far away in time—thus not a very effective contingency.

Teaching Behavior to Others

So far, we've discussed how operant conditioning has taught you particular behaviors, but you can also often be on the other side of the fence and teach behaviors to others. Take a parent, for example. If a child throws a tantrum in a store because she wants a particular object and the parent allows the child to have the object in order to stop the tantrum, that child has just learned that a tantrum will be rewarded with what she wants. It's quite likely the child will throw another tantrum the next time she wants something she is not given immediately. Incidentally, the child has just provided negative reinforcement for parental toy-buying behavior, thus increasing the probability that that behavior will occur again. Perhaps you have employees working for you. How you respond to certain behaviors, such as an employee being consistently late, affects how the person responds. If you choose to ignore the situation, the person will continue the behavior because the experience of being late (getting more time in bed, etc.) is reinforcing. However, if you instead use a punisher or reinforcer in response, the behavior is more likely to change. Of course, operant conditioning works on animals as well. If you have ever tried to train an animal, you understand quite well the effects of reinforcers and punishers.

Understanding how both classical conditioning and operant conditioning aid in a person's learning process and stimulate certain responses and behaviors will help you better understand both yourself and others.

Effective Reinforcement

When done properly, positive or negative reinforcement is much more effective than punishment in changing behavior because it increases the desired behavior (remember, reinforcement increases behavior). Punishment stops behavior, but it doesn't teach what to do instead. If you try to change behavior by punishing everything except the correct behavior, whoever you are training will either give up and stop offering any behavior, or will rebel.

If you want to keep behavior going almost indefinitely, once it is clearly learned, you can put it on an "intermittant, random reinforcement schedule." This means that the behavior is reinforced (positive or negative doesn't matter) at intervals that the trainee can't predict. This works especially if the reinforcer is strong. For example, once you know how to buy and play lottery tickets, you will be reinforced at intervals you can't predict—is it the next ticket? If you win $500, how long are you going to keep buying lottery tickets, hoping for another reward? Welcome to gambling addiction.

If you want behavior to go away, and you are very certain what the reinforcers are that are maintaining behavior, you can extinguish the behavior by witholding all reinforcement when it occurs. For instance, if you continued buying lottery tickets and never, ever again won, eventually you would stop buying them. The problem with extinguishing behaviors is that just before the behavior stops, it gets worse. This is called the "extinguishment burst", and it is deadly for the trainer. So if you're going to withold all reinforcement from your screaming child who wants a toy—hold the line! Do not buy that toy when the volume increases, or otherwise reinforce the behavior. Or you have just reinforced really horrible screaming behavior. If you're going to "try to ignore" bad behavior, and end up reinforcing it by providing attention when you can't stand it anymore (because the extinction burst is torturing you), don't do it. Trying will make it worse.

Learning Through Observation and Imitation

Yet another type of learning is learning through observation and imitation, called *observational learning.* While experience is certainly a great teacher, we needn't experience everything for ourselves in order to learn. We can watch the behavior and actions of others and learn from *their* experiences. In fact, this type of learning is very powerful and prevalent in children, though adults also participate in observational learning.

Because children are greatly affected by observational learning, telling a child to do as you say, not as you do, is not going to produce the behavior you want. The drive to model a parent's behavior is much stronger than the drive to take verbal orders, even if punishers or reinforcers are involved with the warning.

Watch any child and you will see observational learning taking place. Because they are most often around their parents and siblings, children are most likely going to model those family members' behavior. As they grow older, they will also begin to model the behavior of their peers and even the behavior of characters in movies and on television. They will carefully watch the actions and consequences of those actions in others.

If they like what they see and view a potential reward for a particular behavior, they will likely model that behavior, or one that is very similar. For instance, a child watching his father have fun playing basketball in the driveway will likely try to play basketball, too. Of course, modeling behavior doesn't always produce positive results. A child who watches a classmate bully another child into giving up a toy may mimic that behavior because a toy is the reward.

Adults also learn through observation. A med student learns procedures and bedside manner through observing other doctors on rotation in hospitals. An adult may learn how to climb the corporate ladder by watching and learning from the behavior and consequences of her superior. Think of your daily activities and those people you watch and learn from. You may be surprised to find that you participate in observational learning a lot more often than you may think. **E**

Chapter 10

How We Remember, Why We Forget

Our memories are powerful. They allow us to store the information we learn and retrieve it at a later date. They are a major component in creating individuality and are essential in carrying out daily activities. But how does memory work and why are we often unable to recall information we know is stored somewhere in the brain?

Memory—An Overview

Your memory allows you to retrieve a memory. While this may sound simple enough, memory is actually a very tricky and complex thing. Let's first take a look at the basics of how memory works.

Think of memory as a huge selective storage system that is capable of storing an immeasurable amount of information. Memory is reliant upon three components: encoding, storage, and retrieval. Encoding refers to the intake of information and the brain's conversion of that information into a form it is able to process. Storage refers to the placement of this processed information in the brain. The information may be stored as an image, a concept, or within a mental network. Retrieval, of course, refers to the recovery of that information and putting that information to use.

Filling in the Gaps

Most of us would like to think (and may even insist) that we are able to retrieve certain memories with every shining detail in place. For instance, you may swear you remember perfectly well the moment your husband proposed to you, including all details—after all, that was such a special occasion, how could you possibly forget? However, if you were asked to recall the event in detail, you would likely misremember several details and may even make up some others! This is because the retrieval of our memories is a reconstructive process in which we retrieve certain flashes of the event but fill in the gaps for those details that the memory didn't store or process properly.

The memory is selective. It will not store every single event that happens to us or every little detail or bit of information we take in. It has to be selective in order to keep the house clean, so to speak. If it were not, our minds would be cluttered with tons of insignificant and useless information.

Because we are forced to reconstruct the past somewhat when recalling a memory, we often rely on several other sources to fill in the gaps, often without even knowing we are doing it—hence our insistence that we are recollecting that memory perfectly. For instance, we may draw conclusions from photos or video of the event in question; stories others have told about the event; anything you may have said, thought, or felt about the event after the fact; or sometimes even wishful thinking (what we *wanted* the memory to be).

Implicit and Explicit Memory

As you well know, there are some things you work really hard to remember, such as information for an upcoming exam, and other things that you really have no desire to remember, but remember anyway, such as commercial jingles. So what's the difference?

The information that you intentionally work to remember is stored using explicit memory. Because you have spent energy to deliberately remember this information, it makes sense that the memory would store it. The information that you remember but did not intentionally put away for future use is stored using implicit memory. While it seems that this type of information must have affected you in some way, it is not certain exactly why this information is stored in memory.

FACT

The retrieval of explicit memory is usually tested in one of two ways: recall or recognition. Recall refers to the ability to actually retrieve that information you stored, such as in fill-in-the-blank or essay questions. Recognition refers to the ability to recognize the information stored, such as in multiple choice or true/false questions.

Sensory Memory and Incoming Stimulation

The memory as a huge storage system is divided into three storage subsystems, the first of which is sensory memory. This is the entranceway through which all incoming stimulation must pass. This subsystem is divided even further into storage areas for each of the senses: hearing, vision, smell, touch, and taste. For everything you sense, that information is sent directly to one of these memory areas.

The memory of these impressions is stored briefly. Have you ever noticed that after you shut off the radio, you can still hear the sound for a split second? Or perhaps you've looked at the sun (though you know you're not supposed to!) and then shut your eyes: Do you recall the image still being there? These lingering impressions are possible because they are temporarily stored in your sensory memory.

Because you are constantly receiving new information, the sensory memory cannot store impressions for long. For instance, the vision area stores impressions for only a fraction of a second. The hearing area stores impressions for a bit longer, but no more than about two seconds. Amazingly, this is enough time for your brain to decide what to do with this information.

Sensory memory also explains the bird-in-a-cage trick. If you aren't familiar with this "trick," it is where the image of a bird is placed on one side of a card and the image of a cage is placed on the other. When the card is spun rapidly, it appears as if the image you are seeing is the bird inside the cage.

During that short amount of time the impression is stored, the brain decides whether it is important or insignificant information. If it is deemed important, that impression moves on to the short-term memory. If it is deemed insignificant, the brain discards it and it is lost forever.

Short-Term Memory and Working Memory

The impression that makes it through the sensory memory then moves on to the short-term memory. During the transfer, the impression is processed, or encoded, and is turned into a pattern the brain can recognize, such as a word. The information does not stay long in the short-term memory either, only approximately twenty seconds.

The short-term memory deals with only the present time. It stores everything you are conscious of at the moment: the words you are reading, the food you are eating, the sound of a dog barking outside, the telephone number you just looked up, etc. The brain then decides whether to move this information on to the long-term memory or discard it.

Storage Room

The short-term memory can hold only so much information at any given time. But just how many items can it store? For several years, the magic number was seven, give or take two. This gives a good explanation for the number of digits in zip codes (five digits), phone numbers (seven digits), and social security numbers (nine digits). However, not everyone agrees with this number. Some have placed the number of items to be as few as two, while others place the number of items as high as twenty. Regardless, the short-term memory isn't able to hold very many items at one time.

The short-term memory can be a source of frustration for many of us. Depending on how quickly we are receiving new information to replace the information already there, items may be displaced before we are ready to part with them.

Luckily, we are able to combine bits of information into large chunks of information, where each chunk counts as one item. Thus we are able to store more information than we think. For instance, most of us store the term *DVD* as one item, or chunk, rather than three separate items. Along the same lines, you will often see businesses with phone numbers that can be stored as one chunk, such as 555-PETS, instead of seven individual items.

The Working Memory

The short-term memory not only stores new incoming information, it can also hold information that has been retrieved from the long-term memory to be used temporarily. The system within the short-term memory that processes and interprets the incoming information from the long-term memory is referred to as the working memory. For instance, if you are thinking of purchasing a sale item with a particular percentage discounted, your working memory handles the numbers you are working with as well as the instructions brought forth from the long-term memory for completing the mathematical equation to find out the price of the item.

Long-Term Memories and How They Are Stored

Your long-term memory is the final destination. Because it is unable to be measured, the long-term memory is thought to have an infinite capacity. You already have a vast amount of information stored there and are continuously storing more everyday. For instance, your activities of daily living are reliant upon the memories stored in long-term memory. At some point you learned how to shower, brush your teeth, dress yourself, make coffee, drive the route to work, do your job, make dinner, and set the alarm clock. The memories of how to do all these things are retrieved from the long-term memory, even though you may not be conscious of the retrieval. Of course, this isn't the only type of information stored; past experiences that make up your personal history and give you a sense of identity are stored here as well.

Storing and Organizing Information

While the long-term memory holds a great amount of knowledge, it is not just a jumble of bits of information swimming around in chaos. There is an organizational system present that helps both to store and retrieve memories.

When a memory enters long-term memory, it makes associations with memories already present. For instance, words are stored next to other words in your long-term memory that are similar in meaning, sound, or look. To help break it down even further, your mind creates categories for words, so *apple* and *peach* would be stored close to one another since they are both fruits. *Chair* and *table* would be stored next to each other since they are both items of furniture. *Shirt* and *skirt* would be stored close together because they are both articles of clothing. You get the picture. Items can belong to more than one category—for instance, you might want to remember all the pieces of clothing, jewelry, or shoes that you own that are black, in order to put together an outfit.

FACT

As oral storytelling was once the primary way of recording history (before the written word), several cultures relied on the long-term memory of their members to recant and pass on these stories. The *Oddessy* and the *Illiad*, for instance, were both originally oral epic poems that didn't get written down until long after they were composed.

The associations made are very important for both storage and retrieval. If your mind is able to associate a new concept or word with a memory already in long-term, then storage is made easy. Retrieval, also, is easier because as you are searching for that concept or word, your mind can look to the associations for help in bringing it to the consciousness.

Categories of Memories

The long-term memory is able to divide types of memories into three basic categories: procedural memories, episodic memories, and semantic memories. Procedural memories are those that provide information on how to do things. For example, riding a bike, brushing your teeth, tying your shoes, and driving are all procedural memories. Typically, this type of memory becomes so ingrained that it requires very little conscious retrieval or thought to carry out the activity. In other words, procedural memories are implicit.

Episodic memories are those that allow you to recall events and situations that you have experienced. Along with the event itself, the circumstances surrounding the event (location, time, etc.) are also stored. Semantic memories are basically facts you have learned—the date of your father's birthday, the meanings of words, your address, who invented the cotton gin, etc. Episodic and semantic memories are both types of explicit memories. They must be consciously retrieved from long-term memory.

Explanations of Forgetting

A common complaint most of us share is that of forgetting. Forgetting is the inability to retrieve information from the memory due to a problem with encoding, storage, or retrieval. Forgetting can be very frustrating, especially since we are usually aware of forgetting when we need to remember something—such as when taking an exam—or when we should have done something but the moment has passed—such as getting milk from the store before it closed.

Even though forgetting is natural to most of us, if you are fed up with forgetting, there are some techniques you can use to help you remember, such as rehearsal and mnemonics. These techniques will be explained in detail later in the chapter.

Though we don't often think of it as such, forgetting can also be a blessing. For instance, do you really want to remember the pain you experienced in that car accident five years ago? Forgetting allows us to continue our lives without giving focus to past painful, embarrassing, stressful, or unhappy experiences. Even so, most of us still want to know why we forget. Researchers have come up with various theories to explain this.

Replacement Theory

The replacement theory holds that new information entering the memory replaces old information already stored. Studies that support this theory show that misleading information replaces the original memories of people. For instance, one study showed pictures of a car accident to two groups of people. In one group, the researches asked leading questions to make the people think they had seen a yield sign, when the picture had actually shown a stop sign. Those in the other group were not asked leading questions and therefore remembered seeing the stop sign. When both groups were later gathered together, they were told the purpose behind the experiment and asked to guess if they thought they had been part of the group that was misled. Nearly everyone in that particular group claimed that they had truly seen the yield sign and were not misled. This led researchers to conclude that the implanted memory replaced the actual one.

Decay Theory

The decay theory holds that some memories will dissipate if not retrieved every once in a while from the long-term memory. (We already know that memories decay in the sensory and short-term memories.) Why waste space with information you aren't going to use? Fortunately, decay doesn't affect all memories. Many procedural memories will remain in the long-term memory for as long as you live. For instance, even if you haven't ridden a bike in fifteen years, you can still remember how once you get back on. There isn't a specific time limit on when a memory has to be recalled before it decays; some memories will be forgotten the next day, and others may take years to forget.

FACT

Memory loss can also be attributed to brain damage. Were you to suffer a blow to the head, the memories stored in that particular area may be lost. Depending upon the type of damage suffered, the memory loss can be either temporary or permanent.

Cue-Dependent Theory

The cue-dependent theory holds that the retrieval of some memories are dependent upon cues that help to locate that information in the brain; if these cues are missing, then we may not be able to remember.

Because the mind organizes information based on associations with other things, if you are able to recall an association, that increases your likelihood of recalling the particular information you are seeking. For instance, if you have forgotten the last name of a classmate, cues for remembering may be her first name, where she sat in class with you, her nickname, or even the circumstances surrounding the situation in which you first met her. Without these cues, you may not be able to recall her last name.

Interference Theory

The interference theory holds that information within the memory can interfere with other bits of information during storage or retrieval, thus causing us to forget. Incoming information can be similar to already stored information, which can cause confusion when later trying to recall the first-stored information. Or vice versa. The formerly learned information can interfere with the recollection of the recently learned information. For instance, if you've recently met two people with similar names, you might confuse the two names later when meeting one of them again. While this may seem like the replacement theory, it is different in that the new information does not replace the old. Both bits of information are still there; they just become confused.

Psychogenic Amnesia Theory

The psychogenic amnesia theory holds that we forget experiences because of the need to escape the feelings associated with a painful, embarrassing, or otherwise unpleasant experience. In essence, we force the memory to the back of our minds so we do not have to be aware of it. However, this doesn't mean that the memory can never be retrieved. Certain cues can be used to retrieve those memories. This theory began with Freud's theory of repression, which is the involuntary act of moving information that is deemed traumatic or threatening into the unconscious so as to avoid dealing with it. Because the individual is unaware of the memory stored in the unconscious, the individual does not recall the experience or feelings associated with the experience. In other words, it is blocked from the conscious memory, thus making us forget it. The repression theory has become a topic of debate among professionals, as we will soon see.

If you tell someone to "forget it," chances are you have just helped them to remember. While the information may have just resided in short-term memory and then eventually been discarded, your drawing attention to that information may have given it greater meaning and thus helped it to reach the long-term memory.

The Repression Debate

Professionals within the field of psychology have often debated the validity of repressed memories. In the 1980s, some believed that an individual was indeed able involuntarily to push a memory, especially one that was traumatic, to the unconscious, and was thus unaware of its existence. They believed that the individual could retrieve these memories in an altered state of consciousness, such as hypnosis, and recall perfectly the experience or event that took place.

The theory of repressed memories became a hot topic in the 1990s. Certainly, you've heard of at least one case in which an individual was able to recall a repressed memory of sexual abuse years later through psychotherapy and then filed charges against his or her abuser. While some accusations were corroborated with objective evidence, many were not and relied solely on the individual's recall of the repressed memory. Many believed that such recovered memories of abuse should be believed and viewed as accurate.

However, current thinking is that there is no way to know which memories are valid and which are not, other than by outside corroboration, and the client has to learn to live with that reality. The client would never know which recovered memories were real and which were created under hypnosis, and the damage caused by that would be considerable. Because of the way memory works, recovered memories cannot be considered accurate. As stated earlier, memory makes associations, and when recalled, fills in the gaps with information that can come from a variety of sources. Because of this, memory is vulnerable to the power of suggestion. Therefore, a therapist who uses leading questions about sexual abuse may cause a patient to "recover" a memory of abuse that he or she had supposedly repressed. Some believe that because objective corroborative evidence rarely accompanies repressed memories, people and the courts should be skeptical of the authenticity of repressed memories. What do you believe?

Techniques for Improving Your Memory

As you know, our memories aren't always reliable, and often it seems we forget what we need to remember most. So is all hope lost then? Is it all just a game of chance? No. There are strategies you can employ to help preserve that information you want to remember and increase the likelihood of its retrieval. You may already have a few tricks of your own, and by all means continue to use them. If you don't have any or would like to learn more, take a look at the following and see if you can use either of these strategies to help you not to forget.

The SQ3R Method

One of the best ways to trap information for future use is to effectively catch it coming in. The way you encode information determines where it is placed in your long-term memory. If information is encoded in a well-organized and efficient manner, the likelihood of its later retrieval increases. The SQ3R Method is one of the best encoding strategies out there.

Francis Robinson's SQ3R Method was invented during World War II to help military personnel in the Army Specialized Training Program comprehend the material they were learning in the accelerated college courses they took for those specialized skills they needed to fight the war.

In 1941, Francis Robinson, a psychologist, came up with a fantastic strategy for studying (and remembering) written materials. His strategy is called the SQ3R Method—**S**urvey, **Q**uestion, **R**ead, **R**ecite, and **R**eview. The first step is to survey, or scan, the material you will be reading. Take only a few minutes to do this. Look over the material, taking in the headings, subheadings, and any charts or illustrations. This will give you an idea of what you will be reading and will prepare your brain for how it will be organized.

The next step is to create questions that will be answered in your reading. The easiest way to do this is to turn the headings into questions, such as "What is SQ3R?" After you've come up with a list of questions, read through the material and write down the answers to your questions. To help you recall the information in the future, recite the answers and any other key points you encountered in the material. To finish and set the information in your long-term memory, review the material once again, while continuing to recite important points and the answers to your questions.

Mnemonics

Mnemonics are strategies, such as a rhyme or formula, that are used to improve the memory and help you retain and retrieve the information by making use of the information already stored in your long-term memory. Most of us were taught at least a few mnemonics during our school days. For instance, do you remember the rhymes, "In 1492, Columbus sailed the ocean blue" and "Use *i* before *e* except after *c*"? Or perhaps you were taught the formula "**M**y **v**ery **e**ducated **m**other **j**ust **s**erved **us** **n**ine **p**ies" as a trick to help you remember the order of the planets (Mercury, Venus, Earth, Mars, Jupiter, Saturn, Uranus, Neptune, and Pluto). Our teachers used these clever mnemonics to help us store that information for easy retrieval. Word associations, visual images, rhymes, and formulas can all also be used as mnemonics. You can even create a short story including those words or phrases you need to remember to help stimulate the long-term memory. 🝐

Chapter 11

Language and Communication

Communication and language are integral to the study of human psychology. Although there are more than 3,000 languages, spoken and signed, in the world today, all human languages share the same basic components, which will be examined in this chapter. We will also discuss whether language is a uniquely human characteristic.

Grammar and the Vocabulary of Language

Linguistics is the study of language as a complex system of sound or sign, structure, and meaning. Grammar is an integral concept in linguistics. If you are reading this book, you probably remember being taught English grammar at some point. However, we will adopt a technical meaning of the word. In linguistics, *grammar* is used to describe the complex mental system inherent to humans that forms the basis of all human languages. Grammar is composed of several parts that combine to create language: phonology, morphology, syntax, semantics, and pragmatics, which will be discussed in the following sections.

Knowledge of grammar is different from other types of knowledge in that it is largely subconscious. A speaker who learns a language as a first language, from infancy, is known as a native speaker. Native speakers have intuitions about whether or not certain sounds or structural meanings are acceptable in their language. Acceptable forms are grammatical; unacceptable forms are ungrammatical.

FACT

Human language is infinitely creative. We put the parts of our grammars together to form and interpret phrases and sentences that we have never heard or thought of before. In the following sections, we will examine the parts of grammar and how this grammar interacts with other aspects of society.

In order to scientifically approach the study of language, we must dispense with some false but widely held linguistic beliefs. First, many people believe that there are languages with no grammar. All human languages have a grammar. Second, many people believe that some languages or dialects are inferior to others. This is often a point of contention with people who worry about "substandard" dialects of their language. In fact, every person speaks a dialect. "Standard" usage is usually determined by the class of speakers with the most social power. There is nothing inherently superior about one dialect versus another. This also holds for different languages. There is simply no such thing as a primitive language. All languages are complex and creative systems used with full efficiency among their speakers. Finally, some people worry that language is degenerating. All languages undergo change. For instance, if you read Shakespeare, you will see the drastic changes in the English language that have taken place in just a few centuries.

Phonetics and Phonology— The Sound System

Phonetics is the branch of linguistics in which the sounds of language are explored. Humans are capable of creating innumerable sounds. Languages use only a very small portion of the possible range of sounds, called *phones*, or *segments*. Phonetics branches into two main components: articulatory phonetics, which deals with the physical mechanics of sound production, and acoustic phonetics, which deals with the properties of sound waves produced during speech. Humans appear to have innate knowledge that allows them to break down streams of sound input into segments.

Sound Production

Sound production is the result of the combined effects of several physiological processes. The lungs expel air while certain muscles work together to obtain and maintain the correct air pressure needed for speech, especially the diaphragm and the intercostals. Air moves up the trachea and through the larynx, or more commonly, the voice box. The larynx contains sheets of muscle called *the vocal cords*. The space between the vocal cords is the glottis.

The relative openness of the vocal cords is very important for the articulation of various sounds. For example, when the cords are open, air passes through without vibrating them resulting in voiceless segments. Put your fingers on your throat and make the sound "t." You should not feel any vibration. If, however, the vocal cords are brought closer together, air passing through causes them to vibrate resulting in voiced segments. Now, put your fingers to your throat and make the sound "d." You should feel the cords vibrate. Other possible glottal states are whisper and murmur.

After passing through the glottis, the air must pass through the pharynx and the oral and/or nasal cavity.

Vowels and Consonants

Sounds can be divided into classes. You are probably most familiar with the division of sounds into consonants and vowels. Consonants are produced with an obstruction in the vocal tract. Vowels are produced with very little obstruction in the vocal tract.

ALERT!

Consonants and vowels aren't the only classifications of sound. One class of sounds, called *glides,* sometimes pattern like consonants and other times pattern like vowels. Examples of glides would be *y* in "yes" or *w* in "want."

The manner of articulation is how the airflow is restricted. Some segments are nasal. For example, in English the sounds "m" and "n" are nasal. In these articulations, the airflow is blocked from the oral cavity. Oral segments use airflow through the oral cavity as in "b" or "s." Consonants can be divided into classes based on their manner of articulation. *Stops* involve a complete stricture of airflow as in "t" and "b." *Fricatives* have a continuous airflow, such as in "s" and "z." *Affricates* are a stop/release formation, for example "ch" and "dg" as in *judge. Liquids* are segments like "l" and "r."

Vowels, on the other hand, are described by the movement of the tongue and the shape of the lips during articulation. For instance, say the words *he* and *his.* Can you determine the placement of your tongue and the formation of your lips? These words are examples of high front vowels in English. Now say the words *who* and *put.* Where was your tongue and how were your lips formed? These are examples of high back vowels in English. These descriptions refer to the tongue body's location within the mouth. Vowels are described in terms of height (high, mid, or low) and front or backness (front, back, or mid). For something that seems to come so easily to us, language is a very complex structure of sound and meaning!

Phonology

Phonology is the study of the sound patterns of language. Each language selects a set of sounds from the set of all possible sounds of language. The phonological component of grammar determines the possible patterns of sound for a given language. For example, if you are a native English speaker, given the following words *ftornik* and *klants*, you would know that the first word is not possible in English but the second one is possible, even though neither is a real word in English. However, Russian has a different set of phonological requirements, and *ftornik* is a word in Russian meaning "Tuesday."

Morphology—The Formation of Words

Morphology is the branch of linguistics that deals with the formation and structure of words. Words are important in the study of language. As the smallest sound/meaning units that can stand on their own, they provide insight into the structure of the language itself. For example, to an English speaker the word *dog* means "a canine." However, for a Russian speaker *sobaka* has this meaning, and for a French speaker, the word is *chien*.

Morphemes

Words are composed of morphemes. Morphemes are the smallest units into which language can be divided that have systematic sound-to-meaning correspondences. In English, words can be composed of a single morpheme, for example, *dog*. The word *dog* cannot be broken down any further and retain its meaning. However, words may also be composed of several morphemes; take, for example, the word *undoable*. This word is composed of three morphemes: *un, do,* and *able*.

Another method of word formation is onomatopoeia. Onomatopoeia describes the process whereby speakers of a particular language make up words that sound like the thing they represent. Words like *buzz, woof,* and *meow* are onomatopoeic.

Morphemes are classed based on their role in the word. In the previous example, the morpheme *do* is the root, which means it carries the core meaning of the word. The other two morphemes, *un* and *able* are affixes, meaning they are added to the root. Breaking it down even further, *un* is a prefix because it precedes the root; *able* is a suffix because it follows the root. Affixes are added in a certain order to provide meaning. They are added to a base, which is composed of the root and any preceding affixes. Affixes are considered bound morphemes because they cannot stand alone. Morphemes that can stand alone are called *free morphemes*.

Derivation and Inflection

Derivation and inflection are two important morphological processes. In derivation, a word is formed from another through affixation, and the new word has a category (such as noun, verb, adjective, etc.) that is different from its original category. For example, in English, adding the suffix *–able* to a verb results in an adjective: read→readable. Adding the suffix *–ness* to an adjective results in a noun: ugly→ugliness. Inflection, however, does not change the word's category but adds grammatical information. In English, singular versus plural distinction is marked by adding *s*: book→books.

Nonconcatenative Morphemes

So far we have only seen examples of concatenative morphology—that is, end-to-end morphology in which morphemes are attached in a linear order. However, there are many examples of nonconcatenative morphology. For instance, in Arabic, the root *ktb* means "to write." The vowels and their placement act as a morpheme: *katab* means "write" and *uktab* means "being written." An example of nonconcatenative morphology in English is the grammatical change of a word by means of a vowel change: *tooth* to *teeth* and *goose* to *geese*.

Syntax—How We Create Phrases and Sentences

Syntax is the study of the structure and composition of phrases and sentences. Within the linguistic community there are several competing theories about syntax. Syntax is a very complicated and somewhat controversial branch of linguistics. In this section, we will look at a brief overview of syntax and the important concepts in the field without delving too deeply into one theoretical approach or another.

Many people who attempt to learn a new language have a tendency to try to apply the structure of their native language to the new language. However, languages vary in the order and structure of elements. So, as you learn a new language, you will have to adapt your way of thinking about sentence structure.

Creating Phrases and Sentences

Words make up phrases and sentences. They fall into well-known categories such as nouns, verbs, adjectives, adverbs, and prepositions. Of course, there are other less commonly known categories, such as determiners, degree words, qualifiers, auxiliaries, and conjunctions. Determiners are words like *the* and *a*. Degree words are words like *too*. Qualifiers include words like *always*. Auxiliary verbs, often known as helping verbs, are words like *can* or *will*. Conjunctions include words like *and* and *but*.

Words combine to form sentences and phrases. For instance, let's take a look at the following sentence: Harry talked to the doctor on Monday. Phrase structure rules describe the way in which sentences are put together. Breaking down the phrase structure rules for this English sentence, you would get:

- Sentence→Noun phrase plus verb phrase ("Harry" plus "talked to the doctor on Monday")
- Noun phrase→Determiner plus noun ("the" plus "doctor")

- Verb phrase→Verb plus prepositional phrase ("talked" plus "to the doctor")
- Prepositional phrase→Preposition plus noun phrase ("to" plus "the doctor")

In order to describe all the phrase structure rules, we would have to examine many more sentences. This is a small but explanatory example.

Surface and Deep Structure

Even if we follow the phrase structure rules, this does not guarantee a conveyance of a clear meaning. In syntax, there is a distinction between the surface structure of a sentence (meaning the way the sentence is spoken) and the deep structure of a sentence (meaning the way the sentence is to be understood). For instance, the surface structure of the previous example sentence, "Harry talked to the doctor on Monday," conveys one clear meaning, or deep structure. However, consider the sentence "Sally hit the man with the bat." Does this sentence mean that Sally hit the man who held the bat, or does it mean that Sally used the bat to hit the man? This sentence has one surface structure, but two deep structures. We mentally process sentences as we hear them using our knowledge of syntax. Which meaning did you take when you first read the sentence? Because your knowledge of syntax processed that particular meaning, you likely didn't even consider the other meaning until it was related to you.

Semantics and Pragmatics—Meaning and Language in Social Contexts

Language is not merely an abstract system that exists in a mental vacuum. Language is a vehicle for meaning and is highly influenced by the minds of the speaker and listener and factors such as social context.

Semantics is the branch of linguistics that deals with meaning in language. The study of semantics in linguistics is a complex and advanced field combining the disciplines of mathematics, linguistics, logic, and philosophy. Meaning is a complicated idea and is the subject of debate for scientists and philosophers, from the Greeks to modern scholars. However, we will limit our scope to words, phrases, and sentences and define "meaning" as the content of these units.

Semantic Relationships

At the word level, there are several semantic relationships with which you are probably already somewhat familiar. Synonymy is one such relationship. Synonyms are words that have nearly the same meaning. They can often be used interchangeably. For example, to an English speaker, the words *friendly* and *amicable* or *couch* and *sofa* mean almost the same thing. On the other hand, antonyms are words that mean the opposite of one another. Examples of antonyms in English are *dirty* and *clean,* and *tall* and *short*.

FACT

There are also semantic relationships between sentences and phrases. One such relationship is that of a paraphrase. This is a restatement of the meaning of an utterance. For example, the sentence "The ship was sunk by pirates" can be paraphrased as "Pirates sank the ship." Although these sentences mean nearly the same thing, there are slight differences between the two.

Some words are lexically ambiguous—that is, they have more than one possible meaning, depending on context. Homophony results in lexical ambiguity. A homophone is a word that has more than one meaning. For example, the word *rock* has at least two distinct meanings. A "rock" is a noun synonymous with a stone. To "rock" is a verb meaning a swaying or back-and-forth movement. Polysemy also results in lexical ambiguity. Polysemous words have at least two related meanings. For example, the word *smart* can either mean "intellectually outstanding" as in "Mary is smart" or "neat or well dressed" as in "Mary looked smart."

Metaphor is believed to be the source of many words and expressions. Metaphor is the use of one idea to explain another.

Metaphor is not merely a literary device. It is prevalent in every aspect of our lives and is reflected in our speech. For example, we speak about moods in terms of colors: "I was feeling blue."

Truth Conditions

One way to determine the relationship between sentences is to look at each sentence's truth conditions, or the circumstances when the sentences are true. Sentence 1 *entails* sentence 2 when the condition is met that when the first sentence is true the second sentence is also true. For instance, take a look at these two sentences:

Sentence 1: Alex's wife is named Kristin.
Sentence 2: Alex is married.

In this example, sentence 1 entails sentence 2. Notice though that sentence 2 does not entail sentence 1 since it could be true that Alex is married, but his wife is named Cindy.

The opposite of entailment is contradiction. When sentence 1 is true, sentence 2 is false. Consider these sentences:

Sentence 1: Alice is buried in Connecticut.
Sentence 2: Alice lives in Nebraska.

As long as the Alice in sentence 1 is the same Alice as in sentence 2, sentence 2 cannot be true if sentence 1 is true.

Pragmatics

Outside factors such as the beliefs, attitudes, and background of speaker and hearer and the context and cotext of the utterance also affect interpretation. Pragmatics is the study of these other factors and their effect on meaning.

One example of the importance of environment is the use of deictics. Deictics require information about the context in order to be fully interpreted. Take for instance the sentences "This dish has peanuts. That one doesn't." In the preceding sentences, the words *this* and *that* are deictics. A listener would have to have knowledge of the setting in order to properly interpret the sentences.

Discourse

Discourse is the collection of utterances surrounding the speech acts. When perpetrating a speech act, the speaker has assumptions about how much the listener already knows (old information) versus what the listener does not know (new information). For instance:

Mary is taking him to the fair.
Mary is taking George to the fair.

The use of the pronoun in the first sentence indicates that the speaker's listener knows who is represented by "him." This is old information. In the second sentence, "George" replaces "him," so it must be that the identity of the person Mary is taking to the fair is new information.

The Cooperative Principle

In order to be able to enter into and understand a conversation, people must hold certain assumptions. People must assume that the people they are talking to are not just randomly speaking but are actually trying to convey some meaning. The Cooperative Principle, developed by philosopher H. P. Grice, is the assumption that people are attempting to contribute something to the conversation. Grice also developed a set of maxims to further explain the Cooperative Principle:

- **Maxim of Relation:** Be relevant.
- **Maxim of Quality:** Say what is true.
- **Maxim of Quantity:** Be as and only as informative as necessary.
- **Maxim of Manner:** Be clear and orderly.

These maxims are not rules but assumptions people have when they enter a conversation. People flout maxims quite often in conversation. They do this on purpose to convey some sort of meaning. But in order to recognize this meaning, one must recognize the maxim being flouted. For example:

A: Do you want to go to Florida this weekend?
B: I have to work.

Sentence B flouts the maxim of relation. B's answer is not directly relevant to the question, but he assumes that the person he is speaking to is obeying the Cooperative Principle and will therefore get the interpretation that he will not be able to go to Florida for the weekend.

Gestures and Other Nonverbal Communication

The human communication system is not limited to language alone. Nonverbal communication is a very important part of human interaction that is so natural it is often overlooked altogether when discussing communication. Facial expressions and hand gestures are a couple of the more obvious forms of nonverbal communication, but posture, stance, eye contact, and even use of space are often used to convey messages.

ALERT!

While you may think that the gestures you use are universal, many aren't, so be cautious when using gestures in foreign countries. For example, former president George Bush flashed what he considered to be the peace sign in Britain, though there the gesture was an obscene one, akin to the "middle finger" here in the States.

Nonverbal communication adds a flavor to everyday communication that just can't be matched in any other way. Consider facial expressions. If you were to approach someone who is smiling broadly as she says hello, you would interpret this as a sign that you are a welcome sight to the person. However, if you were to approach someone and he said hello but had a let-down or annoyed look on his face, you would interpret this as a sign that you are not a person he is particularly happy to see even though he welcomed you with "hello."

We all use nonverbal communication every day. We nod our heads to convey to another that we understand or the answer is *yes*. We allow others their personal space to convey that we are not a threat. We make eye contact with a speaker to show that we are listening to what is being said. We wave hello and goodbye. The list could go on and on. Pay attention to your use of nonverbal communication and gestures for just one day and you will soon understand how important it is to human interaction and the conveying of messages.

Can Other Animals Learn Human Language?

The short answer to this question is no, animals cannot learn human language. In order to answer this question, we must distinguish between human language and other forms of communication. Language is a creative and infinite system. Many other animals have complex systems of communication. Some bees, for example, can communicate information about their food: where it is and how far, and its quantity. Several species of birds and monkeys are known to have complex signaling systems. These forms of communication are different from language in that they are very limited. Humans can talk about the past, future, or fictional events. They utter sentences that they have never seen or heard before. They have the ability to use language to alter the thoughts and ideas of other humans.

FACT

The Clever Hans controversy involved a horse that appeared to be able to do math and communicate messages by tapping his hoof. It turned out that Clever Hans could not do this when he could not see his trainer. His was a feat of perception only.

There have been many attempts to teach animals language. Usually the pupil is a primate, being our closest relative. One such attempt involved a chimpanzee called Nim Chimpsky after the famous linguist Noam Chomsky. While Nim was quite successful compared to many other attemptees, his linguistic abilities never even reached a level comparable to the level of a four-year-old human child. He could not master syntax and his vocabulary was quite small. Many scientists theorize that the primates are not actually mastering symbolic language but rather are learning behavioral responses to their human trainers. Language is uniquely human. This is not denigrating to animals. Each species has its own communication system. Ⓔ

Chapter 12

Thinking, Knowing, and Solving Problems

You know how information enters and is stored in the brain, but then how do we use that information and apply it to our daily lives? This chapter is going to explore the inner workings of the mind, while focusing on how the units of knowledge in our mind interconnect, our reasoning abilities, and how we solve problems.

The Cognitive Perspective

Cognitive psychology, as mentioned before, focuses on studying the mental processes. In other words, it studies how people think, reason, solve problems, understand language, remember, form beliefs, etc.—all that good stuff that goes on inside your head. The cognitive processes (such as thinking, reasoning, remembering, etc.) are what allow you to understand your environment and how the environment affects you and in turn how you affect the environment.

Studying Thought

You've learned how we learn, remember what we've learned, and where that information is stored. Now, we're going to take a look at how we use that information in our minds to interpret and understand the world around us. Think of the world as a mystery we are constantly trying to solve.

Our minds, in turn, are mysteries cognitive psychologists are constantly trying to solve. However, studying thoughts isn't an easy thing to do. It's not as though a thought is something tangible you can pick up, turn around in your hands, feel, and examine. Even if you were to split open someone's head and examine the brain, you still wouldn't be able to study his or her thoughts.

FACT

One of the first ways researchers tried to study thought was through introspection, in which participants wrote down ideas, images, and feelings as they experienced them. Psychologists tried to study this in order to figure out the mental processes of humans. However, we are too complicated and do not all have the same thoughts and ideas; therefore, introspection did not work.

Researchers, therefore, have built models that are used to explain the inner workings of the mind, the most popular being the information-processing model. This model is a hypothetical representation, somewhat analogous to a computer, in which the thought process can be broken down into components, or units of knowledge, that work together as though along an assembly line to process information.

The Big Picture

In a moment, we'll take a look at those units of knowledge that work together to create thought, but right now, let's take a look at the big picture. First of all, an impression enters your brain through your senses. For instance, let's say you are watching a cooking show on television and a chocolate dessert catches your eye. The brain then manipulates the impression to give it meaning and make sense of it. You love chocolate and the dessert looks scrumptious and certainly like something you would enjoy eating. Next your brain runs through possible responses. You try to recall if you have all the ingredients needed and try to figure out how the cook is making the dessert. Finally, you carry out a response and analyze the results. You run to the kitchen, pull out the ingredients, and try to make the dessert. While this may sound simple enough, the brain is processing several bits of information that must work in conjunction to reach this thought process. Now, let's take a look at those units of knowledge.

Units of Knowledge

As mentioned before, there are units of knowledge that make up the components that work together to process information and create a thought. There are three basic units of knowledge: concepts, prototypes, and schemata.

Concepts

The first unit of knowledge is the concept. This is basically a category that groups together items with similar characteristics or properties. These are the building blocks that are used to create the foundation of thought. Concepts can represent objects, abstract ideas, relationships, or activities. For instance, *dog* is a concept, but so are *love*, *exercise*, *marriage*, and *weather*. Each concept has a list of characteristics that define it. For example, *dog* would have a list that included bark, tail, fur, and four legs. A German shepherd, poodle, Chihuahua, mastiff, and Rottweiler are all examples of this concept.

ALERT!

This isn't to say that all examples must have the exact same characteristics. For instance, not all dogs bark and not all birds fly, but those nonbarking dogs are still examples of the dog concept and those nonflying birds are still examples of the bird concept. All examples of the concept will share a "family resemblance."

Prototypes

Taking the idea of a concept one step further, we come to prototypes. A prototype is basically the most recognizable example of a concept and is therefore the representative of that concept. When your mind is trying to decide where to categorize an impression, it compares that impression with the prototype of a concept. If the impression has similar characteristics to that prototype, it will become an example of that particular concept. For example, your prototype of a chair is likely a piece of furniture used for sitting that has four legs, an upright straight back, and a square or rectangular seat. When you came across a highchair for the first time, your brain processed the impression, comparing it to the prototype of the chair. Once it determined that the highchair had characteristics similar to that prototype, it was filed away as an example of the concept *chair*.

Schemata

Concepts are building blocks, so our brain uses them to build. Concepts are put together to create propositions, which are units of meaning expressing a single idea. Come up with a sentence, any sentence. This is a proposition. Propositions that are related are linked and create a network of knowledge and information that makes up a schema. A schema is basically a mental model of what we expect from a particular encounter.

These schemata are built using our experience and concepts and allow us to have certain expectations when we encounter ideas, beliefs, situations, or people in our environment. We can create schemata about anything from a jog in the park to a particular religion to a race of people.

Formal Reasoning

One of the main things that separates us from animals is our ability to reason. Reasoning is the process of using information (such as facts, assumptions, or observations) to reach conclusions. There are two types of reasoning: formal and informal. All reasoning problems have two major components: premises and conclusions. Premises are those statements of information or observations (those propositions we spoke of earlier) you use to help you reach an answer. The conclusion is basically the answer or the point you have drawn from the premises. Formal reasoning problems are those in which the premises are specified and there is typically only one valid conclusion.

Whether or not the conclusion is valid is determined by whether it is logically based on the truth of the premises. For instance, the following two statements are premises: All quadrilaterals have four sides. A square has four sides. The conclusion drawn from these two premises is that a square is a quadrilateral. Now that you know the components of reasoning, let's take a look at the two major types of formal reasoning: deductive reasoning and inductive reasoning.

Deductive Reasoning

Deductive reasoning uses premises that are guaranteed to be followed by a conclusion of truth. For instance, consider the previous example of the quadrilateral and square. The two premises are generalizations based on fact. Therefore, through deductive reasoning you are able to determine that the conclusion is also factual.

However, the premises have to be in the proper order for this to work. Using the same example, switch the order of the premises: All squares have four sides. A quadrilateral has four sides. You then reach the following conclusion: A quadrilateral is a square. This is not true even though the premises were both facts. The larger category, quadrilaterals, must be within the first premise.

You may not realize it, but you use deductive reasoning quite often, though it is often implicit: "I have to be at work at 8:30 every Monday. Today is Monday. Therefore, I have to be at work at 8:30 today." To help you better understand this, try to think of some examples of deductive reasoning in your daily life.

Inductive Reasoning

Inductive reasoning uses premises to predict an outcome or conclusion that is *probably* true, though there is a possibility the conclusion is false. For example, you may use the premises that most Americans don't speak Russian and that Laura is an American to conclude that Laura doesn't speak Russian. However, it is still a possibility; perhaps she learned Russian in school or from relatives. Or you may recognize a pattern in your observations and use this to draw a conclusion. For instance, you notice that Tom was late to work on Monday, Tuesday, and Wednesday, and therefore you conclude that Tom will be late to work on Thursday. Again, while this is probable, it isn't guaranteed.

Informal Reasoning

Informal reasoning is trickier than formal reasoning, as there is often not one specific correct answer and often not all the premises are supplied. Good examples of informal reasoning problems are those life issues that are controversial, such as abortion or the death penalty. While you may firmly believe in those premises that have led you to reach a conclusion that you feel is the only conclusion, those on the other side of the controversy feel the same way toward their premises and conclusion. In cases such as these, there are often several possible answers to the problem. So how is reasoning applied to such problems?

Dialectical Reasoning

Informal reasoning problems often call for dialectical reasoning. Dialectical reasoning is the process in which you compare and evaluate the opposing points of view to try to resolve the issue at hand. If the issue cannot be resolved, then dialectical reasoning is used to reach the best possible solution. Because controversial topics are often fueled by personal feelings or experiences, it is often difficult to apply dialectical reasoning. For instance, in the case of the death penalty, you would likely be able to list your points of argument rather easily, but when trying to list the points of argument for the opposition, you may have trouble being objective.

FACT

An algorithm is a step-by-step procedure used to guarantee a solution to the problem. While algorithms are useful in solving formal reasoning problems, such as a mathematical equation, they cannot be applied to informal reasoning problems, because the essence of these problems lies in that they typically do not produce a guaranteed correct solution.

While it may seem as though such problems cannot ever be solved, even with dialectical reasoning, there are other types of informal reasoning problems that can benefit from the use of dialectical reasoning. Take for instance the problem facing a jury. This is an informal reasoning problem because not all the premises are always provided and a correct solution is not guaranteed. The jury must apply dialectical reasoning as they compare, contrast, and weigh the points of argument for both sides as they use logic and evidence to reach a best possible solution. Of course, a verdict isn't always guaranteed, but for the most part, dialectical reasoning does help the jury reach a conclusion of guilty or not guilty.

Heuristics

Of course, not all informal reasoning problems are going to be controversial or as weighty as a court trial. There are plenty of other informal reasoning problems we encounter in our daily lives. When time doesn't allow the application of dialectical reasoning, most people resort to using heuristics. A heuristic is basically a rule of thumb that is used to guide your actions toward producing a best possible solution, but this does not mean that the best possible solution will be reached; heuristics are just guidelines and cannot guarantee an outcome.

For instance, those who play chess know that a good rule of thumb is to build up a good defense to protect your king. When you take action to utilize this strategy, you are applying a heuristic. Again, winning the game is not guaranteed from using this heuristic, but it certainly increases your chances! Or perhaps you suspect your significant other of being dishonest with you. While you may not have all the premises to work with, you can use a heuristic to help you solve the mystery: Trust a man's actions before his words. Can you think of any other heuristics you often use to reach a solution to informal reasoning problems?

Strategies in Problem Solving

Solving problems is integral to learning. We began solving problems at a very young age. Granted, those problems may seem trivial (how to get a toy) now compared to the problems we face as adults (how to pay the bills), but they certainly didn't seem trivial at the time. Problems are problems, regardless of the importance or severity; they all have a common goal: to reach a solution. So how do we do that? By employing problem-solving strategies. There are numerous problem-solving strategies out there, but let's take a look at some of the most commonly used.

ALERT!

Not every problem-solving strategy can be applied effectively to each problem. You'll need to determine what kind of problem you are working on and seek out the best strategy to use. For instance, if you are trying to figure out how you're going to pay the bills, then trial and error might not be the best way to go, whereas the other strategies mentioned will work more effectively.

Trial and Error

As children, the most common problem-solving strategy we employed was likely trial and error. For instance, let's say the problem a child faces is how to retrieve a toy his mother has put up on a shelf. The child may try to stretch his arms to reach the toy. That doesn't work. Next, he tries to climb up on the shelf to reach the toy. He falls; that doesn't work. When he can't get it on his own, he asks his mother for the toy. She says no; that doesn't work. Still undeterred, the child cries a bit for the toy. The mother ignores the cries; that doesn't work. Finally, he throws a full-blown tantrum, complete with screams, kicks, and tears. Exasperated, the mother gives the child the toy to appease him. Bingo—the tantrum worked. What do you think he's going to do the next time he faces the same problem?

Puzzles are a great example of problems solved through trial and error. There are several types of puzzle games out on the market to help children learn, and they learn through trial and error. They try to fit a puzzle piece in a particular spot. If that doesn't work, they either keep working with that piece until they find its proper location or they move on to another piece and work with the original spot they were trying to fill.

Brainstorming

Brainstorming is a problem-solving strategy in which you come up with as many possible solutions as you can, usually within a certain period of time. You write down everything that comes to mind, regardless of how ridiculous or implausible it may seem. You simply let your mind go. In using this technique, you are often able to come up with some very creative and imaginative ideas. While not all solutions are going to be able to be employed, chances are you are going to come up with a few that just might work. Once you've created a list and the brainstorming session is over, you can then work through each idea and either discard it or set it aside for closer inspection. By narrowing down the list, you are able to focus your attention on those ideas that are most plausible.

The next time you are facing a comprehensive problem at work, and you just can't seem to come up with a solution, gather a few of your coworkers and suggest a brainstorming session. Brainstorming is even more effective when you are able to tap the minds of more than one person.

Take It Step-by-Step

Probably the best-known, or at least the most-studied, problem-solving technique is that which was introduced by Allen Newell and Herbert Simon (1972). This strategy breaks the problem down into steps that you go through to reach a solution. Though they went into depth with each of the steps, we'll just take a look at the basic principle of each.

The first step is to identify the problem. You must recognize that a problem exists before you can begin to solve it. The second step is to build a representation of the problem, defining it by stating the problem as it was first introduced and the problem's goal. The third step is to create a list of possible strategies and evaluate each. The fourth step is to choose the best strategy out of those possible and to apply that strategy. The final step is to reflect on the effect of that strategy—in other words, see if it worked. Ⓔ

Chapter 13

Personality and Personality Tests

Children often have more personality in their pinkies than some adults have. Television and radio personalities are familiar friends. Agencies specialize in finding the perfect match for your personality type by promising true love. Personality plays a major role in our lives and surrounds us. This chapter explains why and how it not only affects the decisions we make, but defines who we are.

What Is Personality?

How we perceive and react to our environment on a day-to-day basis can be measured by our behavior, thoughts, and emotions. We're "individuals" because a unique combination of these characteristics provides the basic foundation of who we are and makes up the personality that friends and family have come to like (and dislike!).

Characteristics

Characteristics set us apart, yet also bring us together because of the singular diversity each of us adds to the collective mix of life. In other words, each person is his or her own snowflake and no two are alike. Your best friend has qualities you can identify with, whether you admire them or not. It's the unique combination of these characteristics and your acceptance of them that makes the relationship with your friend a positive one.

Types of Behavior

Behavior is how we react to social and physical aspects of our environment based on our personalities. Where one person may never show emotions of anger, joy, grief, or anxiety, another person's responses may be dramatically colored with facial expressions, voice inflections, and hand gestures. Behavior is examined in two ways: internally controlled and externally controlled. Internal theorists believe the individual characteristics of a person dictate the behavioral pattern, while external advocates hold that the behavior is a result of the situation at hand.

Public and Private Personalities

How the world perceives you is a direct reflection of and reaction to how you present yourself to them. Race, age, and gender are qualities you have no control over, but certainly contribute to your personality because of how the world perceives you based on these features. A person who continuously experiences racial discrimination may guard himself against it by at first seeming cold and unfriendly.

But once he or she opens up, you may discover someone completely different inside.

Physical attributes, which you develop over time, also contribute to your personality, and include mannerisms (soft speakers are dubbed "shy" whereas loud speakers are labeled "obnoxious"), gait (purposeful long strides, bouncy sauntering, etc.), eye contact, and facial expressions. How you want the world to perceive you has an effect on how you present yourself to others. Characteristics such as attitude (friendly, outgoing, standoffish, introverted, etc.), response (polite, thoughtful, rude, arrogant, etc.), and general mindset (are you usually upbeat or moody?) create the surface of your one-of-a-kind personality.

Many of us are multifaceted—we project a different personality depending on whom we encounter. For instance, the personality we exhibit to our bosses is likely going to be a lot different than the personality we exhibit to our closest friends.

Dig a little deeper, and the private aspect of your being appears: dreams too bizarre to discuss; experiences too sentimental to reveal; fantasies that may seem childish to others; goals, standards, and morals you aspire to; daily internal dialogue, thoughts, and ideas—all of these elements make up the "you" that only you truly know. And only you can decide when to share these parts of your personality with others. For example, you might be outgoing, courageous, intelligent, and have a lovely voice, but when you step up to the podium to deliver a speech in front of twenty people, you suddenly become anxious, fearful, and at a loss for words.

Heredity, Environment, and Personality

Since the moment you were born, biology has influenced your behavior in ways that may have seemed insignificant then, but are more relevant now. For instance, active babies frequently look around the room and at the people in it, whereas a quieter baby tends to hold a steady gaze in one direction, focusing on a single activity. Granted, these babies may grow up to develop adult personalities that are completely opposite of their newborn personalities, but studies have shown that these characteristics are often a good indicator of who the child will grow to be. In addition to biological factors, both common and unique life experiences help shape your personality.

Biological Factors

Determining the amount of genetic influence that contributes to the makeup of personality has proved to be a difficult task. However, in studying both fraternal and identical twins, we're able to gain some insight into this mystery. After a series of tests, studies have shown that identical adult twins were more likely to answer questions in the same way than fraternal twins were. In subsequent studies, identical twins who were separated for long periods of time compared to those who weren't separated continued to exhibit the same level of personality traits. Similarity in body shapes has also been studied as it may help in understanding why twins who are separated are still alike in an alarming number of ways.

QUESTION?

What is the difference between identical and fraternal twins? Identical twins are produced when a single egg is fertilized by a single sperm (the children share the same set of genes). Fraternal twins are produced when two eggs are each fertilized by a different sperm (the children share approximately half of their genes).

Physiological Differences

Monoamine oxidase (MAO) is an enzyme that functions in the nervous system by breaking down the neurotransmitters said to be a key factor in emotional and motivated behavior. It's an important element to consider, because the levels of MAO in a person's body change due to age and sex hormones. Also, since MAO is an inherited, physiological trait, adventurous parents, for instance, pass that trait along to their offspring and are more likely to have children who are just as adventurous as they are than parents who are not adventurous at all.

Shared Versus Solitary Experiences

Our surroundings and the common belief systems that are established and shared within those surroundings are major contributing factors in the development of our personalities. Culture, religion, education, custom, and family tradition all have something to say about how we should act, especially according to what sex we are. One instance of how adults conform to the general standards of society takes place in the business world. You wouldn't walk into a board meeting of executives wearing jeans and a T-shirt; rather, you'd wear a professional suit or jacket and skirt. Similarly, you're not going to walk into church wearing a bikini top, sarong, and flip-flops, and you probably won't attend a barbecue wearing a prom dress.

Biological and social differences aren't the only factors influencing our personalities. Individual experiences make their marks in our lives especially because of the personal nature in which they are dealt with. If the last jar of honey in the house contains only one drop, Winnie the Pooh views it as a positive experience because there's still one drop left; Piglet is anxious because he's afraid the honey will attract bees; and Eeyore thinks they're all doomed because the food supply has dwindled down to only one drop of honey. How can three individuals be in the same situation yet view it differently?

Although it's not uncommon for women to play sports and for men to become nurses, society still has some pretty clear definitions of what men and women should do, how they should handle situations, and what responsibilities they should take care of.

Past experiences affect attitudes and sway reactions. Pooh realizes there is more honey in the forest, Piglet recalls how much it hurt the last time he was stung by a bee, and Eeyore thinks there won't be anymore honey left in the forest because he is used to never getting what he wants. Surely it will be gone before they get to it! This scenario illustrates how a delicate blend of common and unique experiences, external influences, and inherited characteristics are the makings of a full-bodied personality, unique in its own right, despite the situation. Personality development operates on multiple levels, and can be examined by breaking it down into four different perspectives: traits, psychodynamic, psychoanalytic, or humanistic (phenomenological).

Traits

The trait theory, introduced by Gordon Allport, is the belief that the individual qualities of a person are what determine his or her behavior. The theory also holds that these traits can be measured on dimensions, or scales, each one measuring a characteristic, or trait, of that person. Some examples include rating a person's scale of aggressiveness and emotionality. Is that person quick to get angry? Does she cry easily? How trusting is she? But with all the different types of personality traits available to describe, how do we arrive at determining what traits are most important?

FACT

A trait is considered to be a relatively stable characteristic of our personalities. Though our personalities certainly change somewhat due to the environment we are in, traits, such as race or age, are supposedly those that are always underlying and never affected by changing situations.

Factor Analysis

Factor analysis is the statistical method used to help interpret the scores of multiple personality tests by computing the minimum number of characteristics needed to discover the truest assessment of that personality. For example, when measuring the trait dimension of cheerfulness, you would fall somewhere between serious and enthusiastic, the former having the lowest rating of 1 point and the latter having the highest rating of 10 points. Raymond Cattell (1905–1998), after extensive research, testing, and data collecting, concluded that sixteen factors make up the basic elements of personality. Following is a list of these factors:

- Warm
- Intelligent
- Emotionally stable
- Dominant
- Cheerful
- Conscientious
- Bold
- Sensitive

- Suspicious
- Imaginative
- Shrewd
- Guilt prone
- Experimenting
- Self-sufficient
- Self-disciplined
- Tense

Each trait is rated on a scale of 1 to 10 points in which each level is assigned an adjective, as seen in the previous example with cheerfulness. Cattell also developed a questionnaire of over 100 yes-or-no questions to measure the level at which each person possesses the traits listed and to be able to create as accurate a personality profile as possible for each individual based on his or her answers to the questions.

Problems with the Trait Theory

Although the trait approach succeeds at determining the character of a person based on his or her tendency to lean one way or another regarding certain traits, it doesn't really paint a complete picture. Introversion-extroversion and stability-instability levels prove that behavior can sometimes depend on the situation at hand. Someone who is shy and quiet around acquaintances at the office may let loose and be outgoing on the weekends around her friends. Similarly, a twelve-year-old boy may be nervous and well behaved around his strict parents, but his aggressiveness increases when he's around his friends in the schoolyard. Psychologists have found that developing tests to measure personality is not an easy task, especially since individual experiences and interactions in social situations pave erratic paths that are difficult to follow.

Psychodynamic Views

The main target of trait theorists is the behavior of the individual whereas social-learning theorists believe external elements, such as the environment, hold the key to understanding what causes particular types of behavior. They also believe that both individual and environmental aspects work together by ultimately contributing to each situation indirectly. Understanding how a person handles certain situations based on his personal traits is the first step toward pinpointing behavior patterns.

Aiding and Abetting Behavior

Rewards and punishments—reinforcements—influence our behavior in many ways and are encountered by direct, vicarious, and self-administered learning. Instances of direct reinforcements include concrete rewards of money, plaques, and trophies, as well as punishments that include being yelled at, denounced, or taking something important to the person away from her. Through vicarious learning, we think twice about doing something because we remember observing a similar situation with someone else, or we recall a story a friend or coworker told us that involved the same variables. Our behavior is then affected by our thoughts and conclusions about whether or not the observed behavior was favorable.

If you've been feeling a little blue lately or even if you're just having a bad day, look at yourself in the mirror and (out loud) tell yourself how great you are. It may seem silly and will probably make you laugh (is that such a bad thing?), but it will also likely improve your mood somewhat.

Finally, reinforcements that are self-administered may arguably be the most powerful contribution to our overall demeanor. Statements we administer to ourselves like "I can do it," "Hang in there," "I look good," "I look bad," "I'm too tall," or "This is my color" shape our personalities in that they can either build or crush self-esteem and in return, project a positive or negative image of who we are to the world.

Reacting to Situations

As stated earlier, personality is determined by many factors and functions on many levels. Thus, social-learning theorists contend that our behavior and reactions to situations are the combination of the specifics of the situation at hand, how we see those situations, and what we learned from observing similar situations in the past. Distinctive personal differences come to the forefront of our thoughts when we're preparing to react to a given situation. The following list is a compilation of some of those differences that social-learning theorists think are important:

- **Proficiency**—intellectual, physical, and social skills.
- **Point of view**—interpretation of situations and opinions.
- **Estimation**—determining whether results of behavior will be favorable or rejected.
- **Level of importance**—behavior in one situation may be more important than behavior in other situations (for example, performing acts to impress coworkers and performing acts to impress the boss).
- **Personal goals**—the ability to set realistic goals and act accordingly in order to achieve them.

The relationship between the previous behavioral differences and the situations we encounter on a daily basis follows a give-and-take model. What we contribute is what we get back. Acting disinterested toward people who approach you causes them to stop approaching you, leaving you in a self-created world of solitude. Being friendly and responsive to people will make them feel warm and encourages them to continuously approach you.

Psychoanalytic Approach

In stark contrast to the previous theories, which focused on the public personality and behavioral patterns, psychoanalytic theory turns inward to our private personality where unconscious motives are responsible for the behavior we exhibit.

Free Association

In Freud's *Outline of Psychoanalysis* (1940), he used an iceberg to represent the human mind in describing his analysis of personality structure. The portion that appears just a little above the water is the conscious region of our minds, whereas the massive chunk below the surface represents our unconscious mind where dreams, impulses, and repressed memories are housed. In order to begin to understand these unconscious mysteries, Freud used free association tactics to get a glimpse at what lay beneath. This exercise required the patient to talk about whatever came to mind no matter how relevant, nonsensical, or foreign the thoughts sounded. This technique, along with dream analysis and childhood memory evaluation, attempted to help patients understand themselves and their actions.

FACT

Stream of consciousness is a term applied to a writing exercise utilized by James Joyce, Virginia Woolf, and Beat writer James Kerouac, to name a few, as a means of recording the conscious experience of a continuous flow of ideas, feelings, and images running through the mind at the exact moment they occur.

In addition to free association, Freud's idea that personality is constructed of three components (the id, ego, and superego) is one of the most widely recognized theories in psychology, and is often the subject of cartoons and comics.

Id

The id wants immediate gratification of physical distress such as hunger, thirst, and sexual tension. These biological instincts dictate the id's loyalty to the pleasure principle in that it wants to get rid of pain and discomfort in order to experience satisfaction and relief. The id says, "I seek pleasure."

Ego

The ego is a more mature version of the id. Although it still seeks to gain pleasure, it operates on the reality principle where impulses are controlled when situations aren't favorable for meeting its demands. For example, finding a restroom, rather than using the sidewalk in the middle of a busy city to urinate on, is a decision made by the ego. It says, "I seek pleasure when it's appropriate."

Superego

The superego is best described as the little angel that sits on your right shoulder whispering morals into your ear. The superego censors and restrains the ego, makes value judgments, sets standards, and weighs consequences. It says, "I seek pleasure only if I don't have to do something unpleasurable to receive it."

All three parts of Freud's personality model seem as though they're vying for the spotlight, but usually they share the stage in order to approach a situation with as complete an understanding of it as possible. When they are struggling with each other, feelings of anxiety may become repressed only to show up at a later time, or they may be expressed in other forms such as rigorous exercise or extreme competition. These reactions are called *defense mechanisms* and are put into place to avoid feeling the conflict that goes on among the three impulses.

Humanistic Views

The humanistic approach is often discussed in relation to an individual's phenomenology, the study in which only a human's conscious interpretations and subjective experience of objects and events are relevant to their personality traits. This belief is in direct opposition to the previous theories, because it rejects motivational and subconscious drives. Carl Rogers pioneered this way of thinking and, like Freud, created his beliefs based on his experiences in working with emotionally afflicted people.

Critics of the humanistic approach say that this theory is unstable and unable to be tested. They also state that often, the humanistic approach to study reflects more of the observer than those being observed.

Rogers remains above the surface of the water and encourages a positive, optimistic outlook, believing a person has the ability to change for the better. He practiced person-centered therapy that included sessions in which the client would discuss the problems she was having and what she would like to do about them. As a therapist, Rogers developed the concept of "unconditional positive regard." This means that although Rogers would respond genuinely to patients' behavior even if it angered or irritated him, his essential care and respect for the client was not damaged by negative things the client brought up in a session. Centered around a patient's ideal self, thoughts, feelings, and solutions emerged in order to help the person assess the problem, find a solution, and develop a set of goals and plans that would help her become who she would like to be.

In analyzing one's own characteristics and abilities, self-conscious thought patterns develop and the person begins to ask herself a series of questions. Placing the responsibility of personality traits in the hands of consciousness allows the person to direct her own fate, live up to her real potential, and ultimately feel happy and satisfied with the results.

Popular Personality Tests

No matter what theory is being applied, tests are put into place to prove and disprove it. First impressions are often the most judgmental exchanges humans can have with each other. Stereotypes can be placed upon people based on the kind of clothes they wear, the people they're with, or even the type of food they eat. For instance, upon meeting someone for the first time, you notice his nose is pierced. In just an instant, you conjure up images of punk rockers, motorcycle gangs, and other rebels of society. Sleeves of tattoos must surely be hidden under that long-sleeved sweater! By solely focusing on his pierced nose, you've given it such a high level of importance that all your judgments of him were based on that one aspect of his personality. However, more substantial methods have been developed to assess personality. These include observational methods, personality inventories, and projective techniques.

If you are interested in taking a personality test in your spare time, you can find several on the Internet. However, as many of these are not proved to be accurate, don't put too much faith in the results. Regardless, they can be a fun way to pass time.

Observational Methods

People can be observed by watching them in their natural settings, placing them in difficult situations to see how well they perform, and by conducting an interview. The interview can be unstructured (the majority of the information revealed is decided by the interviewee) or structured (the interviewer covers predetermined topics in order to compare and contrast, for example, multiple job applicants). Rating scales are also popular when conducting job interviews. An example of what might be rated includes but is not limited to self-confidence, poise, emotional stability, interaction with others, personal relationships, and initiative.

Personal Inventories

Self-observations are measured by an individual's personal inventories in which a questionnaire, much like Cattell's factor analysis and yes-or-no test, is presented to the person so their feelings, thoughts, and reactions to situations can be recorded and analyzed. Both the Minnesota Multiphasic Personality Inventory (MMPI) and the California Psychological Inventory (CPI) feature statements that measure personality traits.

The MMPI was initially geared toward people with personality disorders or serious mental illness, but has also been used extensively in examining typical personality traits. The MMPI does not encompass a broad enough range to measure "normal" personalities; therefore, others have been developed that better address that. The CPI, for one, includes a measure of academic capabilities.

Projective Techniques

The most recognizable example of projective techniques is the famous inkblot series that comprise the Rorschach test. Developed by Hermann Rorschach in the 1920s, the test is conducted by presenting a person with an inkblot. The person is asked to look at it and describe everything he or she thinks the inkblot looks like. The idea is to get the person's initial response (open-minded, agitated, insightful, disagreeable) so a personality evaluation can be determined. Extensive training, more than that of any other test, is required in order to make professional assessments.

FACT

Rorschach came up with the idea for the inkblot test after observing a game of "Blotto" that children were playing in a psychiatric hospital. He happened to notice the differences in answers given and how these answers could provide insight into the children's minds; thus the Rorschach test was born.

A similar test called the Thematic Apperception Test (TAT), created by Henry Murray in the 1920s, presents up to twenty photographs of ambiguous subjects to individuals who, in turn, create their own stories about what is taking place or what is about to take place in the illustration. As the story is being told, the psychologist picks up on the underlying messages by looking for clues to the person's motives, emotions, and characteristics.

Both tests are used as a starting point in predicting behavior and are considered in conjunction with further investigation such as the person's observed attitudes, or life history. Ⓔ

Chapter 14

Coping with Life's Difficulties and Achieving Well-Being

Regardless of how successful, healthy, proficient, or happy we are, stress is an unavoidable factor in our lives. How often we experience it and how capable we are of handling it can be examined by exploring some of its main causes, different reactions we have toward it, and the physical dangers we face in coping with it.

Stressors and Stress

First, let's begin with the definition of stress. Stress is a condition in which extreme pressure, hardship, or pain is either suddenly experienced or built up over time. It can be an emotional struggle; a physical obstacle that must be overcome; the result of being pulled in many different directions by demands from family, friends, and work; a response to an unpredicted emergency such as a natural disaster or loss of a loved one; and many other factors that cause unpleasant restlessness, which we'll explore later in this chapter. While there are conflicting ideas as to what stress is—a response to stimulus, the stimulus itself, or the relationship to the stimulus—there are several main categories of stress: conflict, readjustment, daily inconveniences, and individual influences.

Conflict

When we can't have the best of both worlds, such as needing money to buy a car and needing a car to get to the job that will supply the money, a conflict of motives occurs. Finding a working solution to this conflict produces a lot of stress, especially if help from family members or friends is unavailable. In addition to this common conflict, the following are the most common conflict-causing, motivational struggles that we experience, and therefore are the most problematic:

- **Independence/dependence**—Turning to family and friends who we know have the resources to help us is not always an easy thing to do because we want to show them that we are mature enough, intelligent enough, and strong enough to make it in this world on our own.
- **Intimacy/isolation**—The desire to share ourselves and our love with others is often in conflict with our fear of being hurt or disliked. Fear of losing ourselves by relinquishing some of our own independence is another conflict that gets in the way of our need to be close to other people.
- **Collaboration/competition**—It is often emphasized that working together as a team produces the most rewarding results; however, putting our best foot forward in order to be respected and accepted

by society entails showing off our own individual talents and making our abilities known.

- **Impulse/morals**—When we set standards for ourselves, we're able to exercise self-control, restraint, and etiquette as we take our environment into consideration. Conflict emerges when acting impulsively for selfish reasons, as in sexual or aggressive situations, produces guilt and regret.

Operating in intense opposition, these motives induce stressful situations that require extremely difficult choices to be made, usually decided upon after a lot of back-and-forth internal dialogue.

Readjustment

Major life changes involve both positive and negative readjustments. Being offered your dream job in an area that requires you to move 3,000 miles away from home affects stress levels in a physical manner and an emotional one. The Holmes-Rahe Social Readjustment Scale rates events that cause the most stress because of the pressures of time and the level of importance they carry. (You can find the scale at ✑*www.cop.ufl.edu.*) In studying the relationship between stress and physical illness, people were asked to select the events that occurred in their lives during a one-year period. Score totals were then used to predict the odds in which a person would show signs of illness throughout the following year. Scores below 200 resulted in a 30 percent chance for illness; more than 50 percent of people with scores between 200 and 300 had health problems; and approximately 80 percent of the people whose scores totaled more than 300 got ill.

Although these conclusions remain the subject of skepticism, the scale continues to be a model for the development of new scales, as well as for new ways to measure how important a role stress plays in physical illness.

Life's Little Challenges

Daily inconveniences like the alarm not going off in the morning, losing your car keys, contending with traffic, spilling coffee on yourself, bills, and too little time to spend with loved ones may seem small enough on their own; but when encountered repetitively, they can cause enormous distress. The loss of a spouse, while hard enough to deal with on an emotional level, can effect stress in your daily routine because you find yourself having to take care of tasks you're not normally used to taking care of, like maintaining upkeep on your car, tracking finances, etc. These changes can be physically exhausting and learning how to handle them efficiently can produce an extreme amount of stress.

There are several ways in which you can work to de-stress yourself. For instance, you can use relaxation techniques such as yoga, find ways to make yourself laugh such as watching a funny movie or going to a comedy club, and of course, exercise is always a great stress reliever.

A person's general outlook on life can also affect how they respond to small nuisances. A person brimming with optimism might handle being stuck in a traffic jam calmly by realizing "it is what it is" and there's nothing he can do to change it. So instead of becoming frustrated, he tries to come up with alternative methods to pass the time, such as reading. In contrast, the person in the next car might have had an awful day and proceeds to shout, bang his steering wheel, and beep his horn. Why people react differently to the same stressful experience is discussed in the next category of stress.

Individual Influences

While a person's individual assessment of a situation may contribute to her or his reaction to it, the distinctive elements of the stress itself are an important factor in determining the level at which the person experiences the stress. Predictability and controllability affect how this level is felt and dealt with.

Predictability is important because it gives us time to prepare a course of action as well as mentally ready ourselves for the stress that's forthcoming. The results of experiments done with rats, in which signals were used to warn the rats a shock treatment was about to occur, proved that animals preferred to know when a stressful situation was about to happen. By pressing a metal bar, the rats received an audible signal preparing them for the shock; if they didn't press the bar, no warning was received. All the rats learned to press the bar, meaning all the rats preferred anticipating the displeasure rather than experiencing the uncertainty of when it would take place.

ALERT!

If you have a tendency to procrastinate, you'll likely need to keep an eye on your stress levels. Procrastination and stress feed off each other: You put off doing a task because the thought of doing it stresses you; you become stressed because the project is not completed.

Similar studies with humans yielded the same results. Women whose husbands were declared missing in action in Vietnam had more physical and emotional health problems than wives whose husbands were killed or taken as prisoners. Unable to experience "closure," these women lived life wondering about the state of their husbands, waiting for answers from the government, and struggling with when they should make the decision to let go and move on.

Controllability is another element that helps reduce stress. If we know we have the ability to stop the stressful situation, the stress itself won't be as severe. For example, the stress of holiday shopping can be dealt with more easily if we resolve we can always leave the store when it gets too exhausting.

How Stress Affects Physical Health

Physiological reactions to stress include increased heart rate, blood pressure, and breathing rate; tensing of the muscles; dry mouth; and shaking, to name a few. In addition to these biological reactions, physical health begins to deteriorate when stress is continually experienced. Ulcers and heart disease may develop, and the immune system can weaken if the stress isn't treated efficiently.

Ulcers and Heart Disease

Ulcers occur when a hole in the lining of the stomach is caused by the release of too much hydrochloric acid. Hydrochloric acid works with enzymes in order to break down food during digestion. Many factors can cause excessive hydrochloric acid release and stress is one of them. Again, rats were tested using the "warning signal" method before initiating jolts to the rats' tails. And again, the rats that had the good fortune of being warned showed fewer ulcerations than did the rats that were not warned.

Heart disease is another physical ailment that can be brought on by persistent stress. In 1981, the American Heart Association announced that "Type A" behavior should be declared a risk factor in heart disease.

QUESTION?

What is Type A behavior?
Type A behavior is the term used to describe individuals who find it extremely difficult to relax. They're competitive on every level (even when playing games with children), experience anger and impatience with people they feel are incompetent, are always under the restraints of time, and continuously push themselves to achieve more.

Some researchers believe that the hostility characteristic exhibited in Type A individuals is the most crucial contributor to heart disease. Learning to slow down, believing in people's capabilities, and setting realistic goals for oneself can in turn reduce the amount of hostility a person experiences. In some experiments, subjects were told to wait in line, and instead of becoming aggressive (tapping feet, sighing, getting angry at store clerks), were instructed to think about things they don't usually have time to think about or strike up a conversation with the person next to them. Redirecting the energy by turning it into something positive reduces the amount of stress that would normally be amplified by negative reactions to the situation.

The Immune System

Links between the immune system and the nervous system are still being studied, but there is some conclusive evidence that high levels of stress can in fact weaken the immune system's ability to ward off illness. College students studying for final exams, for example, are more susceptible to respiratory infections because the body slows down its production of certain agents needed to prevent the illness.

But not everyone's immune system falls prey to stress. People who feel they are in control of their own life and display positive attitudes and take-charge behaviors perform the actions necessary to solve the problems that cause the stress. This may involve seeking help from other individuals or making changes (small or drastic) to alleviate stress.

How Stress Affects Mental Health

Along with physical illness, psychological reactions to stressful events can hinder our ability to think clearly and logically. In a panic, a person might be so caught up in worrying about the repercussions of a negative end result, that he or she fails to take the steps needed to cause a positive end result. For example, if a nightclub filled with hundreds of people catches fire and everyone's initial panicked response is to run for the same exit, some people can be trampled on or crushed in the process. You might recall that such a tragedy happened in a nightclub in Rhode Island. Some people worry so much about the possible consequences of a decision that they can't make the decision and it gets made for them. Along with cognitive responses to stress, emotional responses such as anxiety, anger, and depression affect how well we cope with it.

Anxiety

Anxiety is the tense feeling you get when you are worried about bad things that might happen in the future. Anxiety is categorized into two types: objective anxiety and neurotic anxiety. Objective anxiety is what Freud described as a person's realistic approach to the situation causing the anxiety. The person is prompted to act in order to get rid of the anxiety he or she feels. Neurotic anxiety, on the other hand, is anxiety that Freud believed to be caused by unconscious-driven intentions that the person does not recognize, therefore is unable to understand or control.

Of all mental illnesses, the disorders that fall under anxiety are the most common. Over 19 million adults, in America alone, suffer from these illnesses. Oddly enough, anxiety disorders are the most undertreated, which could prove why many people take treatment into their own hands by turning to drugs and alcohol.

Anxiety is approached in many ways and believed to appear in many situations. Fear, worry, dread, and a feeling of urgency are all types of anxiety and exist on many levels, some of which can cause serious disorders, which will be discussed in the next chapter. Causes of anxiety are also approached differently. Freud held that neurotic anxiety is caused by the id's conflict with the ego and superego, and since this conflict exists on an unconscious plane, the person has no control of it, and therefore experiences feelings of helplessness.

Anger

Anger is a response to stress that often produces some form of aggressive behavior. The frustration-aggression hypothesis presumes that when something hinders our attempts at getting what we want, we become frustrated, an emotion that causes us to act aggressively by trying to injure the person or thing that is preventing us from getting what we want and causing the frustration. Displaced anger occurs when the anger is directed at someone or something that wasn't involved in causing the frustration. A bad day at work may take the form of a verbal argument with family members, and problems in a marriage may emerge as unusual behavior in social situations.

Depression

When all sense of hope is lost and the desire to live a full, healthy, goal-oriented life has diminished, depression takes over every aspect of the person's being, including disrupting eating and sleeping habits, thought processes, and the ability to form and sustain positive relationships. While signs of depression itself can be identified, what leads up to the depression and who is more apt to become depressed remains yet to be determined. A combination of events as well as a single experience can cause depression, and all personality types are susceptible.

FACT

In just a one-year period, approximately 18.8 American adults suffer some form of depression. Most do not seek treatment, mainly in part because many people do not recognize the signs.

Types of depression include: major depression, a combination of symptoms that interfere with every aspect of a person's life; dysthymia, a less severe form of depression that is not disabling but still produces feelings of despair; and bipolar disorder, also called manic-depressive illness, in which a person experiences an emotional series of extreme highs and lows that are often unpredictable in nature.

Adjustment Disorders

There are several types of adjustment disorders, some of which have already been discussed and some of which are a combination of several disorders. The following are the types of disorders and a few of their defining characteristics: adjustment disorder with depression (hopelessness, crying spells), anxiety (nervousness, excessive worry), depression and anxiety (hopelessness, crying spells, nervousness, excessive worry), disturbance of conduct (acts against society such as vandalism, problems in school, problems with the law), and disturbance of emotions and conduct (all of the above characteristics).

Typically, adjustment disorders last no longer than six months unless chronic stress develops and persists, for example, continuous relationship or work-related problems. Often some form of therapy can be helpful, and medication can be prescribed as part of the treatment involved.

Job Burnout

All of us have experienced stress on the job at one time or another. Some experience the occasional bout, while others deal with it on a regular basis. However, job burnout doesn't occur at the workplace alone. Work-related stress includes being stuck in traffic on the way to work and on the way home from work, noise and air pollution, having to bring work home, struggling with demanding bosses, and contending with uncooperative coworkers. Over time, the combination of these elements can build up and cause an extreme amount of stress in a person's life.

More alarming is the statistical evidence of the frequency with which job stress is encountered. Consider these facts turned up by the 2000 annual "Attitudes in the American Workplace VI" Gallup Poll sponsored by the Marlin Company:

- Eighty percent of workers feel stress on the job, nearly half say they need help in learning how to manage stress, and 42 percent say their coworkers need such help.
- Fourteen percent of respondents had felt like striking a coworker in the past year, but didn't.
- Twenty-five percent have felt like screaming or shouting because of job stress; ten percent are concerned about an individual at work they fear could become violent.

- Nine percent are aware of an assault or violent act in their workplace and 18 percent had experienced some sort of threat or verbal intimidation in the past year.

Additionally, the 2000 Integra Survey reports the following:

- Nineteen percent, or almost one in five respondents, had quit a previous position because of job stress and nearly one in four have been driven to tears because of workplace stress.
- Sixty-two percent routinely find that they end the day with work-related neck pain, 44 percent reported stressed-out eyes, 38 percent complained of hurting hands, and 34 percent reported difficulty in sleeping because they were too stressed-out.
- Twelve percent had called in sick because of job stress.
- Over half said they often spend twelve-hour days on work-related duties and an equal number frequently skip lunch because of the stress of job demands.

So not only are we working longer and harder than ever, the rewards are becoming less frequent and the emotional and physical illnesses are becoming more hazardous.

ALERT!

Stress.org reports that carpal tunnel syndrome is America's highest-costing workplace injury and makes up one-third of worker's compensation distributions. Carpal tunnel syndrome is a condition caused by compression of a nerve where it passes through the wrist into the hand and is characterized especially by weakness, pain, and disturbances of sensation in the hand.

Job burnout, if not detected early, can cause depression, suicidal tendencies, and violent behavior. It can also cause relationship problems, social problems, and physical illnesses, some of which are fatal.

Better Ways of Coping with Stress

Before we examine some of the more efficient ways of coping with stress, let's explore the most unhealthy and unproductive ways of coping with it. These may include but are not limited to drugs, alcohol, overeating, obsessive shopping, gambling, developing an addiction to television, or expressing anger at others. While these may temporarily numb or push away feelings of stress, they may end up causing even more stress in the long run. Healthier and more beneficial ways of coping with stress involve identifying the problem and finding a solution that works.

Problem-Solving Approach

Problem-focused coping is when the problem has been determined and the person develops a plan to solve the problem. If a student is told he is about to fail a required class, he works with the professor to find ways that will help him pass the course. This is the most realistic approach to coping with stress and produces the most positive results. On occasions when natural disasters take place, such as hurricanes or tornados, the community works together to solve the stress-causing problems such as sudden homelessness and loss of clothing and food supply.

Emotional Approach

Emotion-focused coping is when a person tries to deal with the anxiety indirectly. This can involve turning to alcohol or drugs or just avoiding the situation altogether. The college student who learns he is about to fail the class approaches the situation with apathy and resolves to take the class again next semester rather than put in the effort it will immediately require to pass the class now.

FACT

One form of emotion-focused coping, called *defense mechanisms,* involves deceiving the self in ways that can be helpful, but if used as the main resource in problem solving, it can become unhealthy.

Defense Mechanisms

According to Anna Freud, we employ several types of defense mechanisms in order to get ourselves through tough times until we are capable of handling the situation from a more realistic approach. Repression, rationalization, reaction formation, projection, intellectualization, denial, and displacement are all ways in which we engage in some form of artifice. Let's take a closer look at these.

Repression is the most basic and most important mechanism in which painful and frightful memories that incite guilt, shame, or self-worthlessness are kept out of your conscious reach and stored in the unconscious region of the mind. Rationalization is best illustrated by Aesop's fable where the fox decides the grapes are sour only after he can't reach them. You follow the reasoning that sounds good at the time, rather than the reasoning that best reflects the situation, taking on an "I didn't really want it anyway" attitude.

Reaction formation is hiding a motive from yourself by performing acts that display the extreme opposite of that motive. For example, you may hate your mother-in-law, but are ashamed that you feel that way, so you go out of your way to be extra nice to her. Projection is when you assign your own offensive traits to other people in an attempt to avoid disliking yourself. Intellectualization is coping with stressful situations in purely abstract and intellectual terms. People who work in a field where suffering and death are constant must attempt to detach themselves emotionally in order to perform the job successfully (doctors, police officers, firefighters, etc.).

Denial occurs when the reality of the situation is too hard to accept, and therefore you refuse to acknowledge it. Displacement is the defense mechanism in which motives that cannot be fulfilled in the intended way are expressed in other ways such as art, music, or poetry.

Positive Psychology and Subjective Well-Being

A wealth of community resources have emerged as the need for them increases. Halfway houses, youth centers, crisis centers, and telephone hot lines are some examples of how the government has put a considerable amount of funding to use in treating mental health issues.

In addition, promoting your own well-being can be as easy as staying in tune with your needs and desires. Know who you are. Accept who you are. Encourage yourself. Help yourself and ask for help when it's needed. Involve yourself.

Chapter 15

Disorders: When Thinking and Emotionality Go Awry

In this chapter, we are going to take a look at how mental health professionals determine when something is wrong and diagnose a mental disorder. We will also explore some of the major mental disorders affecting our population, including their causes and symptoms. Welcome to the world of abnormal psychology.

What Is Abnormal?

Abnormal psychology is the study of abnormal mental processes and behavior. *Abnormal* is defined as "not normal," but this definition isn't sufficient in the field of psychology. For one thing, normal is a relative term. For instance, what you consider to be abnormal behavior may be considered normal by your neighbor. Society also has its own standards for normal. We each have our own idea of "normal" and thus our own definitions of "abnormal." A mental health professional must be able to define abnormal behavior and then determine when abnormal behavior constitutes a mental disorder. Not an easy task.

Determining Abnormal Behavior

There are several factors a mental health professional must take into account when trying to determine whether a person's behavior is abnormal. One factor is whether the behavior violates cultural standards. Every society has its own set of norms deemed acceptable, and we are expected to conform to those societal norms. Subcultures also have norms; for example, within society in general, wearing extremely baggy pants and bandanas might be seen as abnormal. However, it would be not only considered normal, but would be almost required, in particular subcultures. A behavior that does not conform to the norm of the person's culture is considered statistically abnormal and undesirable. Another factor is whether the behavior is harmful or maladaptive. If the behavior impedes your ability to adjust to the demands of everyday life, it is considered maladaptive. Of course, a behavior that is dangerous and could lead to the harming of oneself or others is considered abnormal.

FACT

Another factor is whether the behavior is distressing to the person. The behavior is only abnormal, however, if the person suffers severe emotional distress or other consequences as a result of the behavior. We all suffer distress from time to time, but this is considered normal. When the behavior becomes extreme or happens on a frequent basis, it is considered abnormal.

Other factors determine whether the behavior is irrational, unpredictable, or inexplicable. In these cases, a person's behavior cannot be understood by others. For instance, someone with anorexia may look as thin as a rail to an outsider, but she believes she looks fat, so she restricts her eating and exercises excessively. This is an irrational behavior that most people cannot understand. Sometimes behavior takes place for no apparent reason. For instance, a person who shouts obscenities at a complete stranger for no apparent reason is considered to be acting erratically. Such behavior is inexplicable and unpredictable and is therefore abnormal.

Making a Diagnosis

Making a diagnosis of mental disorder isn't as easy as just identifying abnormal behavior. Abnormal behavior can be a symptom of a mental disorder, but it does not automatically lead to the existence of a mental disorder. Certainly all of us have behaved irrationally before, but that doesn't mean we all have a mental disorder. These are isolated incidents of a temporary state.

A mental health professional must look at abnormal behavior in terms of length of time and severity. If two or more factors of abnormal behavior apply to a person's behavior, then that warrants a closer look. A person is diagnosed with a mental disorder if the abnormal behavior occurs frequently over an extended period of time and it disrupts a person's normal day-to-day living.

Classifying Mental Disorders

To help identify and diagnose mental disorders, mental health professionals have developed a classification system that describes the symptoms of particular mental disorders. This classification system is found in the *Diagnostic and Statistical Manual of Mental Disorders* (DSM), published by the American Psychiatric Association. This manual contains almost 400 diagnoses of mental disorders classified within sixteen categories:

- **Adjustment disorder.** A person suffering from this disorder will exhibit an unusually intense or sustained emotional reaction to a change that has occurred in his or her life recently.
- **Anxiety disorders.** The disorders within this category all share a symptom of an extreme fear or anxiety. They include phobias, panic attacks with or without agoraphobia, obsessive-compulsive disorder, and posttraumatic stress disorder.
- **Delirium, dementia, amnesia, and other cognitive disorders.** The disorders within this group are a result of brain damage, including damage caused by degenerative diseases, head injury, stroke, or drug use.
- **Disorders usually first diagnosed in infancy, childhood, or adolescence.** These disorders appear before adulthood and include mental retardation, developmental problems, and attention deficit disorders.
- **Dissociative disorders.** These disorders are characterized by the separation of a person's experience from his conscious memory and include dissociative amnesia and dissociative identity disorder.
- **Eating disorders.** These disorders are characterized by excessive overeating, undereating, or purging as a result of a fear of gaining weight. They include anorexia nervosa and bulimia nervosa.
- **Factitious disorders.** These disorders are characterized by a person's attempt to fake physical or psychological illnesses.
- **Impulse control disorders.** These disorders are marked by an inability to resist an impulse to participate in a behavior that is harmful to oneself or others. These include kleptomania, pyromania, pathological gambling, and intermittent explosive disorder.
- **Mental disorders due to a medical condition.** These disorders are a result of a medical cause, such as a psychotic disorder resulting from epilepsy or a change in personality as a result of a brain injury.
- **Mood disorders.** These disorders are characterized by extreme changes in mood, such as major depression, cyclothymia, dysthymia, and bipolar disorder.
- **Personality disorders.** These disorders are a result of maladaptive patterns that disrupt a person's ability to function in everyday life

and/or cause extreme distress. They include narcissistic personality disorder, antisocial personality disorder, borderline personality disorder, obsessive-compulsive personality disorder, and paranoid personality disorder.

- **Psychotic disorders.** These disorders are marked by delusions, hallucinations, or extreme disturbances in thinking (often the sufferer is considered to have lost touch with reality). They include schizophrenia and delusional disorder.
- **Sexual and gender-identity disorders.** These disorders are marked by abnormal behavior regarding sexual functioning. They include sadomasochism, exhibitionism, psychosexual dysfunction, fetishism, and transsexualism.
- **Sleep disorders.** These disorders are marked by a disruption in a person's normal sleeping patterns. They include insomnia, narcolepsy, and sleep apnea.
- **Somatoform disorders.** These disorders are characterized by a complaint of a physical symptom for which no cause can be found. These include hypochondria and conversion disorder.
- **Substance-related disorders.** These disorders are a result of the use of or withdrawl from a drug such as alcohol, caffeine, amphetamines, opiates, or nicotine.

The DSM gives a lot of detailed information concerning each mental disorder to help mental health professionals effectively and accurately diagnose a mental disorder, including symptoms, approximate age of onset (if applicable), prevalence of the disorder, and other pertinent information. In a moment, we will take a closer look at some of the most commonly known mental disorders.

Anxiety Disorders

As mentioned before, anxiety disorders are one classification of mental disorders. We all feel anxious and fearful sometimes—when you're waiting to get your grade back on that big exam, when you board a roller coaster, or when your mother-in-law comes to visit. However, once these situations are over and we've discovered we've lived through them just fine, the anxiety and fear dissipate. For those suffering anxiety disorders, the anxiety and fear doesn't just go away. It may subside for a while, but then suddenly return, or it can hang out in the background, making its mark on the actions and daily life of the sufferer. There are several disorders that fall within this category; let's take a look at a few.

Phobias

We are all afraid of something—snakes, heights, public speaking, clowns—but that doesn't necessarily mean we have a phobia. A phobia is an exaggerated and unrealistic fear that incapacitates the sufferer. Some phobias are more severe than others. For instance, you may have a phobia of clowns, but how often are you confronted with a clown? They are pretty easy to avoid, so you don't have to suffer the physiological responses of this extreme anxiety very often (sweating, nausea, trembling, a racing heart, and/or shortness of breath). In order to be termed a phobia, the efforts to avoid the feared thing or the response to encountering it must severely impact some area of the person's normal functioning.

FACT

Generalized anxiety disorder is a condition in which a person is continuously anxious or worried for a period of at least six months. The chronic anxiety affects their daily lives and they often physically wear themselves out with worry.

People with social phobia are afraid of situations in which they feel that others may judge them. They aren't easily able to avoid their fear unless they want to skip all their classes, never eat at a restaurant, never go out on a date, and basically avoid all social atmospheres (you can forget about their singing karaoke!). Even worse is agoraphobia, which is the fear of being away from a safe place such as your home. It's difficult for most of us to imagine being afraid to leave the house, but this is a very real disorder for some.

Panic Disorder

Panic disorder is another type of anxiety disorder. Those who have panic disorder suffer recurring panic attacks. Panic attacks are a period of extreme fear during which the sufferer may feel as though he or she is dying or going crazy. Panic attacks are often accompanied by shortness of breath, chest pains, dizziness, trembling, and hot and cold flashes. They can last anywhere from a couple of minutes to several hours (though rare). They sometimes seem to appear out of the blue, but they are often first experienced following (sometimes weeks later) a period of heightened stress.

It is possible to suffer a panic attack, or even two or three, without being diagnosed with panic disorder. Many of us will have a panic attack now and then, but those with panic disorder suffer them often and change their behavior or restrict their life in some way to avoid another attack. Because panic attacks happen so unexpectedly and are so upsetting, sufferers often become quite anxious, wondering when the next will occur. This in turn increases the stress in the person's life, thus creating another opportunity for a panic attack. It is a very frightening spiral of anxiety and fear and can be disabling.

Posttraumatic Stress Disorder

Posttraumatic stress disorder (PTSD) is an anxiety disorder that develops following a traumatic experience, such as near-death experiences, rape, war, or natural disasters. The symptoms of PTSD include reliving the traumatic experience in dreams or thoughts, irritability, insomnia and hyperalertness, inability to concentrate, depression, and a detachment from others. While these symptoms are typical following any highly stressful event, a person is diagnosed with PTSD when the symptoms persist for at least six months. The onset of the symptoms may immediately follow the event or occur weeks, sometimes even months, later. This isn't to say that you will develop PTSD if you are involved in a traumatic event; some people are able to recover from the event without developing a mental disorder. However, PTSD is considered to be a normal consequence of having experienced severe trauma.

Many students studying abnormal psychology for the first time relate to some of the symptoms of mental disorders and diagnose themselves as having nearly every mental disorder in the book! Don't allow yourself to get swept up along with them. Keep a sense of humor.

Obsessive-Compulsive Disorder

Obsessive-compulsive disorder (OCD) is an anxiety disorder in which a person is stuck in a cycle of repetitive, unwanted thoughts and repetitive, ritualized behaviors. The repetitive thoughts (obsessions) are often an idea or scenario in which the sufferer is in some kind of danger or inflicts danger upon someone else, which is where the anxiety comes from. While these thoughts are frightening and unwelcome, the person can't help but think them over and over. The repetitive rituals (compulsions) performed are also believed to be out of the sufferer's control. While they may seem excessive (such as washing one's hands fifteen times within an hour) to us, to the sufferer, they are necessary to reduce anxiety. In order to be diagnosed, the symptoms must be understood to be irrational by the sufferer, and must be upsetting.

Mood Disorders

Mood disorders are another classification of mental disorders. Within this category, mental disorders affect a person's mood to the point where it disrupts her or his life. If your significant other or coworkers tells you that you are moody, don't assume this means you have a mood disorder. All of us shift moods from time to time, often due to some kind of stimulus in our environment, such as the bad mood of another. Mood disorders range from extreme depression to extreme mania and last for an extended period of time. A little mood shift here and there, even though it may seem to disrupt your life for the moment (or the lives of others!), is harmless.

Depression

We've all suffered sadness, and we've all been in a bad mood, but when we say, "I'm depressed today," that's not the proper description for our suffering. Depression (technically called *clinical* or *major depression*) is not a twenty-four-hour bug. It is a serious mood disorder in which there are severe changes in an individual's behavior, emotion, cognition, and physical functions. This overwhelming feeling of sadness and/or worthlessness must last at least two weeks and disrupt the sufferer's daily life to be diagnosed as depression.

If you suffer several symptoms of depression, it is a good idea to make a visit to your doctor. If you do have depression, he or she can refer you to a mental health professional who can help. It's possible that you may have a physical illness you were unaware of, as many illnesses share a few of the same symptoms as depression.

The symptoms of depression include a feeling of worthlessness, a lack of desire to do anything, even those things you used to love to do, a feeling of overwhelming sadness, thoughts of death or suicide, a lack of energy, changes in appetite (overeating or not eating), changes in sleeping patterns (inability to fall asleep or sleeping a lot more than usual), difficulty concentrating and making decisions, and a lack of desire to be sociable.

Dysthymia

Dysthymia is another mood disorder. Basically it is a lower level of depression. People with dysthymia suffer similar symptoms of depression, such as a change in appetite, a change in sleeping patterns, a feeling of worthlessness or hopelessness, and a low energy level—over the course of at least two years. However, these symptoms aren't constant all the time. The sufferer may have periods during which he or she feels re-energized and back to normal. Even though the symptoms are milder, dysthymia still disrupts a person's daily life in that it makes activities more difficult to get through.

Bipolar Disorder

Bipolar disorder (formerly called manic-depressive illness) is a mood disorder in which an individual suffers severe mood swings between depression and mania, with periods of normalcy in between. The depression of bipolar disorder is the same depression we spoke of earlier. Mania is the opposite of depression. It is a period of extreme exhilaration wherein the individual is full of energy, high self-esteem, creativity, and ambition. Those in manic states feel as though they could conquer the world—quite different from depression, huh? Imagine how exhausting and confusing it must be to alternate between two such states.

FACT

Many artists, musicians, writers, and scientists have suffered bipolar disorder and said that they were able to create their best work during the manic periods. Mark Twain was one such creative sufferer.

While it may seem like mania is a good thing, it takes its toll. The individual may suffer restlessness so severe that he or she may not sleep for days, rapid and dramatic speech (thus the inability to communicate effectively), extreme irritability, the inability to concentrate (thus the inability to finish anything), paranoia, impulsiveness, weight loss, and possibly hallucinations or delusions. Bipolar disorder is diagnosed when a person has a manic episode; otherwise, it would be diagnosed as depression, as the depression side of the disorder is the same as in clinical or major depression.

Cyclothymia

Cyclothymia is a lower level of bipolar disorder. People with cyclothymia suffer mood swings between mania and depression, but they are not as extreme. They will suffer the same symptoms as those with bipolar disorder, but on a milder level. The major difference between one with bipolar disorder and one with cyclothymia is that a person with cyclothymia never experiences a full-blown manic state, nor will he or she experience a major depressive episode. To be diagnosed, a person must experience these symptoms over the course of at least a two-year period.

Schizophrenia

Schizophrenia is probably the best-known mental disorder, though people often mistakenly confuse it with multiple personality disorder. Someone with multiple personality disorder has two or more personalities that surface; he or she is still in touch with reality and able to function. Someone with schizophrenia, on the other hand, often loses touch with reality and is unable to carry out many daily activities. Schizophrenia is rather difficult to define accurately as it varies in form and sufferers do not have the exact same symptoms. Even so, mental health professionals have come up with a list of common symptoms of schizophrenia, the most prevalent of which are hallucinations and delusions.

Hallucinations and Delusions

Hallucinations are false sensory perceptions that a person believes to be real. While schizophrenics can see things that aren't there or feel things crawling on their skin, the most common hallucinations those with schizophrenia suffer are auditory; they hear voices. The voices are inside the person's head, but the sufferer believes it is just as real as if someone were standing next to him speaking, because his experience is exactly the same as if someone really were. There could be just one voice or several. The voice may give the sufferer orders or insult him or her. Two or more voices could hold a conversation that completely disregards the sufferer altogether. Regardless of what the voices say, the sufferer believes it is real and often will take the advice or orders of the voices.

Delusions are false, and often outlandish, ideas that a person believes to be true. These ideas can be anything the imagination can conjure up, from space aliens living in the bathroom sink to rat poison in their Chap Stick. Oftentimes, schizophrenics will have paranoid delusions in which they believe someone or an agency such as the government is plotting against them. They will think their phones are bugged, people are following them, and their lives are in danger. Sometimes they will believe they are another person, often someone well known such as Jesus, the president, or a celebrity.

ALERT!

Movies and television shows often portray a schizophrenic as being violent toward others. While violence is a possibility, schizophrenics are more likely to turn the violence toward themselves. Suicide attempts are unfortunately common with schizophrenics.

You must understand that as silly as this may seem to us, delusions are as real as the sun to the schizophrenic, and they are just as terrifying as if they were really happening. For instance, one man was hospitalized because he was convinced that the police were after him. He ran from window to window in absolute terror, because he was locked in and was certain that people walking on the hospital grounds were police who were coming to get him. The fact that this wasn't true made no difference to the man; in fact, he understood that other people thought he was crazy, but he believed his worries were true nonetheless.

Disorganization

Other symptoms of schizophrenia include disorganized speech and thought and inappropriate and disorganized behavior. The disorganization of thought manifests itself in speech. A schizophrenic may suddenly begin rhyming or switch from one illogical idea to another without any apparent connection. The sufferer's speech can be scattered and incoherent, unable to be understood. Disorganized behavior can consist of anything from being unable to dress oneself to laughing uncontrollably at a funeral.

Disorganized behavior is inappropriate for the occasion or can result in the sufferer's inability to complete an everyday, simple task.

So Many Symptoms!

Those symptoms we've already discussed are considered "positive" by psychologists. This isn't to be confused with "good." Positive refers to active symptoms that are added to a person's normal behavior; they are symptoms that healthy people do not display. Negative refers to those symptoms that show a lack in some area—ambition, thought, feeling, behavior, etc. Such symptoms include emotional flatness (when a person does not show any emotion whatsoever), an extreme lack of motivation, withdrawal from society, and impoverished thought and speech.

Schizophrenics may also show changes in emotion. They may suffer extreme mood swings rather abruptly or exaggerate a normal feeling, such as laughing too loudly and too long at a joke. They may also become apathetic toward people they had always been close to.

There are so many symptoms, we couldn't possibly list them all here. This is why it is difficult to diagnose schizophrenia. Just as there are no two snowflakes alike, there are no two cases of schizophrenia exactly alike. Mental health professionals must take this very seriously, as it can be a very terrifying and detrimental mental disorder. Fortunately, treatment for schizophrenia has improved over the years. People can now sometimes partially or completely recover from a schizophrenic episode, although others will remain disabled by their condition.

Personality Disorders

As mentioned before, personality disorders are a classification of mental disorders characterized by maladaptive patterns that disrupt a person's ability to function in everyday life and/or cause extreme distress and the inability to get along with other people. As you read, you may recognize someone you know in the symptoms of some of these disorders (of course, you would have none of these yourself), but keep in mind that while a person may have some of the symptoms of a mental disorder, this does not necessarily mean he or she has the disorder itself. So don't go diagnosing your friends with a personality disorder or you just might not have any friends left!

Antisocial Personality Disorder

Probably the best-known personality disorder is antisocial personality disorder. You have probably heard someone called a sociopath or psychopath—well, this is the disorder they were referring to. Someone with an antisocial personality disorder does not connect or bond with other people; he or she is antisocial and can lie, cheat, steal, and kill without feeling any remorse or shame. They are truly frightening members of the community.

The DSM states that in order to diagnose an individual with antisocial personality disorder, he or she must have a history of at least three of seven behavioral problems, as well as a history of similar problems as a child:

- Impulsive and cannot plan ahead.
- Irresponsible and fails to meet obligations.
- Repeatedly gets into physical fights.
- Repeatedly breaks the law.
- Lacks guilt or regret for hurting others.
- Deceitful.
- Has a reckless regard for his or her own safety or the safety of others.

While those with antisocial personality disorder may not give a second thought to killing a child, this doesn't mean that everyone with this disorder is a murderer. Some would much rather con you out of your money than kill you. The point is, regardless of the crime committed, those with antisocial personality disorder simply do not care. They do not have a connection with other people and have no empathy or feelings of regret. Frightening, isn't it?

Narcissistic Personality Disorder

Narcissistic personality disorder is characterized by extreme self-absorption. Individuals with this disorder consider themselves to be better than everyone else. They expect everyone else to shower them with attention and favors, though they very rarely, if at all, return the favor. They are self-absorbed to the point where they are obsessed with their own self-importance, brilliance, and power. They are, essentially, in love with themselves.

FACT

Narcissism comes from the Greek myth of Narcissus. Narcissus was a beautiful young man who came across his reflection in the water one day. He was so entranced with his image that he fell in love with himself and never left the water's edge. (He was eventually turned into the narcissus flower.)

Borderline Personality Disorder

Borderline personality disorder is a personality disorder in which an individual has a history of unstable relationships—one minute the relationship will be passionate and intense as the partner is idealized, but in the next moment, the relationship takes a dive as the partner is suddenly of little or no value. A person with borderline personality disorder is often self-destructive and may threaten to commit suicide. Drugs are sometimes a part of his or her life. Impulsiveness is also characteristic of this disorder, as is emotional instability.

Causes of Mental Disorders

Now that you've been able to take a closer look at some of the more common mental disorders and have seen how they can be debilitating to a person's life, you are likely wondering what could possibly cause such disorders. There isn't a simple and exact answer for this. Mental health professionals and researchers are constantly studying the causes of mental disorders in an attempt to better understand and treat the disorders. Let's take a look at what they have found out so far.

Biological Factors

Some are of the belief that mental disorders are caused solely by problems in the brain and nervous system. As you know, the nervous system is a delicate and complex system in which there is a constant hum of activity that keeps our body alive and functioning well. If there were to be any damage to or a kink in the brain, the executor of the nervous system, the system could be thrown out of whack, possibly resulting in a mental disorder. For instance, the brain's prefrontal cortex is responsible for impulse control and planning. Should this part of the brain be damaged, a person may suffer impulsiveness and an inability to plan ahead, a symptom of schizophrenia.

FACT

Those researchers who believe biological factors are responsible for the onset of mental disorders have contributed greatly to this field of science, particularly in their development of medications that are sometimes able to allow a person suffering a mental disorder to live a normal life.

These people have also shown that some of the biological factors of mental disorders are hereditary and that some people are more susceptible to particular mental disorders than others. For instance, research has shown that major depression is often a heritable mental disorder. Also, as you've surely heard, addiction is thought to originate in a person's biochemistry, and those with a genetic predisposition to addiction are more likely to suffer an addiction.

Psychological Factors

On the other hand, there are those who believe that psychological factors—such as traumatic experiences, past conflicts, the way parents behaved toward a child, etc.—are responsible for the development of mental disorders. For example, posttraumatic stress disorder is a result of a traumatic experience; it is the body's reaction to and coping mechanism for past events of heightened stress. A mental health professional believing in this theory would focus solely on the traumatic event and its effects in an attempt to help the patient overcome this disorder. Certain phobias, also, have shown that they are a result of psychological factors. For instance, someone with the fear of the number thirteen may have developed the phobia due to societal stimulation or cultural tradition.

Working Together

Many mental health professionals and researchers in the field believe that the causes of mental disorders are found among a combination of biological and psychological factors. For instance, someone may have a genetic predisposition toward a certain mental disorder, such as antisocial personality disorder, but the onset of the mental disorder is triggered by a psychological event, such as maternal rejection. Borderline personality disorder is thought to be based in a problem with the emotion regulation system, so that emotions are experienced much more intensely than normal. Because feelings like frustration, hurt, or anger are so much more powerful even over small things, people with BPD elicit reactions such as "Just get over it"; "You're not that upset"; or "You're just looking for attention." While parents of normal children often teach them how to self-soothe and deal with feelings, parents of people with BPD may not have the skills themselves to deal with extra-intense emotions. After a few years, people with BPD learn to hide their feelings—until they can't anymore, and the pain is simply intolerable. That's when they may hurt themselves—which then starts the consequences all over again. As stated before, the causes of mental disorders are continuously being researched and studied, and treatments are continuing to advance every day. Ⓔ

Chapter 16

Psychotherapy and Other Approaches to Treatment

Now that you are familiar with some of the major mental disorders out there, let's take a look at some of the approaches used to treat these disorders. Keep in mind that treatments are constantly evolving as new ones enter the scene and older ones are improved upon. In this chapter, we will take a look at both psychotherapy and biological approaches to treatment.

Psychoanalysis and Psychodynamic Approaches

Psychoanalysis is a form of psychotherapy in which the therapist delves into the patient's unconscious in an attempt to discover an internal source for the problem at hand. Freud was the father of psychoanalysis, as you've probably guessed. He believed that by talking through a person's dreams and memories, he could tap into the unconscious and determine the inner conflict that was causing the psychological problem. By exposing that source, the patient could then experience emotional release and be free of the problem.

Free Association

In this form of treatment, a patient would meet with his or her therapist numerous times and simply talk about dreams, emotions, and pretty much anything that came to mind. Such a situation is often portrayed with the patient lying on a sofa and the therapist sitting alongside the patient in a chair taking notes. As the patient talks freely, the therapist sits quietly, taking in everything that is said in an attempt to make connections and thus search for the source within the unconscious, a technique known as *free association*.

Classic psychoanalysis using free association can be rather pricey considering the number of sessions a patient must pay for before the problem can be worked through. While this certainly isn't the only form of treatment available, many people shy away from seeking treatment due to the cost involved.

There is no quick fix involved. Numerous sessions are required, sometimes even years' worth of sessions, before a therapist can delve deeply enough in to the unconscious to produce emotional release. Of course, this emotional release cannot be guaranteed. Because our society is "quick-fix" oriented, this form of treatment isn't nearly as popular these days, though it is still the most common portrayal of one seeking help for a psychological problem.

Psychodynamic Therapy

Freud's classic psychoanalysis, though not practiced all too often these days, has evolved into other forms of therapy called psychodynamic therapy that are being used more often. In psychodynamic therapy, the therapist still attempts to delve into the unconscious to help the patient discover and face the inner conflict that is manifesting itself as symptoms of a mental disorder. However, this form of therapy is more structured to be acceptable to our quick-fix ideals.

Therapists develop a plan of treatment with their patients, often setting a limit on the number of sessions they will use as well as setting goals for what they want to accomplish. They also participate in the sessions, often guiding the patient to discuss a certain topic or emotion, which is much different from the free association technique used in classic psychoanalysis. In this way, the sessions are more goal oriented and focused on finding a solution to the problem without having to rifle through the insignificant details of a patient's entire life history.

Transference

Both psychoanalysis and psychodynamic approaches make use of transference, which is a process of transferring one's emotions onto another, in this case, the therapist. The therapist will pay close attention to any emotions that you project onto him or her and try to associate those feelings with situations or issues in your life. For instance, if you become jealous of the therapist's other patients, the therapist will start to delve into your current relationships with others, searching for that inner conflict that triggered the transference. Or, if you become enraged with your therapist for going on vacation and not being able to keep the regular schedule of sessions, the therapist will try to find out if you have faced rejection or abandonment in your life. Transference is a way to dig up those past conflicts that are affecting your present living.

Medical Approaches

Some mental health professionals take the stand that mental disorders are diseases that must be treated medically. Researchers have developed many drugs that are being used to treat the symptoms of mental disorders from schizophrenia to depression. However, drugs aren't always able to fix the problem. In which case, other biomedical solutions are sought out, such as brain surgery or electroshock therapy. Let's first take a look at the drugs that are used to treat mental disorders, as they are the most common form of biomedical treatment.

FACT

Research has found that using a combination of medical approaches and psychotherapy has produced excellent results in the treatment of some mental disorders. For instance, it is common for a mental health professional both to prescribe an antidepressant and to schedule the patient for psychotherapy sessions in the treatment of depression.

Antipsychotic Drugs

Antipsychotic drugs are those that are used to treat psychoses such as schizophrenia. These types of drugs have come a long way since they were first introduced. Earlier drugs such as Thorazine helped dull the symptoms of the mental disorder but produced effects that made it just as difficult for the patient to carry out a normal daily life. Antipsychotic drugs these days are beneficial in reducing or getting rid of hallucinations, delusions, and agitation, allowing patients to live their lives outside of a hospital. New drugs such as Restoril are even able to reduce a schizophrenic's apathy and social isolation.

While antipsychotics work wonders for some people, not all will respond to them. Each case needs to be evaluated on an individual basis. Also, some of these drugs can produce side effects that can be debilitating such as uncontrollable trembling or disturbances in motor control.

Antidepressant Drugs

Antidepressant drugs are most often used to treat—you guessed it!—depression. However, some of the newer antidepressants are also effective in treating obsessive-compulsive disorder, some phobias, and sometimes anxiety. You've likely heard of at least a few antidepressants such as Prozac, Zoloft, or Paxil. It has been discovered that depression is often the result of a chemical imbalance in the brain. These drugs target that chemical imbalance and correct it, thus alleviating the symptoms of depression.

Saint John's wort, which is an over-the-counter herbal medication, has been used widely in Europe in the treatment of depression. Studies have shown that this herb can be effective in treating mild forms of depression without as many side effects as common antidepressants. Even so, if you are considering using this, consult your doctor first.

Not all antidepressants will have the same effect on people. For instance, someone who responds well to Zoloft may have shown little or no improvement when using Paxil. Antidepressants also have side effects. While not as severe as those associated with antipsychotics, these side effects can be rather annoying. Common side effects include dry mouth, nausea, headaches, fatigue, blurred vision, weight gain, constipation, and decrease in sexual libido and/or sexual performance.

Antianxiety Drugs

Antianxiety drugs are used in the treatment of anxiety disorders, such as panic disorder and generalized anxiety disorder. Often called tranquilizers, these drugs include Valium, Librium, Xanax, Klonopin, and BuSpar. While these drugs can work wonders for those suffering panic attacks that disrupt their daily lives, they can be rather dangerous as they are highly addictive. They are best used in the short term and patients will need to gradually decrease the dosage to avoid suffering withdrawal and other side effects. Also, while you never want to mix medication with alcohol, this is especially true with antianxiety drugs. The combination can heighten the effects of the alcohol to the point where it is quite possible the person would end up in a coma. Highly effective treatments for phobias, including social phobia, fear of flying, and panic disorders, do exist. A therapist trained in cognitive behavioral exposure–based therapy can often help even severe cases in a relatively short period of time. However, the therapy is intense and scary and requires a significant investment from the client.

Mood Stabilizer Drugs

Mood stabilizers are just as they sound—they are drugs that work to stabilize a person's mood, reducing or getting rid of extreme mood swings. The most common mood stabilizer is lithium carbonate, often used to treat bipolar disorder. Treatment with lithium needs to be monitored closely. If the dose is too small, it may not have any effect; if the dose is too large, it may prove to be fatal. Those taking lithium are required to take toxicity tests regularly. Another problem with lithium is that it can produce side effects such as vomiting, diarrhea, tremors, seizures, and even kidney damage. While lithium has a long history as an effective treatment of mood disorders, there are other drugs being used for mood disorders, such as the antiseizure medications Tegretol and Depakote.

Psychosurgery

Psychosurgery, a method of treatment that involves destroying the part of the brain thought to be responsible for the mental disorder, isn't very common today, but it used to be a popular form of treatment. Psycho-surgery began when physician Gottlieb Burkhardt removed parts of the brain of his schizophrenic patients in the 1890s. While some patients did show calmer behavior following the surgery, some died.

Psychosurgery fell out of favor for a while, but then there was a resurgence in the mid-1930s when prefrontal lobotomies hit the scene. It was discovered that the frontal and temporal lobes controlled aggressiveness and emotional behavior. Holes were drilled into the patient's skull and the nerves connecting the prefrontal lobes were severed or otherwise destroyed. While this operation did reduce the emotional symptoms of mental disorder, it also left most people incapacitated in some way. Some were unable to make plans and follow through, some became severely withdrawn from society, and some could no longer even care for themselves. Remarkably, this continued for nearly twenty years and tens of thousands of people had the surgery.

FACT

The earliest form of psychosurgery was used on patients suffering from schizophrenia. However, as it gained popularity in the 1900s, it was being used to treat a wide range of mental disorders such as bipolar disorder, obsessive-compulsive disorder, pathological violence disorder, and, of course, schizophrenia.

Such lobotomies are not performed today; however, there is a new form of psychosurgery that is currently in use. Cingulotomy is a surgical procedure that burns and destroys a small portion of the brain known to be involved in emotionality. This is used as a last resort for those suffering severe obsessive-compulsive disorder and major depression who have not responded to drugs or forms of psychotherapy. Such surgery has not proved to be as debilitating as former psychosurgeries, though many still question the success reports.

Electroconvulsive Therapy

Electroconvulsive therapy (ECT), commonly called *shock therapy,* is a somewhat controversial procedure used to treat those suffering from severe depression with suicidal thoughts who have not responded to drugs or forms of psychotherapy. ECT involves placing an electrode on either side of the patient's head and sending a current of electricity between the two. The current causes the body to convulse for approximately a minute, and causes the release of many types of neurotransmitters in the brain. Years ago, the current was so strong and lasted long enough that the body sometimes suffered broken bones from the convulsions. Today, patients are given anesthesia and muscle relaxants so that they are able to sleep through the ordeal without pain or muscular contractions; patients wake up after about ten minutes and may have a headache, but generally the side effects are no worse than those of antidepressant medications. Some patients report short-term memory loss in the day following the procedure, and very few patients have more memory loss. Although no one is sure why or how this works, ECT has proved to be effective on almost 70 percent of those undergoing the procedure. Again, this is a controversial procedure. It is often used when someone can't wait or doesn't want to wait the six to eight weeks that antidepressant medications take to start to work. Usually ECT requires a number of sessions spaced a few days apart, followed by monthly or less frequent "booster" sessions.

Humanistic Approaches

The humanistic approach to psychotherapy adopts a philosophy that we each have a desire to be productive, reach our goals, and behave in a healthy manner; we are in control of our destiny and that while we are constantly growing, changing, and being affected by outside factors, we maintain the responsibility for our own happiness. Unlike psychoanalysis, humanistic therapists do not try to find hidden or unconscious past experiences affecting the life of the person today. Rather, they concentrate on the here and now, focus on the current situation or problem, and help the patient (or "client," as humanists prefer) work through, make, and feel good about decisions.

FACT

Client-centered therapy is based on Carl Rogers's idea of unconditional positive regard, in which the therapist provides continuous support without attaching any conditions. In this way, the client feels safe and secure in the support provided and is able to build confidence in his or her ability to solve the problem at hand in the most productive manner possible.

The best-known approach to humanistic therapy is the client-centered therapy strategy developed by Carl Rogers. In this approach, the client is the focus of the session. He or she leads the discussion, talking about the situation or problem at hand. The therapist's job is to actively listen to what the client says and show warmth and empathy. The client is the expert on his or her feelings; the therapist is the sounding board for the client to bounce solutions off of. The therapist must at all times listen with acceptance and not be judgmental in any way, although it is also important that the therapist be honest and genuine in his or her reactions to what the client is bringing up. In this way, the client is able to build self-esteem and the confidence needed to carry out a solution to the problem.

Cognitive-Behavioral Approaches

Cognitive-behavioral approaches to psychotherapy also focus on the "here and now." They are not concerned about what your unconscious may or may not be storing. They want to get right to the point and take action to battle the behavior that is disrupting your daily living. While cognitive therapy and behavioral therapy are technically two separate strategies, they are often combined as they have the same goal of identifying and changing problematic or self-defeating behaviors. Most believe that thought and behavior feed off each other, and therefore approaches that use both are common in practice. Let's take a look at each.

Behavioral Therapy

Behavioral therapy focuses on tackling the problem behavior itself by finding ways to change or stop the behavior. This type of therapy focuses on the principles of classical and operant conditioning as discussed in Chapter 9. Behavioral therapists employ several different techniques for behavioral therapy, depending on which is considered to be the most effective strategy for the type of behavior.

If you have a phobia, a behavioral therapist would likely consider applying systematic desensitization to help you get over that fear. This technique uses a series of steps to help you create a positive conditioned response to the feared object, eventually helping you to confront your fear while feeling relaxed. For instance, let's say you are deathly afraid of dogs. A behavioral therapist would employ systematic desensitization by teaching you to relax as you gradually face the fear from the mildest form to the most terrifying. In this scenario, you would start out by looking at pictures of cute puppies. Once you are able to view these pictures while relaxed, you would then be shown pictures of smaller yet grown dogs, such as a Jack Russell terrier. From there you would move on to medium-sized dogs such as Border collies. Then you would be shown pictures of large and more aggressive dogs such as Rottweilers. The next step would be facing a real dog, though from a safe distance. The ultimate goal is to get you to actually interact with the dog, thus combating your fear and demonstrating that not all dogs are dangerous. All of these steps are done as your body is relaxed. In other words, you will not move on to the next step until you are comfortable and relaxed while in the current step.

If you have a behavior you are considering getting help for, it is a good idea to keep a record of the problematic behavior; in fact, many therapists request this. Identify the behavior, the rewards of the behavior, and when and where the behavior occurs. From this a therapist has a good starting point on which to build a plan for treatment.

Implosion and flooding are two behavioral therapy techniques in which the patient must face his or her problem head-on. In implosion, a person is asked to imagine or is shown a picture of the event or object he or she is afraid of—over and over in a safe environment until the fear no longer has such a hold on or power over the patient. Flooding is a technique in which the person is thrown into the situation they fear most—such as an agoraphobic riding on a crowded subway—alongside the safety of the therapist until he or she no longer feels the panic and anxiety associated with the situation. Both of these techniques focus on immediate exposure, taking away the baby steps of systematic desensitization. The drawback of this kind of therapy is that if the person cannot stay in the intensity of the situation, it can make the fear worse. Most therapists use a combination of education and systematic desensitization, and if done correctly, this treatment is generally highly effective.

Other techniques used in behavioral therapy include skills training, in which the patient is asked to practice a change in behavior in a role-playing situation in preparation for the real event; positive reinforcement therapy, in which the patient is rewarded each time he or she changes the problematic behavior to a more desired behavior; and aversion therapy, in which punishment, such as electric shock, is used to change a problematic behavior. As you can see, there are several forms of behavioral therapy a therapist may choose from, depending on the severity and type of problematic behavior.

Cognitive Therapy

Cognitive therapy employs the premise that rational, realistic, and constructive thinking can reduce the occurrence of or entirely get rid of a problematic behavior. It is also very effective in helping to lessen anxiety or depression that is caused by distorted thinking. Therapists who use cognitive therapy understand that we think before we do, and therefore if we change our thinking, we can change our doing.

One technique used in cognitive therapy is rational emotive behavior therapy, developed by Albert Ellis, in which the therapist counters a patient's unrealistic beliefs or thoughts with rational arguments. Whether the patient is overgeneralizing or catastrophizing, the therapist uses rational thought to make the patient see why his or her thoughts are irrational and leading to the problematic behavior.

The therapist may also have the patient use rational arguments against himself to better understand the irrational or misinformed beliefs. For instance, the patient is asked to identify the thought leading to the problematic behavior. He is then asked to look at that thought from an outside and objective position, listing rational arguments to dispel that thought or belief.

Whichever technique a therapist finds most beneficial (through rational argument or testing beliefs and thoughts against the evidence), cognitive therapy focuses on the idea that to change a feeling or behavior, one must change the thought process that leads up to that behavior. This is, in effect, a way to head off the problem before it has a chance to affect the patient's life.

QUESTION?

What are overgeneralizing and catastrophizing?
Overgeneralizing is taking a thought or belief and irrationally expanding it to areas that would otherwise be unaffected—for instance, believing someone is an entirely evil person just because he made a mistake. Catastrophizing is blowing a small problem out of proportion and turning it into an inescapable disaster—for instance, believing you will be a failure and everyone will hate you if you do not get a perfect score on a test.

Group Therapy

Group therapy in this instance refers to formal therapy in which more than one patient is being treated at a time, such as in couples therapy or family therapy. There are of course several informal group therapies out there that often work as a type of support group in which members suffering from the same type of problem get together and discuss their personal experiences and help each other to find solutions or simply get through the challenges of changing behavior. These groups can be a very powerful form of self-help, as one often encounters people who have lived through the same problem and can offer advice from personal experience as opposed to someone who can understand the problem only from an objective standpoint. Let's take a look at the two most common formal group therapies.

Couples Therapy

Have you ever heard the saying "There are two sides to every story"? This is also the belief of couples therapists. Often, if a relationship is suffering from arguments that never seem to be resolved, helping just one of the partners is not going to be sufficient in healing the relationship. Therefore, therapists prefer to see both participants in an attempt to look at the issue from both sides and help each understand the other's viewpoint in a rational and formal setting.

FACT

There isn't one favored approach to treatment for group therapies. Some therapists may utilize psychodynamic approaches, others may use cognitive-behavioral approaches, and some prefer the humanistic approach. Regardless of the approach used, group therapists all have one thing in common: They focus on the unit and each person is treated as a part of that unit.

As we all know, relationships all suffer inevitable conflicts and require a combined effort of both participants; one person cannot bear all the weight. This is where couples therapy comes into play. Since the therapist has no investment in the relationship, he or she can offer an objective perspective and help weed out the accusations and irrationalities to get to the heart of the matter. The therapist can then help the couple work together to find a way to live with their differences or resolve the conflict.

Family Therapy

It is sometimes recommended that an entire family visit a therapist to seek help for a particular problem. Many people underestimate the influence and effect family can have on a person. The problem of one member can very easily carry over to other members of the family, affecting them in different ways, but affecting them nonetheless. For instance, the eating disorder of a teenager is going to affect not only the teen but the parents and siblings as well. Sometimes problems between the parents are most apparent in the misbehavior of the children, and working on the couple issues resolves the behavior of the child. Other times, the power structure in the family is distorted, and children have more power than the parents, which is not healthy for anyone.

The therapist would help each member recognize the problem for what it is as well as seek out underlying problems that may have contributed to the existence of the problem. The therapist will also help the family recognize and work through the changes that must be made within the unit to best solve the problem at hand. Family dynamics can often be rather complicated and so ingrained in the members that an objective view is sometimes necessary to help the family work together as a unit along the same course of action to face and overcome the problem.

Helping Yourself

Most of us have suffered a symptom of a mental disorder at one time or another. This doesn't mean that we have a mental disorder. Not everything can be perfect in our lives. We all have problems we must deal with, and sometimes they seem overwhelming. Mental health professionals aren't reserved only for those with mental disorders. Anyone can utilize their expertise to help get through a troubling time. Of course, this isn't to say that if you are suffering a troubling time, you have to seek the help of a mental health professional. There are some things you can do to help combat downswings of mental health on your own.

Physical Health

If you are suffering a symptom of a mental disorder, such as loss of appetite, sleeping problems, or mood swings, consider your physical health before assuming it is a mental health problem. For instance, if you seem to be tired all the time lately, take a look at your eating habits. Are you eating healthy foods or junk foods? How often are you eating? Proper nutrition plays a big role in how you feel on a day-to-day basis. Perhaps you have been skipping meals and not acquiring the energy you need to get through the day. Or maybe you are getting your energy from sugar-filled foods, which when the "high" is over cause you to feel even more down and sleepy.

Several symptoms can be attributed to physical problems or changes. For instance, if you suddenly notice you are having muscle twitches, this doesn't necessarily mean you are developing a tick; you could be suffering a vitamin deficiency. Or perhaps you have been quite irritable lately. All that caffeine you are ingesting could be causing you to lose sleep, thus causing you to be more irritable. Whatever the symptom may be, take a look at your physical health. Have you made any recent changes in diet or exercise? Are you suffering any other symptoms? What can you do to improve your physical health?

There are several physical illnesses that have the same symptoms of mental illnesses. Before you self-diagnose a mental disorder, visit your family doctor and get checked out. While you may just be suffering a cold, you could be suffering a life-threatening illness. You know your body. If something is wrong, seek professional help.

Talk to Others

When life's troubles get you down or you are facing a problem you just can't seem to solve on your own, enlist the help of trusted family and friends. Sometimes just talking about a problem makes a solution a little easier to see. Or if you are unable to reach a solution on your own, perhaps your confidant will have a suggestion. The two of you could even brainstorm possible solutions and work together to try to see the problem from all angles. Don't be afraid to show emotion. Bottling up emotion and stress only leads to more problems down the road. Sometimes just talking about a problem allows you the emotional release you need to be able to look at the problem more realistically and find a constructive solution.

Embrace Change

Change can be stressful at times and often unwelcome. However, life throws us in the path of change all the time. If you are able to look at the positive side of change, you can then accept it and make the best of it. Positivity opens the door for optimism, keeps us motivated, and enables us to face our fears. If you find yourself faced with a change and focusing on the negative aspects or possibilities, take the time to create a list of the positive aspects and/or possibilities and redirect your focus.

You may even take this a step further by setting goals to achieve those positive results. By taking charge of the situation, you become more confident in your ability to take command of your own life, thus reducing feelings of helplessness and self-defeating attitudes.

Celebrate Your Uniqueness

Each of us is unique, whether we try to conform to the ideals of others or rebel against conformity. Once you are able to understand that, it becomes easier to accept yourself as an individual. Too often we place value on ourselves according to how we think others view us, even though these thoughts may have no substantial grounding in fact. Accepting yourself and celebrating your uniqueness can only lead to good and positive results. Also, in accepting ourselves, it becomes easier to accept others.

Chapter 17

Social Cognition—
Thinking about
Yourself and Others

Social psychology is the study of how we interact with people, what we think of them, and how we act when we're around them. Beliefs and attitudes mold our perceptions, distort them, and often bias our thought processes. They come into play when we decide who we like or dislike and to what extent we allow society to influence our behavior and perceptions.

Humans as Social Beings

As humans, we perform certain thought processes that help shape our perceptions of people and social situations. First, we observe or collect data (what is the information?); second, we detect covariation (how is the information relative to other information?); and third, we infer cause and effect (what causes the information?). Though we operate on this intuitive level of scientific reasoning, our attitudes and beliefs influence our decisions, as we'll see later in this chapter. Observing data and detecting covariation are explained here, while inferring cause and effect will be explained later when we discuss interpreting behavior.

Observing and Collecting Data

Out of all the many different types of information we collect on a daily basis, the kind of information that seems to stand out the most in our minds is vivid information. Studies have shown that we are more reactive to graphic, dramatic information than we are to less-dynamic information. Even if it is the same information, when presented in a way that stands out more clearly in our minds, we will most likely be influenced by that information.

Mass media plays a major role in this kind of data collection, and is probably the most influential in our decision-making. If a news station dryly reports the results of an abortion survey by simply stating there are more people that believe a woman has the right to choose, we are more likely to remember the vivid, two-second photo spot portraying an antiabortion march than we are the results of the survey. Thus, we might inaccurately conclude that there are more antiabortionists than there are people who are pro choice.

Those warnings against allowing your children too much time in front of the television certainly do have some bearing. If a child grows up watching too much television, she might develop her social reality based on what she is seeing on television.

Another way we collect information is by developing theories of our own, especially concerning subjects such as capital punishment, abortion, and racism. Our theories often distort how we interpret the data we receive, for example, from television or the newspaper. Two people on opposite sides of the capital punishment debate can read the same article that analyzes both the pros and cons of the issue, yet still feel their argument was either strongly supported or strongly biased against. This illustration of how we filter information can also be seen in schemata and scripts, which will be discussed later in the chapter.

Detecting Covariation

When two elements vary in their relationship to each other, such as height and weight, they are said to have a correlation. Part of how we interact socially involves our ability to understand or misread these correlations. For example, we might believe that people who are antiabortionists tend to be against capital punishment as well. A lot of times these correlations are assumed and turn out not to be correct. Thus, a platform for stereotyping and prejudiced judgment evolves.

Beliefs and Attitudes

We tend to make assumptions about a person's attitudes and beliefs based on a known belief. For example, if you know your coworker is against abortion, you might conclude that she believes in gun control, is against capital punishment, and believes marijuana use should be severely penalized. This way of thinking is based on cognitive consistency—the theory that we all try to be consistent in our beliefs and attitudes as reflected by the consistency of our behavior.

FACT

While nurses are busy promoting healthful lifestyles, it's not uncommon to step outside a doctor's office or hospital and see a group of nurses on their break smoking. According to the *Daily Bruin*, 18 percent of nurses smoke cigarettes. And oddly enough, they're not alone. Dentists and physicians are lighting up as well, with 8.2 percent of dentists smoking and 5 percent of physicians smoking.

Consistency Between Beliefs and Attitudes

One way to look at the consistency between beliefs and attitudes is to examine how we rationalize things. If we believe that a particular television produces the best picture, color, and sound, we start to persuade ourselves that they are the most desirable qualities. On the opposite scale, wishful thinking is when we believe that the television is acceptable; therefore, we persuade ourselves that it has the qualities we're looking for and is indeed acceptable. Both rationalization and wishful thinking show how one can affect the other, and in turn, account for how we perceive things on a somewhat unrealistic basis.

Consistency Between Attitudes and Behavior

Attitudes are a combination of beliefs and feelings and can be affected when confronted with social pressures. An example of inconsistency between attitudes and behavior can be seen in R. LaPiere's *Social Forces* in a study conducted during the 1930s. A white professor traveled the United States with a young Chinese couple. At the time, prejudice against Asians was strong and there was no law against denying guests accommodations based on race. The three commuters stopped at over 200 hotels, motels, and restaurants and were served at all the restaurants and all but one hotel without any hassles. Later, a letter was sent to all the businesses that they visited asking them if they would be willing to provide services to a Chinese couple. Of the 128 replies received, 92 percent said they wouldn't. In conclusion, the business owners displayed behavior that was far different from their actual beliefs.

When confronted with a situation, we often do things we don't like, like eat green beans as children. Our behavior is affected then, not only by our beliefs and attitudes, but by social pressures as well.

Similarly, peer pressure can induce actions that aren't consistent with what we believe, but are consistent with our attitudes toward social situations and what others think of us. Teenagers often smoke to "fit in" and put their beliefs aside in order to conform to the social pressure. Although attitudes don't always predict our behavior, attitudes based on direct experience can influence it. For instance, a person whose mother died of lung cancer may advocate a ban on smoking in public places and take part in the annual cancer walk.

Cognitive Dissonance Theory

As attitudes can affect behavior, behavior can affect attitudes. Leon Festinger's theory of cognitive dissonance holds that when our beliefs and attitudes oppose each other or our behavior, we are motivated to reduce the dissonance through changes in behavior or cognition. The theory itself has been influential in predicting behavior that reflects an inconsistency in attitudes. Behaving in such a way that conflicts with one's attitudes causes pressure to change the attitudes in order to be consistent with the behavior.

Social Schemata and Scripts

As mentioned previously, schemata and scripts are a way of collecting data in order to develop our own conclusions and theories about everyday social situations and interactions. Those conclusions and theories can change, however, when new information is introduced.

Schemata

Schemata refer to cognitive structures stored in memory that are abstract representations of events, objects, and relationships in the real world. It is a key ingredient of cognitive theories of psychological phenomena. Schematic processing is the process of retrieving the schema from your memory that is most consistent with the information being received.

Since we already have pre-existing notions and ideas about what a situation or a person should be all about, any new information we receive on the subject is compared with what we already have. Schemata and schematic processing allow us to store and organize the most relevant and striking information, which will surface when the need arises. For example, when you're told you're about to meet someone who is an extrovert, you automatically think of that person as energetic, friendly, warm, loud, and sociable. You then prepare yourself for the meeting based on these schemata that you've collected.

ALERT!

While schemata help us to understand information easily and quickly, they can have a drawback. When you already have information for a particular schema in place, you may have a tendency to pay attention only to new information that fits in with the old information and ignore new information that contradicts or doesn't fit with the old information.

Scripts

Scripts are schemata or abstract cognitive representations of events and social interactions. When you greet someone with "How are you?" the script calls for the person to respond, "I'm fine, thank you." Whereas schemata are the data we've collected for forming impressions of people, scripts represent the data we have for social events and interactions. A greeting script like the previous one can sometimes be misinterpreted and one person might go on and on about how his life is not going well while the person who initially asked the question waits for a chance to escape! The birthday script tells us we should dress a certain way, act a certain way, bring a gift, and expect certain situations like a birthday cake and the blowing out of candles. Scripts break the ice, making it easier to start conversations with people whom we don't know.

Forming Impressions

While first impressions are indeed important, additional information that we receive after the initial impression can change what we think about and how we behave around a particular person. Using the primacy effect, we can determine how much of an impact first impressions have on us and how much they influence any new information we might receive. Primacy effect is the tendency for initial information to carry more weight than information received later (also, in memory experiments, the tendency for initial words in a list to be recalled more readily than later words).

As seen in A. S. Luchins's *The Order of Presentation in Persuasion* (1957), the following paragraph was used in an experiment to determine if the primacy effect was apparent in people's assessment of what kind of person "Jim" was:

Jim left the house to get some stationery. He walked out into the sun-filled street with two of his friends, basking in the sun as he walked. Jim entered the stationery store, which was full of people. Jim talked with an acquaintance while he waited to catch the clerk's eye. On his way out, he stopped to chat with a school friend who was just coming into the store. Leaving the store, he walked toward the school. On his way he met the girl to whom he had been introduced the night before. They talked for a short while, and then Jim left for school. After school, Jim left the classroom alone. Leaving the school, he started on his long walk home. The street was brilliantly filled with sunshine. Jim walked down the street on the shady side. Coming down the street toward him, he saw the pretty girl whom he had met on the previous evening. Jim crossed the street and entered a candy store. The store was crowded with students, and he noticed a few familiar faces. Jim waited quietly until he caught the counterman's eye and then gave his order. Taking his drink, he sat down at a side table. When he had finished with his drink he went home.

The description, when split in half, describes Jim in two different ways. Up until the sentence that begins "After school, Jim left . . . ," Jim is friendly and outgoing. After that point, he's described as a shy, introverted, and unfriendly person. Of the people who read only the first half of the description, 95 percent thought him to be friendly, whereas of the people who read only the last half of the description, 3 percent thought him to be friendly. What's interesting is that of the people who read the entire description with the "unfriendly Jim" description first, only 18 percent thought him to be friendly. This shows that our initial impression of a person has the most significance in our general opinion of a person.

Interpreting Others' Behavior— And Your Own

As mentioned earlier in the chapter, inferring the cause and effect of behavior helps us understand not only the behavior of others, but our own as well. An attribution problem is the attempt to infer the cause of a particular behavior. Distinctiveness, consistency, and consensus are all criteria we use when determining the cause and effect of behavior.

Distinctiveness

One morning you wake up with a runny nose. You look out your window and notice your flowers are blooming, so you assume they are causing the sniffles. You test this hypothesis by leaving the area where the flowers are to see if you still have the symptoms. If the symptoms are still there, you decide that there is nothing distinctive about the flowers and decide they are not the cause. You have just used the criteria involved with distinctiveness to determine the cause of the problem.

Consistency and Consensus

If the symptoms occurred around the same time every year for the past few years, you might be convinced that the flowers are definitely to blame. If it's the first time it's occurred, then the consistency isn't relevant because it never happened before. You then call the doctor and he explains that a lot of people have called to complain about the same symptoms, which is always the case at that particular time of year when flowers are in bloom. Since you're not alone in the situation (others are reacting to the same stimulus), this is the consensus.

We use the same criteria when trying to determine and understand the behavior of other people. When a friend tells us that the food was great at the Chinese restaurant she just went to, we have to determine if our friend said it was great because the food was really great, if it was because our friend is biased toward Chinese food, or if it was because of the social situation—for instance, it was her birthday, everyone was in a great mood, and everything was great. Thus, in an effort to interpret others' behavior, we examine why something occurred and what caused it to occur.

ALERT!

The attribution theory is challenged when one takes into consideration the biases that often lead us to explain behavior. For instance, a lot of us will base our ideas of an individual's personality according to his or her behavior without taking into consideration environmental factors. That particular behavior may not reflect that individual's personality on an everyday basis; rather, it is reflecting the situational factors at hand.

Self-Perception

The theory of self-perception concludes that we make the same judgments about ourselves, use the same processes, and make the same errors as we do when making judgments about others. When an athlete endorses a product, we wonder if he or she really uses that product and believes in its consumer benefits, or if the athlete is just using it as a means to gain wealth and publicity. We often take a look at our own beliefs and attitudes in the same manner. Did you buy the shirt because it was on sale or because you actually liked it?

An induced-compliance experiment was conducted to illustrate how we go about understanding our own behavior. College students were offered money to go into a room, one at a time, and perform repetitive, dull tasks for one hour. After finishing the tasks, some students were given $1 to tell the next student that the tasks were fun and interesting, while other students were given $20 to say the same thing. Subjects who were paid only $1 said they actually enjoyed the tasks, but students who were paid $20 didn't find it any more enjoyable than the control subjects who were given money to say something to the next student.

To help you better understand yourself and your actions, take the time to work through your reasons for a particular behavior, especially if it is an undesirable behavior. Make a list of those reasons for the behavior as well as any patterns that seem to bring about the behavior. In this way you are more self-aware and can take steps to alter that behavior if you so choose.

According to the self-perception theory, the students had to ask themselves why they were saying the tasks were fun and interesting. The student who was next in line observed the previous student getting paid $20 and then saying it was fun, thus he assumed anyone would say the tasks were fun for that amount of money. On the other hand, students who observed the previous student getting paid $1 assumed that he must have really enjoyed the tasks if he only received a dollar for performing them.

Stereotyping and Prejudice

As seen previously in this chapter, first impressions often invoke stereotypical judgments about a particular person. This is based on our beliefs and attitudes and even on our own behavior. Gender, race, political stance, and personality contribute to the stereotypes we place on others.

One kind of stereotype is self-fulfilling stereotypes. When schematic processing causes us to create stereotypes of a person, it's not always with bad intent. Lack of experiences, both socially and casually, often results in a lack of information—information we need to process in order to form our impressions of a person.

When we interact with the very person or group we're stereotyping, we may be doing so in order to self-perpetuate and self-fulfill these stereotypes. Some white people feel uncomfortable around black people because they believe that they have hostility and anger toward white people. Thus, the white person who associates with the black person justifies his own discomfort by hiding behind a stereotype that is neither true nor accurate, but may seem amplified because of his preconceived ideas about black people.

FACT

Stereotypes are also called *implicit personality theories* because, in essence, stereotypes are small-scale theories of covariation, in which one set of traits or behaviors go with another set of traits or behaviors. For example, homosexual males are often assumed to be effeminate, even though that is only true of some homosexual men and is also true of some heterosexual men.

Studies show that we may also act differently with attractive people than we do with people we find unattractive. If the stereotype of an attractive person leads one to believe that the person they just met is sociable, trustworthy, friendly, kind, and fun, then the reaction to that person will lean in a positive direction. But, because of our prejudiced attitude toward attractive people, we may be blinded to the fact that the attractive person we just met is actually obnoxious, arrogant, selfish, and rude.

Chapter 18

Social Interactions and Interpersonal Behavior

Now that we understand something about our own emotions, motives, behaviors, and thought processes, let's look into how we take all of that and relate it to other people—such as in forging friendships, building relationships, and being in love. In addition, we'll explore how our behavior differs within society as opposed to social functions.

The Person and the Situation

One way to gain insight into how and why we relate to others is to look at how the people around us and the society we live in influence our behavior. For example, when you're having a terrible day and you're in a nasty mood, how is it that you can find it in yourself to be extremely courteous, pleasant, and kind to your boss, the store clerk, or your coworker? For one, it depends on how much you want them to like you and how much you want to be accepted by them.

The boss provides an obvious reason to be wary—he's not the guy you want giving you the evil eye all day because you were rude to him in the hallway! But, you might be aware that the store clerk and your coworker had nothing to do with your bad mood, so you treat them as you would want to be treated. Others in this situation don't care if their bad mood is misplaced as they take it out on the wrong person; they're not thinking about how much a person likes them at that particular moment. As we'll see, it only takes one person to distract us from our tasks, interrupt our train of thought, and cause us to behave in ways that don't represent our true form.

The Presence of Another

In 1897, to study how a person works in the presence of another person, psychologist Norman Triplett conducted an experiment to test coaction by monitoring how fast children turned a fishing wheel while they were alone in a room and when another person was present. (*Coaction* is the term used to describe how individuals interact together. In this experiment, it describes the act of two children performing the same task.)

In this study, Triplett placed two children in the same room and gave them both the task of turning a fishing wheel. He monitored how fast the children worked. He compared these results with how quickly the children worked when alone in the room and given the same task. Triplett's findings showed that children worked faster in coaction than when working alone. Psychologists then followed in Triplett's footsteps and conducted similar experiments that tested how well an individual performed in front of a group of people, or an audience. The same outcomes were witnessed, and together, the ramifications of coaction and audience influence were termed *social facilitation.*

Additional studies related to social facilitation have been generated in other animals. In the scientific journal *Physiological Zoology* (1937), S. C. Chen details how ants will dig at a faster rate when they're working in groups than they will when they're working alone.

Monkey See; Monkey Do

While we're affected by the pressure of being driven to work harder and strive for more when another person is performing the same task as we are, we're also pushed outward, prompted to help others in need when we see that the help is coming from someone else.

How we interpret situations is the key element in whether or not we're going to contribute our services. For example, it's become so common to see people sleeping on sidewalks and park benches that we just assume the person is homeless and catching a nap wherever and whenever he can. It's a rare occasion when someone stops to see if the person is really sleeping, if he's extremely ill and in need of care, or if he's dead.

ALERT!

Bystander apathy is common within social situations. Remarkably, the size of the group can affect whether a person will take action, often more so than the typical attitudes or behavior of the person herself. The larger the group, the less likely someone will contribute, because she assumes there are enough people around that surely someone else will act.

But is it "okay" simply to walk by and ignore someone who appears to be sleeping in a public area? The term *pluralistic ignorance* may help in answering the question. Pluralistic ignorance describes a state of thinking in which individuals in a group take their cues from other individuals in a group. For example, if everyone else is being calm about the person sleeping on the sidewalk, and no one is offering assistance, then the situation must not be an emergency and therefore doesn't require my help.

Diffusion of Responsibility

Since most people tend to look to others as models for how they should behave, diffusion of responsibility may take place. Diffusion of responsibility takes place when a group of people are witnessing the same emergency, yet certain people do not offer assistance because other people are present, therefore diffusing their need to act—"someone else will offer help, so I don't need to."

In R. Rosenthal's *Psychological Bulletin* (1964), the murder of Kitty Genovese was reported as having taken over a half an hour to complete because of her resistance. She was attacked in New York City outside of her house. Approximately forty neighbors heard her screaming, yet no one attempted to help her or even called the police. Unlike pluralistic ignorance where one observed behavior affects another's behavior, diffusion of responsibility took place because the neighbors were unable to see the reactions of others; however, no one took action because they thought, "Someone else will take care of it."

Compliance

Yielding to another person's wishes without changing our true beliefs puts us in a situation of compliance. You believe Granny Smith apples make a better apple pie, but your mother-in-law thinks Red Delicious makes the better pie. You agree to make the pie with Red Delicious apples, but you still believe Granny Smith apples are tastier. Though you've submitted to your mother-in-law's request, you haven't given up your own opinion on the subject.

Rebellion often develops when none of the choices presented to an individual are favorable. For example, if the choice is either to conform to the decision at hand or obey the main influencer, a person might choose neither as a complete act of rebellion against the situation as a whole.

Johnny has the choice of either going to school and having to listen to the teacher and actually participate in class discussions, or stay at home with his alcoholic father who will continue to yell at him all day. Not liking either of the choices, Johnny decides to rebel against both of them by neither going to school nor staying at home. Instead, he spends his day hanging out by the river with some of his neighborhood friends.

FACT

There are two types of compliance—conformity and obedience—both of which will be discussed later in this chapter. Both instances involve a main influencer in which a positive (reward) or negative (denunciation) response is elicited from the influencer in reaction to the person's compliant or noncompliant behavior.

Conformity and Peer Pressure

One type of compliance we'll examine is conformity. Conformity is best explained in relation to peer pressure, especially when large groups of people hold the same opinions and beliefs. It's not uncommon to feel uncomfortable in a situation where our opinions and beliefs are not the same as others in our group. As children, we know smoking is bad for our health, and if our parents caught us we'd be in trouble, but when we're standing in that circle with all of our friends and everyone is taking a drag to see what it's like, it's all too tempting to give in to the pressure. We may argue that smoking causes all kinds of diseases, but our friends will argue back that one little drag won't do anything. Do we conform, or do we hold our own? Everyone else thinks it's okay, so it must be. Besides, if we don't conform, our friends might think we're cowards, right?

This way of thinking can be applied to almost any group situation—even as adults. Consider the group of jurors who are given the difficult task of deciding someone's fate—innocent or guilty. If eleven jurors decide on a guilty verdict and the twelfth juror disagrees, how long before he conforms to their verdict, if he ever does? It's possible that he might conform simply because he doesn't think they'll ever see his point since the odds are so stacked against him.

In both the smoking and the jury example, the individual has to re-evaluate information he's already formed an opinion about. Part of growing up is learning how to distinguish between what you believe, what others want you to believe, and how willing you are to understand another point of view. But it doesn't get any easier as adults. With all the information available to us at any given moment, by way of the media and the Internet, we're forced to constantly reassess copious amounts of information in order to form strong, well-rounded choices, beliefs, and opinions. And while "majority rules" in most instances, it's a tough road to follow when you find yourself disagreeing with popular opinion.

The next time you are faced with a situation in which you are feeling peer pressure, think first of your own responsibility for your actions. If you get it out of your head that you can blame peer pressure for bad behavior and there's no one to blame but yourself, you are more likely not to fall prey to peer pressure.

Obedience

Being submissive to authority is an everyday reality that all of us share. Paying taxes, working to earn money, obtaining a driver's license, obeying rules of conduct in public places, and so on are just a few examples of how we obey a higher source. Just as it's important for children to obey their teachers, it's important that teachers follow the principal's rules about curriculum, which in turn follows the standards set by the local school district. There are four elements—social norms, surveillance, buffers, and justifying principles—that help determine what causes us to be (or not to be) obedient:

- **Social norms**—These are rules that have been established and are delegated by the community, government, or other empowered group for individual associates and constituents to follow on a regular basis.
- **Surveillance**—When the delegators of the established rules and regulations are not around to administer them, they aren't always

followed. However, when they are present, obedience levels increase as every effort is made to display how the rules are being followed.

- **Buffers**—A buffer is a device or situation that permits obedience or disobedience to occur more easily. For example, the guard hitting the switch on the electric chair may find it easier to obey his superior's orders because he doesn't have any real contact with the ill-fated convict.
- **Justifying principles**—The guard may not believe it's right to kill another human being, but his duty is justified by the ideals of his superior—the person performed inhumane crimes and therefore must be punished, and the guard believes in following the orders of a superior without question.

Friendships and Romantic Relationships

We're attracted to others in a variety of ways and on a variety of levels: acquaintances, friendships, intimate relationships, and family bonds. While we cannot choose our family, we can choose our friends and life partners. How we choose them and why is what we'll examine next by means of physical attraction and love.

Physical Attraction

First impressions, stereotypes, and behavior are all affected by a person's physical appearance. Whether we like to believe it or not, a person's looks count—*at first*. Once we go beyond the surface and delve into the greater mysteries that define an individual, the importance of appearance seems to fade away. But why do attractive people seem to get more attention than those who are less attractive?

Perhaps one explanation can be found in the following experiment. Male college students were shown a television program that featured several young, striking women. Similarly, a separate group of men and women were shown a picture of a beautiful woman with very attractive features. After watching the TV show, and after being shown the photo of the attractive female, both the male college students and the group of men and women were shown a picture of an average-looking woman. Both groups gave the woman a low rating on the level of attractiveness (Kenrick and Gutierrez, 1980).

The results of this experiment point to the notion that our standards for beauty may be so elevated that recognizing and admiring ordinary beauty can be difficult. Had the groups been shown the photograph of the average-looking woman *before* they saw the images of the extremely beautiful women, they might have given her a higher rating. Thus, the "picture" of beauty in our minds is of the women we see on television, and that is what we're comparing the rest of the world to. This may cause us to treat attractive people better because they represent our ideal of beauty and because we assume they have all the internal qualities we admire.

Likeness

Finding something in common with a coworker, neighbor, or classmate is one of the easiest ways of building relationships. Making friends that like to do the same things we do makes life more fun and interesting and provides a gateway for us to appreciate their differences as well.

FACT

Shy people have a difficult time approaching sociable, outgoing people and find it easy to approach other shy people. This is an example of the expectancy-value theory. For example, an outcast at school who wants a date for the prom isn't likely to ask the most popular boy or girl because he or she is most likely going to be rejected. The outcast might, however, ask someone he or she feels "safe" with, like another outcast, because it's less likely he or she will be rejected.

Love

Once we start building friendships, it's only a matter of time before a serious, loving relationship can start to evolve. Intimacy is shared at a greater level when experiences are exchanged in more depth. Stronger feelings emerge and more is at stake. While everyone has his or her own idea of what love is and what makes us fall in love with one person and not another, the right blend of physical attractiveness, likeness, and intimacy usually does the trick.

It appears that both men and women hold the same opinion concerning romantic love. In a study conducted in 1976, 86 percent of men and 80 percent of women said that marriage was out of the question if they didn't feel they were in love with their partner (Campbell and Berscheid, 1976).

Altruism

Altruism is often perceived as random acts of kindness in which the giver is willing to make a selfless (and sometimes life-threatening) act on the behalf of someone else, even someone unknown to the giver. The founder of sociobiology, Edward Wilson (1929–), holds the belief that altruism in human beings is similar to that seen in other animals in which mothers will risk their own lives in order to save the lives of their offspring and ultimately their genes. Humans are loyal to their kin and many heroic acts can be found in our own soldiers who risk their lives every day in numerous ways to protect the survival of their country's communities. On the other hand, critics of this type of heroism believe they defend their cultural and religious beliefs, as well as their honor.

FACT

Critics argue that there are no selfless acts and therefore altruism in its purest form does not exist. They state that the giver derives pleasure in one form or another from the "selfless act," and thus the giver is rewarded and the act is no longer selfless.

So how is altruism then defined? There are two working definitions. Biological altruism is making a selfless act on the behalf of another in order to attempt to save that person's life, even though your own life may be at risk—for instance, jumping into a rushing river to try to save someone caught in a current. Psychological altruism is making a selfless act to the benefit of another though it does not reward you in any way—for instance, giving up your seat on the subway for someone else to sit down though you know you will be uncomfortable standing in the crowded train. Regardless of how you choose to define altruism, it is a phenomenon that is as of yet inexplicable to social psychologists.

Aggression and Its Causes

Aggression is something that is seen in all walks of life. In fact, it's one of the defining characteristics we have in common with other species within the animal kingdom. Not to be confused with how a bird might kill a rat for its food source, aggression is an act of hostility that one animal displays in front of another animal when it feels threatened, challenged, or an immediacy to protect its territory.

While the cause of aggression in animals is mainly about food supply, land territory, and dominance, human beings usually show aggressive behavior in regards to another type of territory—personal space. Think of the brother and sister who are constantly at each other's throats because the younger sibling won't leave the teenage sibling alone and he certainly can't seem to stay out of her room! Or recall a situation where an acquaintance physically got too close to you during a conversation, in which you felt so crowded you had to take a few steps back.

Not all animals attack in order to eat their prey. When birds flock together to ward off intruders this is called a *mob situation,* in which each aggressive bird aligns with the flock to make the message loud and clear to the unsuspecting prowler.

Certainly human beings act aggressively toward anyone or anything that jeopardizes the well-being of their children, but when finances are compromised because of a mixup at the bank, or when a newly purchased, expensive appliance fails to operate properly after just a few days, things can get pretty heated between the parties involved. So humans not only have a need to protect their personal space and the safety of their children, but humans are very touchy when it comes to their hard-earned financial abundance (or lack thereof!) as well.

The Mentality of Groups

Identifying with a group is the process of adopting its beliefs, attitudes, and standards, as well as complying with its rules and regulations in an effort to gain closeness to other human beings and feel part of something larger than an individual's personal life. In other words, it makes us feel like we belong. We belong to a country, a state, a city, a county, a community, a parish, a family, a credit union, a gym, an art club, etc. Each group helps define who we are and exploits our talents and morals, and in turn we help define the group itself. This symbiotic relationship nourishes our spirit and gives us a sense of society.

The groups we identify with are also called *reference groups* because we refer to them when we need to understand our own opinions and analyze our behavior or reactions to situations.

The importance of groups starts at a young age. Children form groups in their classrooms as well as in their neighborhoods, and groups like the Girl Scouts, Boy Scouts, and the Boys and Girls Club of America help children develop strong personalities, learn skills that boost their confidence, and meet friends who could possibly last a lifetime. Just to give you a basic idea of how important most people think groups are, here are some facts about the Boys and Girls Club of America:

- An estimated 3.6 million boys and girls belong to the club.
- There are 3,300 clubs located all across the nation.
- In addition to all 50 states, these locations include Puerto Rico, the Virgin Islands, and military bases (both domestic and international).
- The club boasts a staff of approximately 40,000 professionals.

Each of us wants to feel like we belong somewhere. That is why groups are so important to our social lives. When we can relate to others, we are able to justify our beliefs and actions even though that justification isn't necessarily needed. Even so, we often feel more secure in our beliefs if we have a support group. Humans rely on the social interactions with others both to learn about their environments and to grow as a person. Ⓔ

Chapter 19

Human Development— Conception to Birth

Developmental psychology helps us understand the physical, cognitive, and social changes that occur in a human life. Beginning with the union of two cells and ending in a full-grown human being, the development of a person is incredibly complex. In this chapter, we'll start with the biological development of the human and advance into the psychological development of a baby.

Genes, Gametes, and Conception

As we all know, the union of two cells, in particular the egg and sperm, beget a baby nine months later. This conception process, however, is very complex and important to understanding human development. Conception begins, as stated previously, with the fusion of an egg cell and a sperm cell, or gametes. At birth, the female has all the immature eggs that she will use throughout the course of her life. The male human being starts producing sperm when he reaches puberty (around 1,000 sperm in a second but this rate slows as the male ages).

FACT

Though a female is born with all her eggs, not all these eggs will reach maturity. Approximately only 1 in 5,000 of a female's eggs reach maturity. When an egg reaches maturity, that egg is then able to produce offspring.

From 200 to 600 million sperm are released in the average ejaculation but a rare few make it to the actual egg, and only one sperm is needed to form a zygote (or a fertilized single-celled egg, the earliest form of human beings). As soon as that one lucky sperm begins to penetrate the jellylike outer coating of the egg cell, the egg becomes defensive and the surface of the egg cell hardens to block out any other sperm cell from penetration. The sperm uses digestive enzymes to work its way through the egg's surface.

Cell Division

Once the zygote is formed, the cell goes into the division process. The first division is called *mitosis*. In mitosis, the zygote divides to form two identical daughter cells. Later, the cell begins another form of division called *meiosis*. Meiosis produces four daughter cells, each daughter cell containing half the chromosomes of the original parent cell. Meiosis is necessary to keep the chromosome number constant from generation to generation. The divisions will continue to form the beginning of a human being. The cells move, or migrate, in relation to other cells forming the first shape of the embryo; this migration is called *morphogenesis*.

Gene Codes

Each gamete (egg and sperm) has twenty-three chromosomes, and when the human is completely developed, she will have forty-six chromosomes. Your genes are located on your chromosomes. A gene is a small piece of one chromosome; it is a code for a specific sequence of amino acids in a protein. Each code is different and very complex, which brings about many different traits.

Most people are familiar with genes as a transportation of hereditary traits. Genes can affect whether or not you will be born with attached earlobes, freckles, or a widow's peak. Genes are the hereditary codes that are passed on to an offspring. Traits, which are caused by your genotype (or genes for a particular trait), can be dominant or recessive. Dependent upon the alleles carried on the chromosomes you received from your parents, your appearance will develop accordingly. For example, if your mother gave you the dominant allele that we will call *W* for a widow's peak, and your father gave you a recessive allele *w*, you would be born with *Ww* and in turn develop with a widow's peak since the dominant trait decides your outcome.

ALERT!

Some diseases are known to be dominant or recessive. For instance, neurofibromatosis and Huntington's disease are known to be dominant disorders. Cystic fibrosis and phenylketonuria (PKU) are known to be recessive.

The ratio for hereditary traits can be figured using a Punnett square. The Punnett square is a prediction of the phenotypic (the outward appearance of a person according to his or her genotype) ratio. Some disorders can be hereditary as well, such as schizophrenia and neuro-fibromatosis (or von Recklinghausen's disease). Some people attempt to use the alleles from other family members to determine how the child will develop (with or without the disease).

The Embryonic Period

The embryonic period lasts from fertilization to the beginning of the third month. The human being begins to develop very distinctly after morphogenesis. Cells begin to take on specific functions and structures in a process called *differentiation*. For the first time, the actual size of the daughter cells begins to grow. Up until this point the cells that were divided were no larger than the parent cells, causing no growth in size.

Development

The cells begin to develop into layers: the upper layer is the ectoderm, the middle layer is the mesoderm, and the lower is the endoderm. Each layer will go on to form different parts of the body. Particularly, the ectoderm becomes the nervous system and the skin. The mesoderm gives rise to muscles, circulatory system, and connective tissue. And finally, the endoderm becomes the linings of the digestive and respiratory tracts.

At this point the extraembryonic membranes begin to develop as well. The most famous extraembryonic membrane is the amnion (more familiar as the amniotic fluid in which the baby develops). Another extraembryonic membrane is the yolk sac. This yolk sac is where the red blood cells begin to form. The placenta also begins to form once the embryo is implanted fully into the uterine wall. This is where the fetal and maternal blood exchange nutrients, gases, and wastes. The umbilical cord comes into play in the placenta. It plays the important role of connecting the fetus to the placenta.

FACT

The effect of the embryonic period on the mother is significant. This is the period when the mother may experience nausea, fatigue, and loss of appetite. The uterus at this time develops from the size of a hen's egg to bigger than an orange and can be felt above the pubic bone.

At this point the fetus also has developed a circulatory system; however, it is slightly different from adults in that it shunts blood away from its unused lungs. Organs like the spinal cord and heart have developed.

Physical Appearance

At the end of the first month, the embryo still has a tail, but the development of arms and legs begins to make it appear more humanlike. By the end of the second month and the end of the embryonic period, the embryo has lost its tail, has developed a form of fingers and toes, has more distinct nose, eyes, and ears, and all major organs have appeared. The heart has begun beating and bone begins to replace cartilage.

The Fetal Period

The fetal period lasts from the third to the ninth month of pregnancy. The fetus is now looking more humanlike and grows to resembling a baby every day. The growth of the body begins to speed up to catch up with the large size of the already developed head (from the embryonic period). The epidermis (outer layer of skin) begins to be polished, developing eyelashes, eyebrows, head hair, and fingernails.

Month-by-Month Breakdown

During the third month of pregnancy, the difference between sexes is visible. By the fourth month, the fetus begins to look much more human. Beginning at the fifth month, the mother is able to feel the movements of the fetus. By the end of the seventh month, the fetus weighs about three pounds and its eyelids are opened. Toward the end of the fetal period, the fetus begins to shift in position, with its head nearing the cervix of the mother. If this turn is not accomplished completely, the baby will most like be birthed by a cesarean section. Fat accumulation beneath the skin causes weight gain in the fetus; it should weigh around seven pounds by the end of the ninth month.

QUESTION?

What is a cesarean section?
A cesarean section is a medical procedure in which an incision is made into the uterus, from which the baby is delivered. This allows the baby to avoid passing through the cervix feet-first, which is dangerous to its survival.

Time for Delivery!

A baby can be born after the sixth or seventh month; however, his or her chance of survival is worse than a full-term baby, due largely to the fact the lungs are not sufficiently developed. A baby born at this time also lacks lung surfactant (a film that protects the delicate linings of the lungs from direct contact with air), which increases the risk of respiratory distress syndrome, or collapsed lungs, upon birth.

The Birth Process

One of the most awesome processes in human life and development is the miracle of birth. Nine months after conception, the baby is ready to greet the world, fully developed. When it is time for the fetus to be expelled from the uterus, androgens released into the blood and production of prostaglandins and oxytocin cause the uterus to contract and force the baby out of the mother's body.

Contrary to popular belief, contractions may happen all throughout pregnancy. The contractions typically occur about every fifteen to twenty minutes and last about twenty to thirty seconds. The start of true labor is marked by contractions that occur regularly every fifteen to twenty minutes and last for forty seconds or more.

The scientific word for the birth of a human being is *parturition*, a stage in which the labor and birth of the fetus occur. When the baby moves down, the cervix begins to disappear in a process called *effacement*. The first stage of parturition is finished when the cervix has disappeared, or dilated, completely. In the second stage of parturition, the uterus contracts every one to two minutes and lasts about sixty seconds.

This is the stage in which the mother is overcome with a desire to push while the baby's head travels down to the vagina.

An episiotomy is sometimes performed since the woman's vagina cannot expand enough to accommodate the baby's head for passage. An episiotomy is an incision that helps widen the vagina for the baby's head to go through; the incision prevents tearing of the delicate tissue and limits bleeding.

The baby's head emerges and once the baby is breathing well, the doctor will cut and tie the umbilical cord. In the third stage or parturition, the placenta (or afterbirth) is expelled from the mother's body around fifteen minutes after the baby is delivered. The expulsion of the placenta is the completion of the final stage of parturition.

Maternal Health and Nutrition

An expectant mother has many things to worry about while her child is solely dependent on her. A fetus has no other way of maintaining its health than by the attentive care of its mother. An expectant mother must care for not only her child's health but her own as well; if she allows her own health to fall, her child's will inevitably be harmed.

When people think of a pregnant woman, one of the first things to come to mind is the outrageous cravings we have all heard tell of. While these cravings may seem bizarre, such as a craving for pickles and ice cream, they may reflect the nutritional needs of the pregnant mother. Supporting both herself and her baby, an expectant mother has to balance the nutritional needs of both. A mother who has a bad diet will develop a placenta that is not up to par. An undernourished placenta cannot perform its transportation of nutrients as well as a well-nourished one, thereby leaving the fetus of an undernourished woman in want of nutrients and oxygen.

Iron

Pregnant women need many more minerals and nutrients than the average woman. An expecting mother's blood volume increases by about 30 percent. Because of this increase, a pregnant woman needs much more iron than a normal person. Usually, unless the mother has another sort of health problem, her health care professional will recommend iron supplements of 30 to 60 milligrams since it is difficult to fit the ideal amount of iron needed for both mother and fetus into a normal American female's diet.

ALERT!

If a woman does not meet the adequate requirements for iron during her pregnancy, she can develop iron-deficiency anemia. This anemia lessens the mother's ability to fight off infections.

A normal woman is able to absorb 10 percent of the iron in her food; however, a pregnant woman is able to absorb almost twice this much, making it a little easier to obtain as much iron as needed to sustain two lives in one person's diet. A person can get iron from many foods, but the best sources of it are meat (especially liver), eggs, and legumes.

Folic Acid and Vitamins

During pregnancy a woman will also have an increase in need for folate, or folic acid. Folic acid is highly present in green leafy vegetables, some fruits, and liver. A severe lack of folic acid in an expecting mother's diet can result in megaloblastic anemia. This disorder occurs during the last trimester of pregnancy, causing the mother's heart, liver, and spleen to become enlarged and thus threatening the life of the fetus.

B_6 and B_{12} vitamins are very important to a pregnant woman. These vitamins can be found in whole grains, milk, and organ meats. B_{12} is most often found in foods that come from animals. A lack of vitamins found in animal products can cause brain damage or learning disorders.

Calcium and Sodium

Along with B_6 and B_{12}, an expectant mother should increase her intake of calcium to about an extra 400 milligrams a day. Four hundred milligrams is about 50 percent more calcium than is recommended for the average adult female twenty-five years of age and older. The huge increase in calcium in a mother's diet goes most directly to helping her baby's bones develop sufficiently. Nature allows the increase of calcium absorption just as it does with iron.

A pregnant woman's sodium intake must also be altered. It is suggested that a pregnant women should take in about 2,000 to 8,000 milligrams of sodium daily, as opposed to a normal female intake of 1,100 to 3,300 milligrams a day. However, sodium must be carefully watched like all the other vitamins and minerals mentioned in this section; a sudden, drastic increase in any can cause problems for the mother as well as the fetus.

Weight Gain

A pregnant woman should not be scared of gaining weight while carrying. The average and expected weight gain for an expecting mother is from twenty-five to thirty pounds. Although this seems like a lot of weight, keep in mind that the increase in weight includes not only the baby but also the increase in breast size, the placenta, amniotic fluid, enlarged uterus, increased blood volume, stored fats, and water retention.

Vegan and vegetarian mothers must be very careful when eating for two. The fetus needs many vitamins and minerals found mainly in animal meats and products. A vegetarian and especially a vegan mother should consult with her doctor or nutritionist to find the best way to suit her child's needs through her diet.

If a pregnant woman strictly limits her calorie intake, which is a popular way of dieting, she can establish the production of ketones in her blood and urine. Ketones are produced when an animal goes into a starvation-like state. An overproduction of ketones can affect the baby's brain, so badly in fact that the baby could be born mentally retarded if the production is high enough.

The nutrition should be most carefully watched in the final three months of pregnancy. Before these last months, the weight gain in the woman is due mainly to the fact that the baby's body is increasing in tissue, blood volume, and fat stores, and also from the mother's enlarged breasts and uterus.

Maternal Diseases and Drug Use

As we have learned, the placenta carries the nutrients and wastes to and from the body of the baby and the mother. Any harmful things that the mother ingests are transported into the baby through the blood. Although the placenta has the ability to screen and block certain harmful substances from entering the unborn baby's blood, it allows some harmful substances to slip by unnoticed, some particularly harmful things.

Teratogens are harmful agents, particularly drugs and viruses, that the placenta allows to pass through. Many people know that an expectant mother with the AIDS virus will most likely pass the virus on to her unborn child. Also, if the mother happens to be addicted to heroin, the baby will also receive her frequent heroin doses, and in turn, be born a heroin addict.

The relationship of an unborn child to its mother is the closest human relationship that a person will ever have due to the fact the baby is biologically dependent on the mother for survival. The mother must be very careful about what she lets enter her system and that of her baby's.

Women smokers also have a great impact on their baby's health. The baby receives the nicotine that the mother brings into her system. This substance causes the baby to be unable to receive as many nutrients and thereby causes unhealthy weight loss. Very heavy smoking may also cause brain defects in the fetus.

Fetal Alcohol Syndrome

One of the most common and notorious problems caused by a mother's insufficient monitoring of what enters her body is fetal alcohol syndrome (FAS). What most people do not understand is that even moderate drinking can affect a fetal brain. When alcohol enters the bloodstream of the expectant mother, it depresses both the mother's and the child's central nervous system. Fetal alcohol syndrome causes physical and cognitive abnormalities in children. Some of the more serious fetal alcohol syndrome babies include small and disproportional heads and brain abnormalities. This problem of fetal alcohol syndrome has become the leading cause of mental retardation in children.

While fetal alcohol syndrome is theoretically 100 percent preventable, there are mothers whose personal problems or difficult social environments make it more likely that they will drink more than is good for them and their fetus. The extent to which the behavior of pregnant women should be controlled by the state for the protection of their fetuses is controversial; for instance, do you think that a pregnant woman who is alcoholic should be committed to a hospital to prevent her harming her fetus? Or should her rights to do as she wishes be respected, with the consequence that society will have to address the extensive medical, educational, and social problems of her child as it grows?

Diabetic Mothers

An expectant mother with diabetes is to be very closely monitored to see that her blood sugars remain at a normal level. If the mother's blood sugar becomes too high, the fetus may become large, overdeveloped, and have blood sugar problems itself when it is born. Diabetic mothers also have problems maintaining the appropriate nutrients needed to sustain a dependent fetus and fight off infections.

A pregnant woman should take great care in monitoring what she allows into her body. Unprotected sex, drug use, and even the wrong amount of caffeine can put the dependent fetus in great danger of deformities or even death. While managing substance abuse or dependency is very difficult under any circumstances, some women manage to find the additional motivation and support they need to quit when their child's health is at stake. Other women cannot do it even then, and they live with the knowledge that their behavior has harmed their children as their children grow and try to deal with the world. Ⓔ

Chapter 20

Human Development— Infancy and Childhood

As we learned in the last chapter, infants are reliant upon their caregivers for survival. However, this doesn't mean that they are not learning and growing on their own. The growth and development of infants and children is simply remarkable. These first formative years are of the utmost importance to a child's development. Let's take a look at how a child begins to learn about its world and how to function.

Physical Growth

During infancy and childhood, the human goes through many changes physically. Humans are born with most of the brain cells that they will develop in their lifetime, though a few brain cells develop after birth. When a child is born, he is without a mature nervous system. As an infant grows, he develops complicated nervous structures enabling his ability to perform functions as he grows such as walking and talking.

Maturation

Infants go through a process called maturation in which the biological growth processes enable changes in behavior in an orderly fashion. A simple example of maturation is that certain actions are performed in a certain order by all humans, such as standing before walking. If a child is severely abused, however, she may not develop at the same pace as other children.

Memory

Most children are unable to place things in their long-term memory before the age of three, which is why most people do not remember happenings before their third birthday. The human infant lacks the neural connections to keep the memory of experiences for a long period of time.

FACT

Studies have shown that babies can remember things for short periods of time, however. In different studies testing their ability to remember actions that have been performed in front of them, infants have been found capable of remembering certain things (such as recognizing pictures they had been shown at a previous time) from one day up to three months later.

All the time parents spend taking care of their babies (i.e., changing diapers, feeding, and doctors visits) is not likely to be remembered by the child. An older child will accept the stories of their parents staying up with her all night without sleep, but will not remember a moment of it. This lack of memory does not, however, affect the attachment a child feels to the nurturers surrounding her when she is a baby.

Development of Motor Skills

After birth, a human's body begins to develop a more mature nervous system. With this more complicated nervous system come more complicated actions. The development of motor skills causes much grief among mothers. Many mothers will worry if their child is not sitting up or walking when his peers are; however, children in general, unless they have been abused or have some kind of inhibiting disability, tend to develop at nearly the same rate as far as motor skills are concerned.

There are two different kinds of motor skills: fine motor skills and gross motor skills. Fine (or small) motor skills use small muscles such as the eyes and the fingers, and also use more than one part of the body at the same time. Gross (or large) motor skills involve, obviously, the larger muscles like the arms and legs, and also include balance and coordination.

Developing at Different Rates

It is important to understand that a child's brain develops in sections, and that development of different capabilities may happen at different rates. If a child is speaking and reacting to speech better than his peers but still lacks the motor development of his peers, there is no problem with the child in question. Children's brains develop the motor skills portion later on, so a child could be talking quite effectively and not yet walking.

Children in different cultures tend to develop at slightly different rates. For example, 90 percent of babies in the United States will walk by the age of fifteen months, but most babies will be able to walk by the age of ten months in Uganda. But even blind children will begin to walk nearly the same time as their peers in their culture because of the maturation process.

A human being is born with the ability to suck, swallow, spit up, eliminate, and breathe, but other functions develop as the baby's nervous system further develops. The human body matures from the top to the bottom. First an infant will move her head, neck, and shoulders, then onto the arms, trunk, and eventually the legs. An infant should be able to turn her head at two weeks, sit on her own at eight to nine months, and skip by age five, but as mentioned earlier, that is just a generalized outline of development.

Don't try to force your child to develop skills earlier than he or she may be ready. Biologically speaking, our cerebellum develops very rapidly at this time, giving children the ability to learn to walk at nearly the same age. Genes also affect the maturation process of children's motor skills, causing slight differences in timing, but on the whole these differences usually even out within a short period of time.

Increasing Development of Motor Skills

Some doctors suggest things, which most people take for granted as just being part of child's play, to increase the development of motor skills. For example, toddlers who play with stackable toys, turn pages in books, and scribble are helping to develop their motor skills. Preschoolers who cut paper with scissors, finger-paint, and play with Play-Doh are helping along their motor skill development. These activities will eventually develop into tying shoes, buttoning clothes, and later on to playing tag and skipping.

Cognitive Development—How Infants and Children Think

As you know, cognition refers to all the mental processes associated with thinking. In this section we will rely heavily on Jean Piaget's research on the development of children's cognitive abilities. Although some of his findings have been proved different by later research, his theories about the basic process of development are still useful.

Schemata

Piaget's work used the concept of schemata to understand the cognitive processes of children. Basically, Piaget suggested that we as children make a mold for an experience and will put everything similar to that experience in the same mold. For example, a child will be familiar with the family dog and the proper word for it, but when she sees a dingo on television, she still calls the dingo a dog, assimilating it into her schema for dogs. Later on in the cognitive development of the child, she will understand that there are different *kinds* of dogs, and even later that a dingo is not a dog and accommodate for this change.

Stages of Cognitive Development

Piaget categorized the cognitive development into four stages: the sensorimotor stage, the preoperational stage, the concrete operational stage, and the formal operational stage. The transitions between these stages do not occur abruptly but rather are gradual.

The first stage, the sensorimotor stage, begins at birth and lasts until the child is about two years old. In this stage, a child experiences the world solely through his five senses. The second stage, the preoperational stage, lasts from around two years old to six years old. This stage is the stage in which a child learns to use language but doesn't yet understand concrete logic, even though children in this stage do possess the ability for symbolic thought. Egocentrism is introduced in this stage as well. Egocentrism is, according to Piaget, "the inability of the preoperational child to take another person's point of view."

People who abuse children do not understand egocentrism. They find a child who stands in the way of the television to be stubborn and therefore punish the child, not realizing that the child thinks his parents can see the television simply because he can.

For example, if a child draws a picture and shows it to his mother, he will expect her to know exactly what is drawn on the page, because in his eyes, the picture is as plain as day. Egocentrism also explains why a child who hides her eyes thinks her mother cannot see her—which leads to countless rousing games of "peekaboo!"

The next stage, the concrete operational stage, lasts from when a child is about six years old to around eleven years old. In this stage, children are able to use the mental operations needed to think logically about concrete events. In the concrete operational stage, children begin to grasp the concept of jokes and arithmetic problems. The final stage, the formal operational stage, begins around age twelve. This stage is when children are able to think logically about abstract concepts. Although there are certain pieces of Piaget's theory that are being challenged, the general cognitive development of human beings seems to follow the basic outline of his model.

Language Development—Part Prewired, Part Learned

Language may not seem like an important part of psychology, but some psychologists see language as what sets humans apart from the rest of the animal kingdom. Language is also something that psychologists continue to learn more and more about.

A behavioral psychologist, like B. F. Skinner, would say that language is learned because children get positive reinforcement for speaking the correct words. Parents will hug, kiss, and smile when a child says "mommy" or "daddy" for the first time, prompting the child to do so again.

Children will rarely make gross grammatical errors such as saying "ball my" instead of "my ball" even though they have not yet learned the proper subject, verb, object rule. This knowledge suggests that Chomsky is right in thinking humans are predisposed to language.

Psychologist and linguist Noam Chomsky looked at language from a biological standpoint. His claim is that humans are biologically born to speak, prewired for language. Chomsky noticed that all languages share common characteristics (such as the fact that the most commonly used words are generally the shortest) and said that languages developed this way because humans are predisposed to these characteristics.

Development of Language

Children from different cultures seem to follow, in general, the same development of language. At around four months, children will look in the same direction as parents when parents begin to point and label things. At twelve months, children usually start to speak, saying variations of words like "mom" or "dad." It is at this stage in their development that children make the mistake of overextension. An example of overextension is when a child refers to all males as "dad." A child also uses holophrastic speech around the twelve-month mark. Holophrastic speech is the use of a single word to express a complete idea. For example, a one-year-old may say "car" when she really wants to go for a ride.

QUESTION?

What is overregularization?
Overregularization is when a child overapplies the rules of grammar. For example, a child might say, "I hidded the watch" and find nothing grammatically incorrect in that statement because the child is overapplying the rules of past tense that he has learned.

At eighteen to twenty-four months, children develop telegraphic, or two-word, speech. In this stage, children delete the nonessential words, speaking in a very Tarzan-like way. For example a child wanting to say, "Hand me the cup" would merely say, "Give cup." After twenty-four months, a child's language develops rapidly. Once a child learns grammatical rules, however, it is common for her to make the mistake of overregularization.

Critical Period for Language Acquisition

There is a critical period for language acquisition, which seems to go from infancy to early adolescence. This time is when the brain is particularly receptive to speech. Children not taught properly during this time will never catch up with the average adult who has been taught how to speak and been around other people who speak. A child who grows up without being spoken to cannot fully acquire or understand the rules of language.

A big part of learning a language is for children to be around people who speak it. Although children are taught in school the right way to form sentences and new words, living with their families helps the children to develop proper language acquisition from the start. Children whose parents are deaf sometimes have delays in learning spoken English, but they are usually exposed to enough hearing adults in their environment or on the television or radio that they are familiar with spoken language. Many children of deaf parents learn American Sign Language as a first language and are as fluent as native speakers of any other language.

Brain Functioning

Two parts of the brain function in developing and maintaining language skills. Wernicke's area is the area of the brain, usually in the left temporal lobe, involved in language comprehension and expression. Broca's area is the area of the brain, usually in the frontal lobe of the left hemisphere, that directs the muscle movements involved in speech. If either of these areas is damaged, due to injury or stroke, specific problems with language occur. Damage to Wernicke's area causes a person to be able only to form nonsensical words, from an outsider's viewpoint, which sound normal to the injured person. Damage to Broca's area leaves a person struggling to form words but able to comprehend speech.

Developing a Sense of Self

Self-concept is a sense of an individual's identity and personal worth. Self-concept develops by around age twelve. Developmental psychologists are not able to determine an infant's self-concept since that question is too difficult for someone barely speaking to understand. However, these psychologists use the behavior of infants and children to hypothesize about their sense of self.

ALERT!

Don't underestimate the importance of a child's self-image. Children with positive self-images are more confident, sociable, and independent, and often have an optimistic outlook. Children with a negative self-image are typically the opposite.

By around fifteen to eighteen months, a child begins to recognize himself in a mirror. When children begin to attend school, they describe themselves according to comparisons with their peers. And finally around age eight or ten years, stable self-images are fully developed, for better or for worse.

Types of Parenting

A child's self-image is influenced by his or her caretakers' parenting style. Psychologists have identified three different types of parenting styles: authoritarian parents, permissive parents, and authoritative parents. Authoritarian parents are those who develop rules and lay down the law, so to speak. If the rules are not followed, the parent punishes the child. The permissive parent does what the child wants and rarely punishes her for doing wrong. The authoritative parent is a comfortable in-between stage. The parent sets and enforces rules to exert appropriate control but also explains the reasons for the rules. The parent is open to (and in fact encourages) discussion and will consider a compromise or exception when making rules.

How Parenting Affects Development

Many studies have shown that authoritative parents have children who are well adapted and happy. Children with authoritative parents had the highest self-esteem, self-reliance, and social competence. Those with a somewhat controlled upbringing are more motivated and self-confident. Children of overly permissive parents are often found to be more helpless and incompetent, with difficulties in dealing with frustration or limits.

Keep in mind that the studies surrounding these parenting styles are correlational. Many introductory psychology classes clearly state "correlation is not causation." Other causes such as education and stress levels can result in a child who is less competent and outgoing.

Social and Emotional Development

It is not a secret that infants develop a strong emotional attachment to the people who provide them with a caring and nurturing relationship. Infants are familiar with the faces of family members and react positively to seeing their faces and being held by them. However, the situation is very different when the infant comes in contact with Great Aunt Bertie, who the baby has never seen before. When the baby is passed from its familiar mother to caring but unfamiliar Great Aunt Bertie, the baby will most likely not react in the same manner as she did with her mother. Instead the infant will cry and reach for the more familiar mom. This fear is called *stranger anxiety*, and it occurs in babies between six months and two years old.

Attachment

Attachment is an emotional tie with another person. In young children attachment is shown by their desire to be held by their parents or other familiar caregivers and by their becoming upset or distressed when separated. Attachment is a survival impulse. Just as you would see cubs following the mother lion around in Africa, a baby stays close to its mother for protection.

Attachment comes from three key factors in the mother-child relationship: body contact, familiarity, and responsive parenting. An infant seeks body contact with the mother, or main caregiver. This soft, warm body gives the infant a safe haven from which to explore his or her surroundings and also a place to go to when upset. A mother's or caregiver's body is very important in attachment with the infant because it allows a sense of security.

FACT

Although it is thought to be the mother's job to provide the most nurturing for her children, the father's presence is important to the development of his child. Studies show that children who grow up without a father can be at an increased risk for various psychological and social pathologies. Of course, single parents of either sex are often exposed to poverty, increased stress, and more limited resources, which impact what they can offer their children.

Familiarity is based on the critical period of infants, which is that period of time shortly after birth in which the infant is exposed to stimuli that will produce proper development. Attachments based on familiarity must happen during the critical period. It is not necessary for a child to be in contact with her main caregivers right at birth to develop an attachment to them, as is seen in adopted children, but human attachment develops very slowly and is helped along when an infant is in contact with her main caregiver from the beginning.

Forms of Attachment

Attachment comes in two different forms: secure attachment and insecure attachment. Secure attachment is shown when a baby can happily play in and explore a new environment in his mother's presence. An insecurely attached baby will not be eager to explore the surroundings, but rather will stick to his mother. One explanation for the secure and insecurely attached babies is the mother's actions.

Responsive mothers who act with sensitivity and attentiveness toward their children most likely have securely attached infants. Mothers who are insensitive toward their children and ignore them will most likely have babies with insecure attachments. A child's temperament may also influence the parent's behavior. For instance, a child who is generally more anxious, less cuddly, and more easily upset will elicit different parenting behavior than a cheerful, calm, relaxed child. It goes both ways.

Much of this chapter has been mentioning the child's attachment to the mother. Though the mother's attachment seems to be a very, very important role in the development of a child, the father's presence also makes a big difference. However it need not be a biological mother or father to satisfy the child's need for attachment. The presence of safe, caring, responsible adults in a child's life is what seems to be important in nurturing healthy development. Ⓔ

Chapter 21

Human Development—Adolescence

For many Americans the word *adolescence* brings forth memories of the teenage years: fights with their parents, trying to establish themselves as individuals, and contradicting this newfound individuality by acting in a herd animal–like fashion, sporting the trendiest of clothing worn by their peers. This turbulent period is the one we will explore in the next chapter.

The Growth Spurt and Entrance into Puberty

Human adolescence begins with the onset of puberty. What is puberty exactly, besides that most awkward of times for teenagers? It is the point at which a person becomes physically able to reproduce. A huge rush of hormones begins puberty and a two-year period of rapid physical development ensues. Puberty, as we have all seen in educational videos, comes to people at different times. However, puberty *usually* begins in a girl around age eleven and around age thirteen in boys.

Characteristics of Puberty

Puberty is most noticeable by the growth spurt almost every kid goes through, leaving them in awkward shape, generally growing faster vertically than other parts of their bodies. Girls enter puberty before boys, causing a brief period of time when a boy's female counterparts are taller; however, when the boys reach puberty (near age thirteen or fourteen), they will catch up to and most likely become taller than girls their age.

During puberty, humans develop primary and secondary sex characteristics. The development of primary sex characteristics involves the rapid growth of the reproductive organs and external genitalia. The development of secondary sex characteristics includes the development of traits such as breasts and wider hips in girls and deep voices and facial hair in boys. Both boys and girls develop hair under their arms and in the pubic region.

Sexual Attraction

At this time, boys and girls begin to feel the beginnings of sexual attraction to each other. In this stage, the reproductive organs not only develop rapidly but also start acting out their functions as part of the growing process. Boys will experience their first ejaculation around age fourteen, usually through nocturnal emissions (or wet dreams as they are commonly called). Girls typically experience their first menstrual period around age thirteen, though some girls experience this as early as age nine. This first menstrual period is called *menarche*.

Effects of Developing Quickly

Studies have found that boys who develop more quickly than their peers are found to be more popular and independent as their muscular development prompts them to be proud. However, girls who develop earlier than their peers are more likely to be seen as outcasts since the development of breasts and a period is not something that can be used in sports or to gain popularity (regardless of what one would think). Girls who develop earlier than their peers are more prone to teasing than a boy who is developing faster than other boys.

Current research suggests that girls tend to become markedly less assertive around ages nine to eleven, and tend to put the needs of others, particularly boys, ahead of their own needs. This change has an impact on girls' self-esteem, self-confidence, and relationships with other girls.

Cognitive Development—How Adolescents Think

Adolescence seems to be a very troublesome stage, especially for parents. After reaching puberty and becoming more aware of their surroundings, adolescents will begin trying to break away from their parents' influence and begin developing into their own person—however much turmoil this creates depends on the household.

Adolescents begin to develop abstract reasoning skills. It is during this part of life that humans, as teenagers, are capable of exploring abstract thoughts. Along with trying to figure out who and what they are, adolescents begin to criticize others as well as themselves. They begin to spot hypocrisy in other people, especially their parents, leading to many typical fights between parents and adolescents.

Preconventional Morality

Adolescents also start developing a sense of morality, learning to distinguish right from wrong, and developing their character around their choices. Psychologist Lawrence Kohlberg (1927–1987) examined the moral development of children and adolescents and placed them in three general categories. The first stage, he suggests, is the preconventional morality. In this first stage, children, or adolescents even, will only obey the rules and choose to do right to either avoid punishment or gain a reward for acting "good." This first stage is mostly referring to children under nine years of age.

Conventional Morality

The second stage, the conventional morality stage, is the stage in which adolescents will begin to uphold laws because they understand the concept of rules and that they should be obeyed. This is also the stage in which adolescents start doing good out of caring for others. In this stage, acceptance in the social order by doing good is key. If an adolescent chooses to do wrong, he or she will not be accepted by the social order as a positive influence and therefore will either be punished accordingly or pushed to the outside of the group.

FACT

Adolescence is a period in which, although much of our moral thinking is developed, we may not choose to follow the voice in our head solely due to the decisions being made around us by our peers. Studies have shown that although teenagers have a set of standards, they may cross these in order to fit into the crowd.

Postconventional Morality

The third and final stage of moral thought processes is post-conventional morality. This is an advanced stage (most likely not reached by very early adolescents) in which an adolescent will act according to his or her own basic ethical principles. This stage is fully separated from parents, friends, and authoritative figures, although the child's development might have been influenced by the aforementioned people. This is the stage where adolescents make decisions based solely on their ideals in their own mind. However, many psychologists have debated over the postconventional level, saying this level is only blatant in adolescents raised in Western countries that promote individualism.

Differences in Moral Development

There are differences in moral development between boys and girls. Some interesting research by Carol Gilligan suggests that, in general, girls develop a different kind of morality than boys do. In the Heinz' dilemma, in which a man must decide whether to steal medicine to save his dying wife, girls tended to move toward an ethic of caring—what is "right" means what is good for people and relationships, even if it stretches the law. Boys at an equivalent stage believe that "right" means how closely behavior adheres to the law, or rules that govern society. While Kohlberg identifies decisions based on caring as an inferior stage of development, Gilligan argues that girls and boys are equally developed in their moral understanding, but that because women in our culture are generally responsible for caretaking and men for defending life and property, we develop along parallel but different tracks. Of course, this is an overgeneralization in both cases, but it bears thinking about.

Developing a Sense of Identity

Adolescence is a very important part of human development. It is at this point that people will summarize their entire life and decide who they want to be. Teenagers will test different roles until deciding which identity they fit most comfortably in, perhaps the preps or maybe the jocks. Teenagers may try on different roles with different people, behaving in different ways around their school friends and their sports friends.

While attempting to develop a set identity, teenagers also develop the capacity to experience intimacy with others. This is where gender roles become very separate. Girls tend to have a few very good friends while boys will hang around groups of other boys. Females begin to become the one with whom both women and men share feelings. Boys will tend to begin to become domineering and unexpressive.

Developing an identity is also very taxing on relationships with parents. Adolescents tend to break from their strong childhood connections with parents in order to find their appropriate identity. Peer influence begins to replace parental influence. Teenagers seem to lean toward friends for advice in matters while breaking the bonds with their parents.

This change in behavior could be explained through a biological stance. A human at this point is looking for courtship or possibly more than that, and in doing so, will display the appropriate biologically important aspects in order to gain a mate: men as protective creatures and women as nurturers.

Discovering Sexuality

As stated before, the hormones of adolescents are running rampant, making this a rather confusing and frustrating time for many. They are now able to procreate and feel that urge, but they aren't sure what to do with that urge. Society, parents, educational administrations, and peers all have their own input on the matter of sexuality, and adolescents must sort through all of this information to find meaning in their newfound sexuality. Two major issues related to adolescent sexuality are masturbation and sexual experimentation.

Masturbation

Masturbation is a natural process of self-exploration. Though it is rarely discussed with peers or with parents, most adolescents will begin to masturbate upon reaching puberty. This is a healthy way for adolescents to become familiar with their reproductive organs and experiment with the different feelings and sensations they can experience.

While there are certainly some people who frown on the practice of masturbation, there are many health professionals who encourage it. Masturbation not only allows adolescents the opportunity to explore their own body, but will also help prepare them for some of the components of intercourse with another person.

Many people have found that through the practice of masturbation, they develop the capacity for heightened pleasure in sexual relationships. Because those who masturbate typically know what they like and how they want to feel, they are better able to convey this to their partner, thus deriving a more pleasurable experience from the act.

Sexual Experimentation

Of course, masturbation isn't going to be quite enough for many adolescents. Curiosity about sex is strong, and they will want to know what it is like to partake in sexual acts with another person. This isn't to say that every adolescent is going to rush out and have sex with the first person he or she comes across. However, it isn't unnatural for an adolescent to explore some sexual acts (anything from kissing to touching to intercourse) with another adolescent. An adolescent may even experiment with someone of the same sex, though this doesn't necessarily mean that he or she is gay. Experimentation is just that— testing to satisfy curiosity and find answers.

These are also the years when some teens begin to identify feelings of attraction for members of their own sex. While some people who are gay report that they have always felt "different," and only put a name to the difference in adolescence, others discover their interest in midadolescence or even early adulthood. Gay teens who feel they have to conceal their interest from parents and peers often miss out on the skills in developing intimacy that most teens practice during this time.

Teenage Pregnancy

Although the rate of teenage births has been declining since 1991, our society is still having a major problem with it. Whether it be due to lack of education on contraceptives, lack of funding for contraceptives, or pure laziness, as many as 1 million teenage girls are pregnant each year and about 485,000 teenage girls give birth a year, many out of wedlock.

Teenage pregnancy is a cause for concern for the health of mother and child. Teenagers don't always have the healthiest eating habits, which does not benefit a teenager feeding two people at once. A teenager who is with child faces a higher percentage of risk for anemia, high blood pressure, and premature birth. The baby also suffers a higher rate of health problems such as cerebral palsy, epilepsy, and in rare cases mental retardation. A teenage mother is least likely to receive regular prenatal care.

ALERT!

Somewhere around 3 million teenagers have contracted sexually transmitted diseases, and a teen mother with an STD puts the health of herself and her child at risk. Some STDs prominent among teenagers and particularly harmful to both mother and child are chlamydia, syphilis, and AIDS.

Dropping out of School

Not only is the teen mother's health affected, her life has to be put on hold while she cares for the newborn baby. Around 80 percent of student teenage mothers still drop out of high school because of the pressure of academic work, eating and caring for two people, and having to deal with the social atmosphere of being the only, or nearly the only, pregnant student in the school. Teenage mothers who drop out of high school may find it hard to go back, and those who do finish their education usually end up in the GED program.

Stressful Situations

Around 75 percent of unmarried teenage girls go on welfare in the five years after their first child is born, depending on whether or not the father of the child is responsible about paying child support. Because welfare provides only a basic level of subsistence, most mothers on welfare live under conditions of severe poverty, in unsafe housing, with inappropriate food, and with limited access to day care or medical care. E

Chapter 22

Human Development—Adulthood, Aging, and Dying

We've reached the last stage of human development, as well as the last chapter of this book. In this chapter we are going to explore the changes that occur during adulthood. While many people look on aging with a sense of fear, this chapter will show that the elderly are quite capable of enjoying fulfilling, healthy, and active lives.

Physical Health

When people think of aging, most tend to think first of the changes in physical health. Many associate aging with numerous medications, disease, inability to function on one's own, and a body waiting to die. However, this is a misconception, especially in today's society in which people are living longer, healthier, and more productive lives.

There are three stages of adulthood: young adulthood (twenties and thirties), middle adulthood (forties and fifties), and later adulthood (sixty and older). In none of these stages is it inevitable that all people will suffer the aforementioned afflictions associated with aging. There are physical changes that take place with aging, but even these do not necessarily have to lead to a sedentary and unhealthy lifestyle in later years. A major factor in how well your body functions in later years is how well you treat it in the younger years.

Be Healthy Now; Be Healthy Later

Studies have shown that many diseases resulting in death or debilitation in later years begin during young adulthood. How you treat your body during those early adult years will have a direct impact on how well your body functions in later years.

As we all know, nutrition is very important for our physical health, young or old. By developing healthful eating habits now, you will not only be more likely to maintain those habits in later years, but you also may stave off diseases that could very well affect your well-being later in life. Whether you are an adolescent or already into later adulthood, it is never too late to adopt a healthful lifestyle. Not only will it make your quality of life better, but it can also prolong your life.

Be Energetic Now; Be Energetic Later

As a typical young adult, you are living in the prime of your life, at least as far as physical fitness, health, strength, and stamina go. Even though this may be the prime, it doesn't mean that you cannot maintain energy levels into middle and later adulthood. Studies have shown that many people who were active in their earlier adulthood years, creating a pattern and the body's expectation for activity, have grown into quite active and energetic elderly adults. Granted, there are outside factors that can inhibit activity levels such as diseases like osteoporosis, arthritis, and various diseases of the organs. But even so, regular exercise increases one's chances of living a healthy and disease-free life.

ALERT!

Living a sedentary lifestyle in your younger years is likely to carry over to your later years. Because later adults do suffer some deterioration in physical ability, such as strength and flexibility, it is of the utmost importance that they do not aid that deterioration by living a sedentary lifestyle.

If you are able to incorporate a regular exercise routine, whether it be walking or spending an hour at the gym every day, in your younger years, your body comes to expect that exertion and you will feel like you are in a slump if you slack off. By building this into your routine now, the likelihood that you will continue exercise patterns into your later years increases. There is nothing out there that says elderly people cannot exercise. In fact, it is highly recommended, as those who do get regular exercise find that they are able to live more active and enjoyable lifestyles than others who do not exercise. While later adults may not have the heightened energy levels, strength, and stamina of young adults, physical exercise can keep these qualities up to par for the activities you wish to participate in.

Changes During Middle Adulthood

People within the years of middle adulthood are going through several changes that can drastically affect their ways of life. While most people typically think of this time period as being the most stressful and unpleasant of all, if you ask those who are living it, you may receive a different answer.

If you think about it, this is the time period in which the children generally leave the house and the parents now have their lives back to themselves. Granted, some parents go through the empty-nest syndrome in which they have difficulty adjusting to life without their children, but this is temporary and once that newfound freedom is discovered, adults in the middle years may very well act as giddy as children again!

Many use this time to re-evaluate their lives (which may be where the misconception of midlife crises comes into play, though we will discuss that later) and take stock of what they have accomplished and what they yet want to accomplish. This is often a period of new adventures, hobbies, and sometimes more community involvement.

Menopause

Menopause is a hot topic for women during middle adulthood. This is a time of great physical change in which menstruation ceases and the ovaries stop producing estrogen. While you will often hear horror stories of menopause, most women typically view it indifferently or positively. Most women are relieved not to have to worry about pregnancy and deal with monthly cycles. Granted, there are some physical symptoms that accompany menopause as the body adjusts to the decrease of estrogen. The most common symptom is hot flashes. Regardless of what you may have heard, menopause does not throw a woman into depression, make her irritable, or cause irrational behavior. Some women do experience severe physical symptoms, but the percentage is very low.

Midlife Crises

A popular misconception is that men often experience midlife crises during middle adulthood, in which their personalities seem to change overnight and they may suddenly regress to their earlier years. There is absolutely no foundation for this belief. Men do not suffer any type of crisis pertinent to a particular age period, other than the re-evaluation of priorities and goals that normally happens during these years.

FACT

The aging process does not bring about a midlife crisis. Those things that may bring about a "midlife crisis" are drastic and sudden life-altering events such as the death of a loved one or the loss of employment.

While men may have the time, money, and inclination to delve into new hobbies or purchase expensive toys during this time, this is in no way associated with a crisis. Instead, it is considered a productive period of mental well-being. Men are no more susceptible to a midlife crisis than women.

Changes in Sexuality

Many people are under the assumption that once you reach a certain age, sex is no longer an important part of your life, if it is a part of your life at all. This is simply not true. Granted, elderly people may not be as rambunctious as young adults when it comes to sexual exploits, but they do still have the desire to have sex, even into their late eighties. Sex is an important part of any relationship and does not exclude itself from the relationships of older people. However, men and women do undergo changes in their sexuality as they age.

Changes in Men

One of the main concerns of men as they age is that their ability to achieve erection is affected. In some men, it may take longer and require more stimulation to achieve erection, and even then it may not be as firm as it was in their young adult years. Some men are unable to achieve erection at all. This is referred to as *impotence*. Impotence doesn't only affect elderly men; younger men will also likely suffer this at least once in their lives.

If you are experiencing erectile dysfunction, you may want to look into the possibility of Viagra. This relatively new medication has proved to be quite effective in cases of impotence. It also has very few side effects, but possible side effects include headaches and queasiness of the stomach. Men who have heart conditions cannot take it. Because impotence may be related to other medications, it's important to discuss it with your doctor.

Impotence is thought to stem primarily from psychological causes, though it can also be caused by some physical problems. An inability to perform is rather embarrassing and frightening for a man. As he feels more and more pressure to perform or feels anxiety about the changes in his body, a man may psyche himself up so much that he is unable to achieve erection. While impotence is usually only temporary, some men may become so frustrated with it that they begin to fear sexual experiences and thus feed the pressure to perform, in turn causing erectile dysfunction.

Another change a man faces as he ages is the decrease in the stimulation felt. Whereas a young man can be turned on rather easily, it may take an older man more time and more effort to achieve an erection. Even when he does achieve erection, he may need a constant flow of stimulation in order to maintain it. There are several products on the market to aid in the achieving and maintaining of an erection, so while this may be a little embarrassing, it is not a hopeless problem.

Changes in Women

As you've learned, menopause is probably the greatest change a woman will undergo during middle adulthood. Menopause is the most common cause for sexual changes in women as they age. Following menopause, a woman's vaginal canal may be shortened and thinned and sometimes even becomes smaller all around. Many women also experience a decrease in lubrication. The combination of a smaller vagina and less lubrication can make sex a rather uncomfortable act. Of course, there are lubricants that can be used to counteract this effect of aging. And often, women do not mind the changes in the vaginal structure, as they can actually increase stimulation and pleasure.

Cognitive Growth and Decline

Unfortunately, certain mental functioning aspects do decline with age, such as memory, reasoning, and complex problem solving. This isn't to say that these abilities necessarily disappear; they sometimes just take a little longer to process. For instance, you may notice that it takes elderly people longer to think of names or other information than it does for younger people. The information may still be there, but the speed of cognitive processing has slowed, making it difficult at times to retrieve that information. The ability to utilize deductive reasoning and/or to use new information in problem solving also declines with age. While this may seem as if a large portion of your mental processes is vulnerable to deterioration, it really isn't as bad as it sounds. It may be annoying, but this doesn't mean that an elderly person becomes incapable of taking care of him or herself.

Many people assume that to get older means to get depressed and lack interest in activities that used to be stimulating. This is simply not true. While depression can certainly affect the elderly, the two do not go hand in hand. There are many elderly people living their lives the happiest they've ever been.

Not all aspects of mental functioning decline with age. Some skills that you have consistently used throughout the course of your lifetime, such as the ability to define words or solve mathematical equations, tends to remain stable and retrievable throughout the later years. The best part is that it is even possible that these skills will improve! Of course, this depends on the education you've received and the amount of experience you've had with the particular skill.

Treatable Cognitive Conditions

Thankfully, researchers have been able to dispel some of the preconceived notions of senility and other conditions formerly associated with old age. Not only are some of these conditions *not* brought on by the aging process, but they are also treatable, ultimately improving the quality of life for the elderly.

For instance, senility was once thought to be just an accepted byproduct of old age. However, recent studies have shown that many cases of senility aren't senility at all, but rather side effects of certain types of medication or combinations of medications. As stated before, exercise and proper diet can do a lot for a person's energy levels, strength, and stamina. Therefore, whereas frailty was once considered an inevitable effect of aging, it is now known that frailty and weakness do not have to be accepted. Doctors can help set their patients on exercise and diet regimens that will help them to live more active lives.

Alzheimer's Disease

Alzheimer's disease often crosses the minds of those who worry about aging, and with good reason. Alzheimer's disease is a degenerative disease that results in the loss of brain cells. Those with Alzheimer's suffer a variety of symptoms, including memory loss, disorientation, problems with reasoning, personality changes, agitation, anxiety, delusions, hallucinations, and an inability to perform routine tasks. Such a disease is incredibly frightening both for the sufferer and for his or her family.

The duration of the disease can last anywhere from three to twenty years. While there is no cure as of yet, there are several drugs being employed to slow down the degenerative process, thus adding up to several years of independence to the patient's life. Eventually, however, the disease progresses to the point where the patient will require twenty-four-hour care and could even possibly lead to death due to the loss of brain function.

FACT

According to the Alzheimer's Association, approximately 10 percent of those age sixty-five and older have developed Alzheimer's disease. Approximately 50 percent of those age eighty-five and older have the disease. Obviously, age does play a role in a person's risk of developing the disease.

No one knows exactly what causes Alzheimer's disease; however, it is pretty commonly known that age plays a role in its development. This isn't to say that everyone who reaches age sixty-five and beyond will develop the disease. Of course, some people are more susceptible than others, especially those with a family history of the disease.

Retirement

Retiring from full-time employment is considered one of the major events in an individual's life. As much as we may complain about our jobs, they are an important part of our lives, for social, economic, and personal identity purposes. After having worked forty-plus years, an individual may feel a significant loss once he or she retires. The workplace affords consistency, routine, social atmosphere, and employment of time in a constructive manner. Once that is gone, an individual may feel the same psychological effects as he or she would in losing a loved one. All of a sudden the individual is left with lots of time on her hands, less money in her pocket, and sometimes even a feeling of worthlessness.

This isn't to say that everyone who retires will feel this way. How individuals cope with retirement depends on numerous factors, including family life, how prepared they are for retirement, social tendencies, and physical health. Those who have supportive families, have saved up enough money as to not have to worry about financial hardship, have social structures outside the workplace, and are in good physical condition, are more likely to deal well with retirement and view it as a freedom that can be enjoyed. However, those without families, with limited funds, with no social groups outside the workplace, and in poor health are more likely to view retirement as a loss that cannot possibly be replaced. These individuals may slip into depression and otherwise simply feel miserable. They may wander around, feeling as though they no longer have a purpose in or use for life.

If you find yourself facing retirement, take a few moments to write down a list of activities you enjoy, projects you would like to complete, or new hobbies you would like to try out. Those who are able to find productive ways to employ their time after retirement are more likely to make a smooth and positive transition.

Stress accompanies any type of life-altering event and making the transition from employment to retirement may be a struggle for many. However, you can help combat this struggle and any psychological disturbances you may face by being as prepared as you can be for the event. Understanding the loss and having a plan of action in place will ease your mind a bit when the time comes. Of course, you will have to go through an adjustment period, but if you are able to look on the event with a positive light, your years spent in retirement will likely be more enjoyable and productive.

Death—The Final Stage in Development

Death, of course, is the inevitable final stage of human development. While death may occur at any age, those who are in later adulthood focus more on death than do most others. They know that they cannot live forever and often begin making plans for their death. Not to say that they begin to plan suicide, though some do, but rather that they review their assets and prepare ways in which to provide for their families once they are gone, preplan funeral arrangements, or create/update wills and trusts.

While the thought of planning for death might seem rather morbid to some, it can actually create peace of mind in some of the elderly. If they are in later adulthood, it is likely that they have experienced the death of a loved one at one time or another during their lives. They understand the effect it can have on those family and friends left behind. By preparing for their death, they are able to rest assured knowing they have done what they can to make the process of burial, funeral arrangements, and divvying up the assets as smooth as possible. Some may even go to the extent of detailing the plans down to the songs they want sung or verses read so as to take the burden of making decisions under bereavement away from loved ones.

This isn't to say that all are ready to accept the fact that they will die. Some fear death and will never be prepared to go. However, studies have shown that those who believe in some form of afterlife are more accepting and at peace during their later years than those who believe in the finality of death. Regardless of your beliefs, death is inevitable, so for the sake of your mental health, do all that you can do to make your last years of life the most enjoyable they can be. Ⓔ

Appendix A

Glossary of Psychological Terms

abnormal psychology: The study of abnormal mental processes and behavior.

agoraphobia: The fear of being away from a safe place, such as your home.

Alzheimer's disease: A degenerative disease that results in the loss of brain cells, typically occurring in the elderly.

amnesia: Loss of memory, whether partially or completely.

anorexia nervosa: An eating disorder in which an individual starves him or herself in order to lose weight.

antianxiety drugs: Drugs that are used in the treatment of anxiety disorders, such as Valium or Xanax.

antidepressants: Drugs that are most often used to treat depression, such as Prozac, Zoloft, or Paxil.

antipsychotic drugs: Drugs that are used to treat psychoses such as schizophrenia, such as Restoril.

anxiety disorders: A category of mental disorders in which all share a symptom of an extreme fear or anxiety. They include phobias, panic attacks with or without agoraphobia, obsessive-compulsive disorder, and posttraumatic stress disorder.

attribution theory: A psychological theory that offers explanations of social or individual behavior.

awareness: How conscious you are of yourself or materials and things within your environment.

behavior therapy: A form of therapy in which conditioning techniques are applied to change or eliminate a problematic behavior.

biological altruism: A selfless act made on the behalf of another in order to attempt to save that person's life, even though your own life may be at risk.

bipolar disorder: A mental disorder in which a person experiences a series of extreme highs and lows that are often unpredictable in nature, formerly called manic-depressive illness, usually occurring over months rather than within one day or week.

brainstorming: A problem-solving strategy in which you come up with as many possible solutions as you can, usually within a certain period of time.

bulimia nervosa: An eating disorder in which an individual eats large amounts of food and then purges in order to lose weight.

catastrophizing: Blowing a small problem out of proportion and turning it into an inescapable disaster.

central nervous system: A system of the body consisting of the spinal column and the brain.

chromosomes: The structures within every cell that carry the genes.

chunk: A unit of information containing smaller bits of information stored in the memory.

cingulotomy: A surgical procedure that burns and destroys a small portion of the brain known to be involved in emotionality. This is used as a last resort for those suffering severe obsessive-compulsive disorder and major depression who have not responded to drugs or forms of psychotherapy.

classical conditioning: The process by which a normally neutral stimulus becomes a conditioned stimulus, eliciting a response in an individual due to its association with a stimulus that already elicits a similar response.

client-centered therapy: A humanistic therapy approach in which the client is the focus of the therapy session.

cognitive processes: Processes (such as thinking, reasoning, remembering, etc.) that allow you to understand your environment and how the environment affects you and in turn how you affect the environment.

cognitive therapy: A form of therapy that employs the premise that rational, realistic, and constructive thinking can reduce the occurrence of or entirely get rid of a problematic behavior.

compliance: Yielding to another person's wishes without modifying our true beliefs.

compulsion: A repetitive ritual behavior in obsessive-compulsive disorder that is used to reduce anxiety.

conditioning: A learning process in which an environmental stimulus elicits a response, and an individual learns from the association between that stimulus and response. The association is what conditions, or modifies, our behavior and we therefore learn to behave in a certain manner toward the same stimulus in the future.

conscious: The term used to describe your active awareness.

consciousness: Level of awareness.

conventional morality: The second stage of the moral thought process in which adolescents begin to uphold laws because they understand the concept of rules and that they should be obeyed. This is also the stage in which adolescents start doing good out of caring for others.

cyclothymia: A milder form of bipolar disorder. People with cyclothymia suffer mood swings between mania and depression, but they are not as extreme.

deductive reasoning: A form of reasoning that uses premises that guarantee to be followed by a conclusion of truth.

delusions: False, and often outlandish, ideas that a person believes to be true, not consistent with the person's cultural context.

diffusion of responsibility: An event that takes place when a group of people are witnessing the same emergency, yet certain people do not offer assistance because other people are present, therefore diffusing their need to act.

dissociative disorders: A category of mental disorders in which the disorders are characterized by the separation of a person's awareness from his conscious memory. These include dissociative amnesia and dissociative identity disorder.

dysthymia: A less severe form of depression that is not disabling but still produces feelings of despair and pervasive lack of pleasure.

eating disorders: A category of mental disorders in which the disorders are characterized by excessive overeating, undereating, overexercising, or purging as a result of a fear of gaining weight. They include anorexia nervosa and bulimia nervosa.

ego: A component of personality that seeks to gain pleasure, it operates on the reality principle where impulses are controlled when situations aren't favorable for meeting its demands.

electroencephalograph: A device used to measure brain waves, otherwise known as EEG.

event-related potential: Minute electrical changes that are studied to localize brain activity.

explicit memory: The storage location for information you intentionally work to remember.

factitious disorders: A category of mental disorders in which the disorders are characterized by a person's attempt to fake physical or psychological illnesses.

free association: An exercise used in therapy that required the patient to talk about whatever came to mind no matter how relevant, nonsensical, or foreign the thoughts sounded. This technique, along with dream analysis and childhood memory evaluation, attempted to help patients understand themselves and their actions.

habituation: The most basic form of learning in which an individual turns his attention to new objects and away from already discovered objects.

hallucinations: False sensory perceptions that a person believes to be real.

hypnosis: A procedure meant to create an altered state of consciousness in which a hypnotist suggests changes in feelings, perceptions, thoughts, or behavior of the subject.

id: A component of personality that wants immediate gratification of physical distress such as hunger, thirst, and sexual tension.

implicit memory: The storage location for information you remember but did not intentionally store for future use.

impulse control disorders: A category of mental disorders in which the disorders are marked by an inability to resist an impulse to participate in a behavior that is harmful to oneself or others. These include kleptomania, pyromania, pathological gambling, and intermittent explosive disorder.

inductive reasoning: A form of reasoning that uses premises to predict an outcome or conclusion that is *probably* true, though there is a possibility the conclusion is false.

long-term memory: The memory that stores all information the mind wishes to keep for the long term, information that may be retrieved and used in the future.

major depression: A mood disorder involving interruptions in an individual's behavior, emotion, cognition, and body function.

mania: A period of extreme exhilaration wherein the individual is full of energy, high self-esteem, creativity, and ambition.

menopause: A time of physical change in women (typically during middle adulthood) in which menstruation ceases and the ovaries stop producing estrogen.

mnemonics: Strategies, such as a rhyme or formula, that are used to improve the memory and help you retain and retrieve the information by making use of the information already stored in your long-term memory.

mood disorders: A category of mental disorders in which the disorders are characterized by extreme changes in mood, such as major depression, cyclothymia, dysthymia, and bipolar disorder.

mood stabilizers: Drugs that work to stabilize a person's mood, reducing or getting rid of extreme mood swings.

operant conditioning: A process by which an individual's response is followed by a consequence (either positive or negative) and that consequence teaches her either to repeat the response or to decrease its occurrence.

overgeneralizing: Taking a thought or belief and irrationally expanding it to areas that would otherwise be unaffected.

panic disorder: An anxiety disorder in which an individual suffers recurring panic attacks.

personality disorders: A category of mental disorders in which the disorders are a result of maladaptive patterns that disrupt a person's ability to function in everyday life and/or cause extreme distress. They include narcissistic personality disorder, antisocial personality disorder, and paranoid personality disorder, as well as borderline personality disorder, obsessive-compulsive personality disorder, and avoidant personality disorder.

phobia: An exaggerated and unrealistic fear that incapacitates the sufferer.

postconventional morality: The third stage of moral thought in which an adolescent will act according to his or her own basic ethical principles.

posttraumatic stress disorder: An anxiety disorder that develops following a traumatic experience, such as near-death experiences, rape, war, or natural disasters. The symptoms of PTSD include reliving the traumatic experience in dreams or thoughts, irritability, insomnia, inability to concentrate, depression, and a detachment from others.

preconscious: The part of the mind that stores memories that you do not have a use for at the present moment, but that you can retrieve in the future if needed.

preconventional morality: The first stage of the moral thought process in which a child will obey the rules and choose to do right only to avoid punishment or gain a reward for acting "good."

psychological altruism: A selfless act made for the benefit of another though it does not reward you in any way.

psychosurgery: A method of treatment that involves destroying the part of the brain thought to be responsible for the mental disorder.

psychotic disorders: A category of mental disorders in which the disorders are marked by delusions, hallucinations, or extreme emotional disturbances (often the sufferer is considered to have lost touch with reality). They include schizophrenia and delusional disorder.

reference group: Groups we identify with when we need to understand our own opinions and analyze our behavior or reactions to situations.

reinforcement: Rewards and punishments.

REM sleep: A stage of sleep in which your brain is just as active as it is when you are wide awake during the day.

repressed memory: A memory that has been involuntarily pushed to the unconscious and the individual is unaware of it.

schemata: Cognitive structures stored in memory that are abstract representations of events, objects, and relationships in the real world.

schizophrenia: A mental disorder in which an individual loses touch with reality, suffers hallucinations and delusions, and is unable to carry out many daily activities.

scripts: Schemata or abstract cognitive representations of events and social interactions.

self-perception: A theory that concludes that we make the same judgments about ourselves, use the same processes, and make the same errors as we do when making judgments about others.

sensory memory: The memory that briefly stores incoming impressions.

sexual and gender-identity disorders: A category of mental disorders in which the disorders are marked by abnormal behavior regarding sexual functioning. They include sadomasochism, exhibitionism, psychosexual dysfunction, fetishism, and transsexualism.

short-term memory: The memory that deals with only the present time. It stores everything you are conscious of at the moment.

sleep disorders: A category of mental disorders in which the disorders are marked by a disruption in a person's normal sleeping patterns. They include insomnia, narcolepsy, and sleep apnea.

somatoform disorders: A category of mental disorders in which the disorders are characterized by a complaint of a physical symptom for which no cause can be found. These include hypochondria and conversion disorder.

stimulants: Drugs that speed up the activity in the central nervous system. Stimulants include, but are not limited to, cocaine, methamphetamine hydrochloride (speed), and amphetamines (uppers).

stimulus generalization: Occurs when an individual has the same conditioned response to a stimulus that is similar though not the same as the conditioned stimulus.

stress: A condition in which extreme pressure, hardship, or pain is either suddenly experienced or built up over time.

stressors: Those stimuli that produce stress.

subconscious: The part of the mind that handles the information and mental processes needed to perform routine activities that do not require conscious thought.

substance-related disorders: A category of mental disorders in which the disorders are a result of the use of or withdrawal from a drug such as alcohol, caffeine, amphetamines, opiates, or nicotine.

superego: A component of personality that censors and restrains the ego, makes value judgments, sets standards, and weighs consequences.

transference: The process of transferring one's emotions toward a figure from one's past onto another person, often a therapist.

trial and error: A problem-solving strategy in which an individual tries out several solutions until she or he finds the correct one.

unconscious: The part of the mind that stores those memories we are unaware of.

Appendix B

Resources

Further Reading

Abnormal Psychology with Infotrac: An Integrative Approach, by David H. Barlow and Vincent Mark Durand.

Biological Psychology with Infotrac, by James W. Kalat.

Casebook in Abnormal Psychology, by Timothy A. Brown and David H. Barlow.

Case Studies in Abnormal Psychology, by Thomas F. Oltmanns, John M. Neale, and Gerald C. Davison.

Case Studies in Child and Adolescent Psychopathology, by Robin Morgan.

Diagnostic and Statistical Manual of Mental Disorders, by American Psychiatric Association.

Doing Psychotherapy, by Michael Franz Basch.

Exploring Psychology, by David G. Myers.

Genetics of Mental Disorders: A Guide for Students, Clinicians, and Researchers, by Stephen V. Faraone, Ming T. Tsuang, and Debby W. Tsuang.

Mental Disorders in Older Adults: Fundamentals of Assessment and Treatment, by Steven H. Zarit and Judy M. Zarit.

Mental Health Disorders Sourcebook, edited by Karen Bellenir.

Obsessive-Compulsive Disorders: A Complete Guide to Getting Well and Staying Well, by Fred Penzel.

Personality: Theory and Research, by Lawrence A. Pervin and Oliver P. John.

Psychology, by David G. Myers.

Social Psychology, by Robert A. Baron and Donn Byrne.

Understanding Psychotherapy, by Michael Franz Basch.

What's Going on in There?: How the Brain and Mind Develop in the First Five Years of Life, by Lise Eliot.

When Someone You Love Has a Mental Illness: A Handbook for Family, Friends, and Caregivers, by Rebecca Woolis and Agnes Hatfield.

Associations

Academy for Eating Disorders
6728 Old McLean Village Drive
McLean, VA 22101
703-556-9222
✍ *www.aedweb.org*

American Psychoanalytic Association
309 East 49th Street
New York, NY 10017
212-752-0450
✍ *www.apsa.org*

American Psychological Association
750 First Street, NE
Washington, DC 20002
800-374-2721
✍ *www.apa.org*

American Psychological Society
1010 Vermont Avenue NW, Suite 1100
Washington, DC 20005
202-783-2077
✍ *www.psychologicalscience.org*

American Society on Aging
833 Market Street, Suite 511
San Francisco, CA 94103
800-537-9728
✍ *www.asaging.org*

Association for Advancement of Behavior Therapy
305 7th Avenue, 16th Floor
New York, NY 10001
212-647-1890
✍ *www.aabt.org*

Association for Humanistic Psychology
1516 Oak Street, #320A
Alameda, CA 94501
510-769-6495
✍ *www.ahpweb.org*

The Federation of Behavioral, Psychological, and Cognitive Sciences
750 First Street, NE
Washington, DC 20002
202-336-5920
✍ *www.thefederationonline.org*

International Psychogeriatric Association
5215 Old Orchard Road, Suite 340
Skokie, IL 60077
847-663-0574
✍ *www.ipa-online.org*

International Society for the Study of Dissociation
60 Revere Drive, Suite 500
Northbrook, IL 60062
847-480-0899
✍ *www.issd.org*

Society for Personality and Social Psychology
University of Rochester
Department of Psychology
Rochester, NY 14627
585-275-8724
✍ *www.spsp.org*

Society for the Psychological Study of Social Issues
208 I Street, NE
Washington, DC 20002
202-675-6956
✍ *www.spssi.org*

Index

A

Abnormal psychology, 178, 277. *See also* Disorders; *specific disorders*
Actin, 34
Adjustment disorders, 171–72, 180
Adolescence. *See* Human development, adolescence
Adrenaline, 32
Advertising, 104
Afferent neurons, 31
Aggression-learning experiment, 16–18
Aggressive behavior, 70–73
   causes of, 232–33
   frustration-aggression hypothesis, 71
   as learned process, 72
   physiological causes, 71–72
   TV violence and, 72–73
Aging. *See* Human development, adulthood/beyond
Algorithms, 145
Alleles, 34
Allport, Gordon, 154
Altruism, 38, 231–32
Alzheimer's disease, 274, 277
American Psychological Association (APA), 5
Amnesia, 180, 277
Anal, 8
Anaphylaxis, 68
Anger, 170–71
Animal impulses, 7
Antianxiety drugs, 199–200, 277
Antidepressants, 199, 277
Antipsychotic drugs, 198, 277
Antisocial personality disorder, 190–91, 193
Anxiety, 170
Anxiety disorders, 180, 181–84, 277
Associations, 284
Attachments, 256–57
Attitudes/beliefs, 213–15
Attribution theory, 219, 277
Auditory perception, 59–60
Auditory sensation, 57–58
Autonomic nervous system, 31–32, 42, 65–66
Autosomes, 34

B

Bandura, Albert, 16–18, 23
Behavior
   abnormal. *See* Disorders; *specific disorders*
   beliefs, attitudes and, 214–15

consistency, consensus and, 218–19
   defined, 2
   distinctiveness and, 218
   interpersonal. *See* Social interactions
   interpreting, 218–20
   self-perception and, 219–20
   teaching to others, 107–8
   types of, 150
Behavioral adjustments, 77
Behavioral neuroscientists, 4, 12
Behavioral therapy, 203–5, 277
Behaviorism (strict), 8–10
Beliefs/attitudes, 213–15
Biological altruism, 231–32, 277
Biological perspective, 27–38
   autonomic nervous system, 31–32, 42, 65–66
   central nervous system, 29–30
   endocrine system, 32–33, 42
   genetics, 33–36
   human evolution, 37–38
   mental disorders, 192
   neurons, 28–29
   peripheral nervous system, 30–32
   somatic nervous system, 31
Biological psychology, 12
Bipolar disorder, 186, 187, 193, 277
Birth process, 240–41
Blood temperature, 79
Bobo dolls, 16–18
Body temperature, 76–78
Borderline personality disorder (BPD), 191, 193
Brain, 39–48
   body temperature and, 76–78
   central nervous system and, 30
   cerebrum, 42–43
   corpus callosum, 42
   emotions and, 67
   evolution, 40
   forebrain, 41–42
   hindbrain, 41
   imaging technologies, 44–46
   language development and, 254
   lobes, 42–43
   midbrain, 41
   mind and, 46–48
   modern study approach, 44–46
   motivation and, 76–78
   origins, 40–41
   sensory processing, 42–43
   traditional study approaches, 43–44

Brainstorming, 147–48, 277
Brainwaves, sleep and, 80–81
Broca, Paul, 43
Burkhardt, Gottlieb, 200
B vitamins, 242
Bystander apathy, 225

C

Caffeine, 97
Calcium, 243
Case histories, 19–20
Catastrophizing, 205, 206, 278
Cat experiments (of Thorndike), 8–9, 105
Cattell, Raymond, 155
Central nervous system, 29–30, 278
Cerebrum, 42–43
Cesarean section, 240
Change, embracing, 209–10
Characteristics, 150
Chomsky, Noam, 253
Chromosomes, 34, 237, 278
Cingulotomy, 201, 278
Classical conditioning, 101–4, 278
Client-centered therapy, 202, 203, 278
Clinical psychologists, 3
Coaction, 224–25
Cognitive decline, 272–74
Cognitive development, 250–52, 261–63, 272–74
Cognitive disorders, 180
Cognitive dissonance theory, 215
Cognitive neuroscientists, 4, 12
Cognitive psychologists, 4
Cognitive psychology, 11–12, 140–41
Cognitive therapy, 205–6, 278
Collagen, 34
Color perception, 56–57
Communication. *See* Language
Compliance, 226–27, 278
Computerized tomography (CT) scans, 44
Concepts, 141–42
Conditioned stimulus (CS), 102
Conditioning
   classical, 101–4, 278
   defined, 101, 278
   operant, 104–9
Conformity, 227–28
Conscious, 88, 278
Consciousness
   defined, 278
   dreaming and, 92–93

THE EVERYTHING SERIES!

BUSINESS & PERSONAL FINANCE

Everything® Accounting Book
Everything® Budgeting Book, 2nd Ed.
Everything® Business Planning Book
Everything® Coaching and Mentoring Book, 2nd Ed.
Everything® Fundraising Book
Everything® Get Out of Debt Book
Everything® Grant Writing Book, 2nd Ed.
Everything® Guide to Buying Foreclosures
Everything® Guide to Fundraising, $15.95
Everything® Guide to Mortgages
Everything® Guide to Personal Finance for Single Mothers
Everything® Home-Based Business Book, 2nd Ed.
Everything® Homebuying Book, 3rd Ed., $15.95
Everything® Homeselling Book, 2nd Ed.
Everything® Human Resource Management Book
Everything® Improve Your Credit Book
Everything® Investing Book, 2nd Ed.
Everything® Landlording Book
Everything® Leadership Book, 2nd Ed.
Everything® Managing People Book, 2nd Ed.
Everything® Negotiating Book
Everything® Online Auctions Book
Everything® Online Business Book
Everything® Personal Finance Book
Everything® Personal Finance in Your 20s & 30s Book, 2nd Ed.
Everything® Personal Finance in Your 40s & 50s Book, $15.95
Everything® Project Management Book, 2nd Ed.
Everything® Real Estate Investing Book
Everything® Retirement Planning Book
Everything® Robert's Rules Book, $7.95
Everything® Selling Book
Everything® Start Your Own Business Book, 2nd Ed.
Everything® Wills & Estate Planning Book

COOKING

Everything® Barbecue Cookbook
Everything® Bartender's Book, 2nd Ed., $9.95
Everything® Calorie Counting Cookbook
Everything® Cheese Book
Everything® Chinese Cookbook
Everything® Classic Recipes Book
Everything® Cocktail Parties & Drinks Book
Everything® College Cookbook
Everything® Cooking for Baby and Toddler Book
Everything® Diabetes Cookbook
Everything® Easy Gourmet Cookbook
Everything® Fondue Cookbook
Everything® Food Allergy Cookbook, $15.95
Everything® Fondue Party Book
Everything® Gluten-Free Cookbook
Everything® Glycemic Index Cookbook
Everything® Grilling Cookbook
Everything® Healthy Cooking for Parties Book, $15.95
Everything® Holiday Cookbook
Everything® Indian Cookbook
Everything® Lactose-Free Cookbook
Everything® Low-Cholesterol Cookbook

Everything® Low-Fat High-Flavor Cookbook, 2nd Ed., $15.95
Everything® Low-Salt Cookbook
Everything® Meals for a Month Cookbook
Everything® Meals on a Budget Cookbook
Everything® Mediterranean Cookbook
Everything® Mexican Cookbook
Everything® No Trans Fat Cookbook
Everything® One-Pot Cookbook, 2nd Ed., $15.95
Everything® Organic Cooking for Baby & Toddler Book, $15.95
Everything® Pizza Cookbook
Everything® Quick Meals Cookbook, 2nd Ed., $15.95
Everything® Slow Cooker Cookbook
Everything® Slow Cooking for a Crowd Cookbook
Everything® Soup Cookbook
Everything® Stir-Fry Cookbook
Everything® Sugar-Free Cookbook
Everything® Tapas and Small Plates Cookbook
Everything® Tex-Mex Cookbook
Everything® Thai Cookbook
Everything® Vegetarian Cookbook
Everything® Whole-Grain, High-Fiber Cookbook
Everything® Wild Game Cookbook
Everything® Wine Book, 2nd Ed.

GAMES

Everything® 15-Minute Sudoku Book, $9.95
Everything® 30-Minute Sudoku Book, $9.95
Everything® Bible Crosswords Book, $9.95
Everything® Blackjack Strategy Book
Everything® Brain Strain Book, $9.95
Everything® Bridge Book
Everything® Card Games Book
Everything® Card Tricks Book, $9.95
Everything® Casino Gambling Book, 2nd Ed.
Everything® Chess Basics Book
Everything® Christmas Crosswords Book, $9.95
Everything® Craps Strategy Book
Everything® Crossword and Puzzle Book
Everything® Crosswords and Puzzles for Quote Lovers Book, $9.95
Everything® Crossword Challenge Book
Everything® Crosswords for the Beach Book, $9.95
Everything® Cryptic Crosswords Book, $9.95
Everything® Cryptograms Book, $9.95
Everything® Easy Crosswords Book
Everything® Easy Kakuro Book, $9.95
Everything® Easy Large-Print Crosswords Book
Everything® Games Book, 2nd Ed.
Everything® Giant Book of Crosswords
Everything® Giant Sudoku Book, $9.95
Everything® Giant Word Search Book
Everything® Kakuro Challenge Book, $9.95
Everything® Large-Print Crossword Challenge Book
Everything® Large-Print Crosswords Book
Everything® Large-Print Travel Crosswords Book
Everything® Lateral Thinking Puzzles Book, $9.95
Everything® Literary Crosswords Book, $9.95
Everything® Mazes Book
Everything® Memory Booster Puzzles Book, $9.95

Everything® Movie Crosswords Book, $9.95
Everything® Music Crosswords Book, $9.95
Everything® Online Poker Book
Everything® Pencil Puzzles Book, $9.95
Everything® Poker Strategy Book
Everything® Pool & Billiards Book
Everything® Puzzles for Commuters Book, $9.95
Everything® Puzzles for Dog Lovers Book, $9.95
Everything® Sports Crosswords Book, $9.95
Everything® Test Your IQ Book, $9.95
Everything® Texas Hold 'Em Book, $9.95
Everything® Travel Crosswords Book, $9.95
Everything® Travel Mazes Book, $9.95
Everything® Travel Word Search Book, $9.95
Everything® TV Crosswords Book, $9.95
Everything® Word Games Challenge Book
Everything® Word Scramble Book
Everything® Word Search Book

HEALTH

Everything® Alzheimer's Book
Everything® Diabetes Book
Everything® First Aid Book, $9.95
Everything® Green Living Book
Everything® Health Guide to Addiction and Recovery
Everything® Health Guide to Adult Bipolar Disorder
Everything® Health Guide to Arthritis
Everything® Health Guide to Controlling Anxiety
Everything® Health Guide to Depression
Everything® Health Guide to Diabetes, 2nd Ed.
Everything® Health Guide to Fibromyalgia
Everything® Health Guide to Menopause, 2nd Ed.
Everything® Health Guide to Migraines
Everything® Health Guide to Multiple Sclerosis
Everything® Health Guide to OCD
Everything® Health Guide to PMS
Everything® Health Guide to Postpartum Care
Everything® Health Guide to Thyroid Disease
Everything® Hypnosis Book
Everything® Low Cholesterol Book
Everything® Menopause Book
Everything® Nutrition Book
Everything® Reflexology Book
Everything® Stress Management Book
Everything® Superfoods Book, $15.95

HISTORY

Everything® American Government Book
Everything® American History Book, 2nd Ed.
Everything® American Revolution Book, $15.95
Everything® Civil War Book
Everything® Freemasons Book
Everything® Irish History & Heritage Book
Everything® World War II Book, 2nd Ed.

HOBBIES

Everything® Candlemaking Book
Everything® Cartooning Book
Everything® Coin Collecting Book
Everything® Digital Photography Book, 2nd Ed.

Everything® Drawing Book
Everything® Family Tree Book, 2nd Ed.
Everything® Guide to Online Genealogy, $15.95
Everything® Knitting Book
Everything® Knots Book
Everything® Photography Book
Everything® Quilting Book
Everything® Sewing Book
Everything® Soapmaking Book, 2nd Ed.
Everything® Woodworking Book

HOME IMPROVEMENT

Everything® Feng Shui Book
Everything® Feng Shui Decluttering Book, $9.95
Everything® Fix-It Book
Everything® Green Living Book
Everything® Home Decorating Book
Everything® Home Storage Solutions Book
Everything® Homebuilding Book
Everything® Organize Your Home Book, 2nd Ed.

KIDS' BOOKS

All titles are $7.95
Everything® Fairy Tales Book, $14.95
Everything® Kids' Animal Puzzle & Activity Book
Everything® Kids' Astronomy Book
Everything® Kids' Baseball Book, 5th Ed.
Everything® Kids' Bible Trivia Book
Everything® Kids' Bugs Book
Everything® Kids' Cars and Trucks Puzzle and Activity Book
Everything® Kids' Christmas Puzzle & Activity Book
Everything® Kids' Connect the Dots
Puzzle and Activity Book
Everything® Kids' Cookbook, 2nd Ed.
Everything® Kids' Crazy Puzzles Book
Everything® Kids' Dinosaurs Book
Everything® Kids' Dragons Puzzle and Activity Book
Everything® Kids' Environment Book $7.95
Everything® Kids' Fairies Puzzle and Activity Book
Everything® Kids' First Spanish Puzzle and Activity Book
Everything® Kids' Football Book
Everything® Kids' Geography Book
Everything® Kids' Gross Cookbook
Everything® Kids' Gross Hidden Pictures Book
Everything® Kids' Gross Jokes Book
Everything® Kids' Gross Mazes Book
Everything® Kids' Gross Puzzle & Activity Book
Everything® Kids' Halloween Puzzle & Activity Book
Everything® Kids' Hanukkah Puzzle and Activity Book
Everything® Kids' Hidden Pictures Book
Everything® Kids' Horses Book
Everything® Kids' Joke Book
Everything® Kids' Knock Knock Book
Everything® Kids' Learning French Book
Everything® Kids' Learning Spanish Book
Everything® Kids' Magical Science Experiments Book
Everything® Kids' Math Puzzles Book
Everything® Kids' Mazes Book
Everything® Kids' Money Book, 2nd Ed.
Everything® Kids' Mummies, Pharaoh's, and Pyramids
Puzzle and Activity Book
Everything® Kids' Nature Book
Everything® Kids' Pirates Puzzle and Activity Book
Everything® Kids' Presidents Book
Everything® Kids' Princess Puzzle and Activity Book
Everything® Kids' Puzzle Book

Everything® Kids' Racecars Puzzle and Activity Book
Everything® Kids' Riddles & Brain Teasers Book
Everything® Kids' Science Experiments Book
Everything® Kids' Sharks Book
Everything® Kids' Soccer Book
Everything® Kids' Spelling Book
Everything® Kids' Spies Puzzle and Activity Book
Everything® Kids' States Book
Everything® Kids' Travel Activity Book
Everything® Kids' Word Search Puzzle and Activity Book

LANGUAGE

Everything® Conversational Japanese Book with CD, $19.95
Everything® French Grammar Book
Everything® French Phrase Book, $9.95
Everything® French Verb Book, $9.95
Everything® German Phrase Book, $9.95
Everything® German Practice Book with CD, $19.95
Everything® Inglés Book
Everything® Intermediate Spanish Book with CD, $19.95
Everything® Italian Phrase Book, $9.95
Everything® Italian Practice Book with CD, $19.95
Everything® Learning Brazilian Portuguese Book with CD, $19.95
Everything® Learning French Book with CD, 2nd Ed., $19.95
Everything® Learning German Book
Everything® Learning Italian Book
Everything® Learning Latin Book
Everything® Learning Russian Book with CD, $19.95
Everything® Learning Spanish Book
Everything® Learning Spanish Book with CD, 2nd Ed., $19.95
Everything® Russian Practice Book with CD, $19.95
Everything® Sign Language Book, $15.95
Everything® Spanish Grammar Book
Everything® Spanish Phrase Book, $9.95
Everything® Spanish Practice Book with CD, $19.95
Everything® Spanish Verb Book, $9.95
Everything® Speaking Mandarin Chinese Book with CD, $19.95

MUSIC

Everything® Bass Guitar Book with CD, $19.95
Everything® Drums Book with CD, $19.95
Everything® Guitar Book with CD, 2nd Ed., $19.95
Everything® Guitar Chords Book with CD, $19.95
Everything® Guitar Scales Book with CD, $19.95
Everything® Harmonica Book with CD, $15.95
Everything® Home Recording Book
Everything® Music Theory Book with CD, $19.95
Everything® Reading Music Book with CD, $19.95
Everything® Rock & Blues Guitar Book with CD, $19.95
Everything® Rock & Blues Piano Book with CD, $19.95
Everything® Rock Drums Book with CD, $19.95
Everything® Singing Book with CD, $19.95
Everything® Songwriting Book

NEW AGE

Everything® Astrology Book, 2nd Ed.
Everything® Birthday Personology Book
Everything® Celtic Wisdom Book, $15.95
Everything® Dreams Book, 2nd Ed.
Everything® Law of Attraction Book, $15.95
Everything® Love Signs Book, $9.95
Everything® Love Spells Book, $9.95
Everything® Palmistry Book
Everything® Psychic Book
Everything® Reiki Book

Everything® Sex Signs Book, $9.95
Everything® Spells & Charms Book, 2nd Ed.
Everything® Tarot Book, 2nd Ed.
Everything® Toltec Wisdom Book
Everything® Wicca & Witchcraft Book, 2nd Ed.

PARENTING

Everything® Baby Names Book, 2nd Ed.
Everything® Baby Shower Book, 2nd Ed.
Everything® Baby Sign Language Book with DVD
Everything® Baby's First Year Book
Everything® Birthing Book
Everything® Breastfeeding Book
Everything® Father-to-Be Book
Everything® Father's First Year Book
Everything® Get Ready for Baby Book, 2nd Ed.
Everything® Get Your Baby to Sleep Book, $9.95
Everything® Getting Pregnant Book
Everything® Guide to Pregnancy Over 35
Everything® Guide to Raising a One-Year-Old
Everything® Guide to Raising a Two-Year-Old
Everything® Guide to Raising Adolescent Boys
Everything® Guide to Raising Adolescent Girls
Everything® Mother's First Year Book
Everything® Parent's Guide to Childhood Illnesses
Everything® Parent's Guide to Children and Divorce
Everything® Parent's Guide to Children with ADD/ADHD
Everything® Parent's Guide to Children with Asperger's
Syndrome
Everything® Parent's Guide to Children with Anxiety
Everything® Parent's Guide to Children with Asthma
Everything® Parent's Guide to Children with Autism
Everything® Parent's Guide to Children with Bipolar Disorder
Everything® Parent's Guide to Children with Depression
Everything® Parent's Guide to Children with Dyslexia
Everything® Parent's Guide to Children with Juvenile Diabetes
Everything® Parent's Guide to Children with OCD
Everything® Parent's Guide to Positive Discipline
Everything® Parent's Guide to Raising Boys
Everything® Parent's Guide to Raising Girls
Everything® Parent's Guide to Raising Siblings
Everything® Parent's Guide to Raising Your
Adopted Child
Everything® Parent's Guide to Sensory Integration Disorder
Everything® Parent's Guide to Tantrums
Everything® Parent's Guide to the Strong-Willed Child
Everything® Parenting a Teenager Book
Everything® Potty Training Book, $9.95
Everything® Pregnancy Book, 3rd Ed.
Everything® Pregnancy Fitness Book
Everything® Pregnancy Nutrition Book
Everything® Pregnancy Organizer, 2nd Ed., $16.95
Everything® Toddler Activities Book
Everything® Toddler Book
Everything® Tween Book
Everything® Twins, Triplets, and More Book

PETS

Everything® Aquarium Book
Everything® Boxer Book
Everything® Cat Book, 2nd Ed.
Everything® Chihuahua Book
Everything® Cooking for Dogs Book
Everything® Dachshund Book
Everything® Dog Book, 2nd Ed.
Everything® Dog Grooming Book

Everything® Dog Obedience Book
Everything® Dog Owner's Organizer, $16.95
Everything® Dog Training and Tricks Book
Everything® German Shepherd Book
Everything® Golden Retriever Book
Everything® Horse Book, 2nd Ed., $15.95
Everything® Horse Care Book
Everything® Horseback Riding Book
Everything® Labrador Retriever Book
Everything® Poodle Book
Everything® Pug Book
Everything® Puppy Book
Everything® Small Dogs Book
Everything® Tropical Fish Book
Everything® Yorkshire Terrier Book

REFERENCE

Everything® American Presidents Book
Everything® Blogging Book
Everything® Build Your Vocabulary Book, $9.95
Everything® Car Care Book
Everything® Classical Mythology Book
Everything® Da Vinci Book
Everything® Einstein Book
Everything® Enneagram Book
Everything® Etiquette Book, 2nd Ed.
Everything® Family Christmas Book, $15.95
Everything® Guide to C. S. Lewis & Narnia
Everything® Guide to Divorce, 2nd Ed., $15.95
Everything® Guide to Edgar Allan Poe
Everything® Guide to Understanding Philosophy
Everything® Inventions and Patents Book
Everything® Jacqueline Kennedy Onassis Book
Everything® John F. Kennedy Book
Everything® Mafia Book
Everything® Martin Luther King Jr. Book
Everything® Pirates Book
Everything® Private Investigation Book
Everything® Psychology Book
Everything® Public Speaking Book, $9.95
Everything® Shakespeare Book, 2nd Ed.

RELIGION

Everything® Angels Book
Everything® Bible Book
Everything® Bible Study Book with CD, $19.95
Everything® Buddhism Book
Everything® Catholicism Book
Everything® Christianity Book
Everything® Gnostic Gospels Book
Everything® Hinduism Book, $15.95
Everything® History of the Bible Book
Everything® Jesus Book
Everything® Jewish History & Heritage Book
Everything® Judaism Book
Everything® Kabbalah Book
Everything® Koran Book
Everything® Mary Book
Everything® Mary Magdalene Book
Everything® Prayer Book

Everything® Saints Book, 2nd Ed.
Everything® Torah Book
Everything® Understanding Islam Book
Everything® Women of the Bible Book
Everything® World's Religions Book

SCHOOL & CAREERS

Everything® Career Tests Book
Everything® College Major Test Book
Everything® College Survival Book, 2nd Ed.
Everything® Cover Letter Book, 2nd Ed.
Everything® Filmmaking Book
Everything® Get-a-Job Book, 2nd Ed.
Everything® Guide to Being a Paralegal
Everything® Guide to Being a Personal Trainer
Everything® Guide to Being a Real Estate Agent
Everything® Guide to Being a Sales Rep
Everything® Guide to Being an Event Planner
Everything® Guide to Careers in Health Care
Everything® Guide to Careers in Law Enforcement
Everything® Guide to Government Jobs
Everything® Guide to Starting and Running a Catering Business
Everything® Guide to Starting and Running a Restaurant
Everything® Guide to Starting and Running a Retail Store
Everything® Job Interview Book, 2nd Ed.
Everything® New Nurse Book
Everything® New Teacher Book
Everything® Paying for College Book
Everything® Practice Interview Book
Everything® Resume Book, 3rd Ed.
Everything® Study Book

SELF-HELP

Everything® Body Language Book
Everything® Dating Book, 2nd Ed.
Everything® Great Sex Book
Everything® Guide to Caring for Aging Parents, $15.95
Everything® Self-Esteem Book
Everything® Self-Hypnosis Book, $9.95
Everything® Tantric Sex Book

SPORTS & FITNESS

Everything® Easy Fitness Book
Everything® Fishing Book
Everything® Guide to Weight Training, $15.95
Everything® Krav Maga for Fitness Book
Everything® Running Book, 2nd Ed.
Everything® Triathlon Training Book, $15.95

TRAVEL

Everything® Family Guide to Coastal Florida
Everything® Family Guide to Cruise Vacations
Everything® Family Guide to Hawaii
Everything® Family Guide to Las Vegas, 2nd Ed.
Everything® Family Guide to Mexico
Everything® Family Guide to New England, 2nd Ed.

Everything® Family Guide to New York City, 3rd Ed.
Everything® Family Guide to Northern California and Lake Tahoe
Everything® Family Guide to RV Travel & Campgrounds
Everything® Family Guide to the Caribbean
Everything® Family Guide to the Disneyland® Resort, California Adventure®, Universal Studios®, and the Anaheim Area, 2nd Ed.
Everything® Family Guide to the Walt Disney World Resort®, Universal Studios®, and Greater Orlando, 5th Ed.
Everything® Family Guide to Timeshares
Everything® Family Guide to Washington D.C., 2nd Ed.

WEDDINGS

Everything® Bachelorette Party Book, $9.95
Everything® Bridesmaid Book, $9.95
Everything® Destination Wedding Book
Everything® Father of the Bride Book, $9.95
Everything® Green Wedding Book, $15.95
Everything® Groom Book, $9.95
Everything® Jewish Wedding Book, 2nd Ed., $15.95
Everything® Mother of the Bride Book, $9.95
Everything® Outdoor Wedding Book
Everything® Wedding Book, 3rd Ed.
Everything® Wedding Checklist, $9.95
Everything® Wedding Etiquette Book, $9.95
Everything® Wedding Organizer, 2nd Ed., $16.95
Everything® Wedding Shower Book, $9.95
Everything® Wedding Vows Book, 3rd Ed., $9.95
Everything® Wedding Workout Book
Everything® Weddings on a Budget Book, 2nd Ed., $9.95

WRITING

Everything® Creative Writing Book
Everything® Get Published Book, 2nd Ed.
Everything® Grammar and Style Book, 2nd Ed.
Everything® Guide to Magazine Writing
Everything® Guide to Writing a Book Proposal
Everything® Guide to Writing a Novel
Everything® Guide to Writing Children's Books
Everything® Guide to Writing Copy
Everything® Guide to Writing Graphic Novels
Everything® Guide to Writing Research Papers
Everything® Guide to Writing a Romance Novel, $15.95
Everything® Improve Your Writing Book, 2nd Ed.
Everything® Writing Poetry Book